Teaching Transformative Life Skills to Students

Gratitude for your support
Bidyut

Norton Books in Education

Teaching Transformative Life Skills to Students

Evidence-Based Lessons in
Stress Resilience, Self Awareness,
Emotion Regulation, and
Healthy Relationships

Bidyut Bose

Danielle Ancin, Jennifer Frank, and Annika Malik

W. W. Norton & Company
New York •London

Copyright © 2017 by Niroga Institute

For information about permission to reproduce selections from this book,
write to Permissions, W. W. Norton & Company, Inc.,
500 Fifth Avenue, New York, NY 10110

For information about special discounts for bulk purchases, please contact
W. W. Norton Special Sales at specialsales@wwnorton.com or 800-233-4830

Manufacturing by Edwards Brothers Malloy
Book design by Vicki Fischman
Production manager: Christine Critelli

Library of Congress Cataloging-in-Publication Data

Names: Bose, Bidyut, author.
Title: Teaching transformative life skills to students : a comprehensive dynamic mindfulness
curriculum / Bidyut Bose, Danielle Ancin, Jennifer Frank, Annika Malik.
Description: First edition. | New York : W. W. Norton & Company, [2017] | Series: Norton books in
education | Includes bibliographical references and index.
Identifiers: LCCN 2016018234 | ISBN 9780393711929 (pbk.)
Subjects: LCSH: Transformative learning. | Life skills—Study and teaching. | Mindfulness (Psychology)
Classification: LCC LC1100 .B67 2017 | DDC 370.11/5—dc23 LC
record available at https://lccn.loc.gov/2016018234

W. W. Norton & Company, Inc.
500 Fifth Avenue, New York, N.Y. 10110
www.wwnorton.com

W. W. Norton & Company Ltd.
15 Carlisle Street, London W1D 3BS

1 2 3 4 5 6 7 8 9 0

To our students, who are our greatest teachers.

GETTING STARTED: THE TRANSFORMATIVE LIFE SKILLS CURRICULUM

UNIT 1. STRESS RESILIENCE

UNIT 2. SELF-AWARENESS

UNIT 3. EMOTION REGULATION

UNIT 4. HEALTHY RELATIONSHIPS

*Transformative
Life Skills
Curriculum*

TRANSFORMATIVE LIFE SKILLS
An Overview for Instructors

What Is Transformative Life Skills?

Transformative Life Skills (TLS) is a multimodality intervention that includes active yoga postures, breathing techniques, and centering meditation. Within the TLS curriculum, we refer to these three core practices as the ABC's (action-breathing-centering). TLS is a strengths-based approach that sits firmly among the cognitive-behavioral therapy (CBT) emerging interventions. It enables students to learn integrative skills for self-awareness, impulse-control, and managing anxiety and stress. The skills learned in TLS affect all aspects of life. They are transformative because if practiced regularly, they actually change the connections in the brain, becoming not only skills but, ultimately, habits and traits.

Why TLS for Youth?

Stress is endemic in our society, and our children are carrying it as well. Students come to school with day-to-day stress from their environment, chronic stress, and even traumatic and posttraumatic stress. The impact of stress on the brain and learning is clear: when a person is under stress, the parts of the brain responsible for memory, listening, language, and thinking are impaired. How can we expect young people to learn without first helping them to manage their stress?

People, including youth, take action in order to seek safety and to feel better. When seen through this lens, "negative" classroom behaviors take on new meaning. The purpose of teaching TLS in schools is to provide students with ways to manage their stress, understand their mental and emotional states, and find a sense of safety in their own bodies, as well as to provide teachers with tools for managing their own stress and meeting challenging behaviors with skill and empathy. TLS covers the five core competencies of social and emotional learning: self-management, self-awareness, responsible decision-making, relationship skills, and social awareness. Young people need these tools in order to engage in school, learn, and have positive relationships. Yet schools often do not provide these tools.

The latest research in brain development and learning points to an integration of the cognitive, emotional, and kinesthetic for optimal information processing, which in turn enables emotion regulation. As shown in the figure below, TLS maps elegantly into this framework with the ABC's—mindful action addressing the kinesthetic, mindful breathing addressing the emotional (given intrinsic connections between our respiratory and nervous systems), and mindful centering addressing the cognitive (through meditation practices that include focused attention as well as open monitoring).

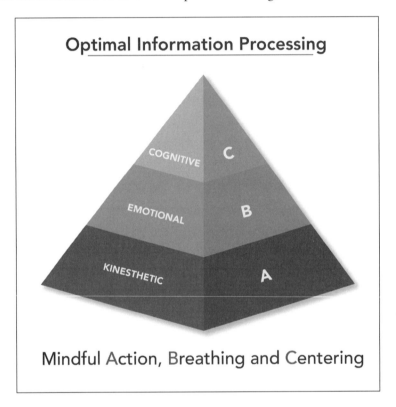

If we are sincerely interested in closing the achievement gap in U.S. schools, we must look at the needs of all our students. Statistics show that African-American and Latino children are at much greater risk of being affected by poverty, abuse, and toxic levels of stress. Schools traditionally have focused on punishing rather than healing students, resulting in an achievement gap that, by the time the student reaches high school, is often insurmountable. There is a clear need to dismantle structural inequities in education and beyond, and a part of this work is developing schools that are responsive to the social and emotional needs of children dealing with inequity and hardship.

Features of TLS

1. TLS is inclusive. Any person, regardless of age, ethnicity, class, or physical or mental ability can practice TLS anywhere, as it requires no formal equipment. TLS concepts can be readily adapted to all levels of physical health and various conditions. The skills can be used in the classroom, individual and group therapy, family settings, group living, or by individuals for their own personal practice.

2. TLS can reach youth who do not respond positively to traditional CBT, such as adolescents and those dealing with complex trauma, head trauma, learning disabilities, or emerging personality disorders. The student is offered choices and invited to participate at her/his own pace, which can build a sense of self-determination and agency.

3. TLS is self-sustaining and empowering. It offers adults and adolescents skills that they can apply on a daily basis with no ongoing cost. Once they learn the basic practice, they can continue to utilize the techniques throughout their lives. TLS elevates mood and engagement in other skill building and therapeutic processes, creating a platform from which motivation is enhanced to address challenges. There is no end point to TLS: the more it is practiced, the greater the benefits.

4. TLS is trauma-informed. As such, it is meant to be not only accessible but also healing for students who have suffered acute or complex trauma. Trauma is an experience of not being in control of what happens to one's body. Unreleased trauma often results in a disconnection from the body and a hyperaroused nervous system. TLS invites students to reengage with their bodies in a way that gives them control, choice, and tools for calming the nervous system and managing triggers.

5. TLS is simple and flexible. It can be quickly learned by professionals to utilize with their students or clients in full 20-minute sessions or broken into smaller doses throughout the day.

How Does TLS Work?

Chronic stress disrupts prefrontal cortical processing, negatively affecting attention control, emotion regulation, adaptive coping strategies, and empathy. Neuroscientific research has shown that mindfulness practices mitigate those very same effects (Jha, Krimpinger, & Baine, 2007). TLS is a *dynamic mindfulness* practice because it incorporates the elements of movement and physical postures, providing an important point of access for people dealing with trauma and chronic stress. The centuries-old techniques of physical postures (action), breathing techniques, and meditation (centering) are known to reduce tension, relax and focus the mind, and energize the body. TLS works by incorporating these three components in unison: moving with full attention on the present experience while using the breath to calm the nervous system. This integration of the physical, emotional, and cognitive leads to optimal information processing and enables the cortical area of the brain to better regulate the entire brain-body system.

Below the ABC's are broken down to show how each component works, but keep in mind that the sum of the ABC's is much greater than its parts.

❖ **Action:** The action component of the ABC's includes both mindful movement and holding various postures, increasing our ability both to notice sensations and tolerate discomfort, and providing us with opportunities to make healthy choices for our bodies. Because chronic stress and trauma are often held in the muscles and tissues, we need to use the body in order to release them. In addition, trauma often has a debilitating effect on the insula, the part of the brain responsible for processing pain and emotions, sensing the body, and several socioemotional functions. Studies of the brain using MRI have shown an increase in insular activity among people practicing yoga and meditation. Thus, the practice of yoga postures coupled with awareness of the body and breath can not only release muscular tension and prevent chronic pain, but may also increase our self-awareness and our ability to maintain healthy relationships with self and others.

❖ **Breathing:** Perhaps the most effective component of the ABC's for managing stress is the breathing. The calming breathing techniques practiced in TLS directly affect the parasympathetic nervous system, activating the relaxation response. They decrease the power of the fight-or-flight centers in the mind and restore the centers of self-control, language, listening, and thinking. Coordinating the movement with the breathing is an important tool to help students focus the mind on the present and calm the nervous system.

❖ **Centering:** The centering component of the ABC's refers to a nonjudgmental focus of attention on present moment experience. When we are centered, we are aware of what is happening in the present moment. We notice our body sensations, thoughts, and feelings without feeling swept away by them. This can also be referred to as concentration or meditation. When we meditate, we use and strengthen a part of the brain called the medial prefrontal cortex (PFC), which enables self-observation and allows us to choose appropriate responses to situations. The larger the medial PFC, the more control the person has over their actions. The medial PFC has a direct pathway to the amygdala, which is the fight-or-flight center of the mind, and thus plays an important role in stress management and emotional regulation.

Given that TLS affects the very structure and wiring of the brain, the lessons and skills learned through the practice become habits and behaviors over time. When students practice TLS regularly, they begin to see changes in the way that they feel and act even without consciously trying. They do not just memorize ways to have better stress management, self-awareness, self-regulation, and healthy relationships—they change their ability and behavior from the inside out.

TLS can be effective in meeting specific challenges commonly faced by youth:

1. **Trauma:** Students may experience trauma from various sources, including a recent event, repeated childhood experiences, violence and insecurity in their environment, and historical trauma reinforced by systemic injustices. Trauma can lead to a disconnection from the body and from the present moment, as the nervous system responds to stimuli from the past rather than what is right here. Trauma can disrupt the body's basic systems, lead to a hyper- (or hypo-) aroused nervous system, and affect our relationships and the very way we see ourselves and the world. Practicing TLS regularly helps youth develop a sense of safety in their own bodies, reestablish biological rhythms, learn ways to calm themselves using the breath, regain control over their reactions to events, and practice making healthy choices. The Department of Veterans Affairs is increasingly using yoga to treat PTSD, and preliminary research has shown yoga to have a higher rate of effectiveness than CBT in the treatment of complex trauma (van der Kolk et al., 2014).

2. **Mood regulation:** Through the practice of TLS, one's mood can be enhanced, and symptoms of depression and anxiety can be reduced. Dynamic mindfulness increases alpha and theta waves in the brain, which are needed to access and process emotions and pressures in life. Research by Luders found that the brains of those who meditate have more gray matter and thus process information more quickly, making them better at managing their emotions (Luders, Toga, Lepore, & Gaser, 2009).

3. **Stress and anxiety:** Stress generates the hormone cortisol, which can lead to a wide variety of health problems when present in high quantities or over a prolonged period of time, as is the case in chronic stress. After a yoga class, cortisol levels have been found to be reduced. A study by Harvard University and Massachusetts Hospital on 28 highly stressed adults who did an 8-week yoga and meditation course documented that the brain became less reactive and more resilient (McGonigal, 2010).

4. **Self esteem and motivation:** TLS allows for self-empowerment; practitioners develop not only physical strength but also courage and willpower that can be used in everyday life when faced by challenges. Those

who practice dynamic mindfulness learn that they have the capacity to learn and succeed at new activities. They gain confidence and mood regulation skills that boost their motivation and ability to engage in activities and face challenges.

5. **Alcohol and other drugs (AOD):** TLS incorporates mindfulness, which, broadly interpreted, refers to focusing fully on the present moment with an attitude of nonjudgmental acceptance. TLS assists youth in identifying physical sensations that occur during movements and poses, and increasingly tolerating any discomfort that arises without immediately reacting. This widening of the window of tolerance for discomfort can be beneficial in many aspects of life. TLS's use of physical postures, breathing, and meditation together create powerful tools by which those in recovery can disrupt the craving response, as well as affect metacognitive processes, which have broad and long-term effects on the abuse of AOD (Segal, Williams, & Teasdale, 2002).

Empirical Support for TLS

A randomized, controlled study was conducted in 2012 in an urban school with sixth and ninth grade students to measure the effectiveness of the TLS program that appears in these pages, originally developed by the Niroga Institute in Oakland, California. The findings and implications are compelling, and span three interconnected domains of social function: education, mental health, and violence prevention. Researchers found that students participating in the TLS program showed lower levels of perceived stress, greater levels of self-control, school engagement, emotional awareness, and distress tolerance, and altered attitudes toward violence (Frank, 2012). This increases students' personal capacity to deal with systemic inequities, evidenced by the academic achievement gap and the school-to-prison pipeline, and benefits not only the students but the school as a whole.

The aim of a second study that had a quasi-experimental prepost design was to assess the effectiveness of TLS on indicators of adolescent emotional distress, prosocial behavior, and attitudes toward violence in a sample of students in high-risk conditions. Participants included 49 students in grades nine to eleven attending a diverse alternative high school in an inner-city school district. Results indicated that students who participated in the TLS program demonstrated significant reductions in anxiety, depression, global psychological distress, rumination, intrusive thoughts, and physical and emotional arousal (Frank, Bose, & Schrobenhauser-Clonan, 2014). Students exposed to TLS reported being significantly less likely to endorse revenge-motivation orientations in response to interpersonal transgressions and reported overall less hostility than did students in the comparison condition. Results of this pilot study provide evidence of the potential for TLS to influence important student social-emotional outcomes among youth exposed to violence and high-risk environments.

In a study involving over 1,000 students in three inner-city schools, independent researchers found statistically significant improvement in reading and math scores, school engagement and academic motivation, empathy, and prosocial behavior (Frank & Peal, 2015). They also found statistically significant reductions in hyperactivity, inattentiveness, bullying, and conflicts within student-teacher relationships. These results indicate benefits for academic and social-emotional learning, and the possibility of dynamic mindfulness to transform school and classroom climate.

These studies confirm the findings of earlier studies on TLS. A controlled study conducted in an ethnically and economically diverse high school (n = 543) revealed statistically significant improvements in student self-control and concurrent reductions in perceived stress. Improvement was particularly strong for female students. Follow-up interviews with program participants revealed a high degree of intervention acceptability and social validity among both students and teachers. A similar study of TLS in a juvenile detention center yielded the same results of reduced perceived stress and increased self-control, further demonstrating that TLS can be employed with youth of various cultures, backgrounds, and experiences (Ramadoss & Bose, 2010).

ABOUT THIS CURRICULUM
Program Goals and Outcomes

The goals of the TLS curriculum can be organized according to the curriculum's four units: stress resilience, self-awareness, emotion regulation, and healthy relationships. Learning objectives are cumulative, in that one builds upon the other, but they are not linear. Each component of TLS affects and augments the others, as indicated in the figure below.

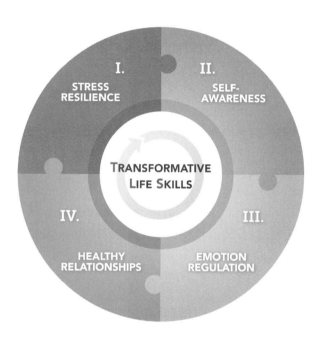

Students do not graduate from TLS, but can continue to use the practice to enhance their stress management skills, self-awareness, self-regulation, and relationships throughout their lives. Thus, the TLS curriculum is a catalyst to life-long personal development.

Stress resilience is a necessary gateway to self-awareness, emotional regulation, and managing healthy relationships. When we are overcome by stress (whether everyday stress, chronic stress, traumatic stress, or posttraumatic stress), the part of the brain that governs inhibition, logical thinking, and self-control is temporarily debilitated. This part of the brain also controls language and listening. It follows that students unable to manage their stress will have obstacles to learning. The first premise of TLS is to calm the nervous system to bring this part of the brain back on line.

As students learn to reduce and manage their stress, they will be increasingly able to engage in classroom activities, listen to instructions, and remember what they have learned. Researchers have shown that anxiety can play an important role in attention disorders; providing students with tools for managing anxious feelings is essential for helping them manage their attention. Learning to manage and reduce feelings of stress and anxiety when they come up can thus have a direct positive impact on learning readiness. It can also contribute to a safer and more engaged classroom climate and a positive school-wide learning environment.

Self-awareness includes being aware of your body sensations, emotions, actions (including reactions), and thoughts. It is the essential difference between being subsumed by a powerful emotion and the ability to witness it: "I am sad or mad," versus "I am feeling sad or mad." The practice of dynamic mindfulness builds self-awareness by slowing down the action and breath and focusing the attention on what's happening in the present. When engaged in this type of mindful movement and breathing, our thoughts slow down as well, making it possible to observe them without becoming absorbed in them. As we practice, we build neurological connections to support increased self-awareness, and we become more aware of our body's signals, our emotions, and our thought patterns in everyday life. Self-awareness affects our self-care, relationships, and self-regard; in fact, it affects every aspect of our lives.

Emotion regulation is similar to self-control: the ability to experience emotions as they come up without them negatively altering our behavior or health. When we regulate our emotions, we still feel them, but we are more able to choose our response. Research by Tagney and others has shown low self-control to be a risk factor for a broad range of social and psychological problems (Tagney, Baumeister, & Boone, 2004).Likewise, higher self-control is correlated with better grades, less binge eating and alcohol abuse, better relationships and interpersonal skills, secure attachment, better adjustment (less incidence of psychopathology and higher self-esteem), and more optimal emotional responses. In other words, better self-regulation positively affects all areas of life.

Emotion regulation includes managing our reactions to our emotions as well as managing our emotions themselves. In TLS, we practice mindful action combined with calming breathing, enabling us to increase our tolerance for discomfort and act deliberately rather than reacting to impulse. Mindful breathing calms the nervous system while we evoke sensations through our movement. We notice the sensations, which can sometimes be uncomfortable or stressful, and we pause to decide whether we maintain or change the action. With practice, we build new connections in the brain that enable us to have more self-awareness and self-control, even in stressful situations.

The ability to tolerate uncomfortable feelings allows us to notice and be with emotions without rushing to change them. This is an important skill for processing and releasing emotions and past experiences. In addition, TLS includes postures and breathing exercises that relax or energize the body. The relative tension or relaxation in the body has a direct impact on our emotions. As they practice relaxing and stimulating the body, students learn that they can do things that help them feel a sense of calm (or energy), and thus a sense of control over their experience.

The intrapersonal nature of the first three units gives way to the interpersonal in the final unit on **healthy relationships**. In this unit we not only explore what it means to have healthy relationships, but we also lead students, through the practice of TLS, to gain a sense of their own interconnectedness and interdependence with one another.

TLS can be challenging, but it is a noncompetitive activity. It allows students the chance to build a sense of accomplishment and strength not by "beating" someone else or being better than them, but by practicing and getting better at something difficult. Thus, we can all learn and improve, and support each other in our learning. Through exploring the body and the world of emotions, students celebrate their differences and appreciate their commonalities. Students are offered the opportunity to work together to master poses in a group, and in doing so see how their actions affect the outcome for everyone.

Without stress management, self-awareness, or self-regulation, it would be very difficult to maintain healthy relationships. Healthy relationships, in turn, support students in managing their stress and developing self-awareness and self-regulation. All four aspects of the TLS curriculum support each other, buoying the student up toward healthier behaviors and enhanced inner resources as they continue to practice.

As you map social-emotional learning (SEL) competencies (as outlined by the national Collaborative for Academic, Social and Emotional Learning or CASEL) to TLS in the figure below, you find that *self-awareness* shows up in both. Emotion regulation is the essential capability of acting rather

than reacting, for choosing what is good in the long term instead of what is merely pleasant in the short term. Therefore, self-regulation is the powerful catalyst for *self-management* and *responsible decision making*. And as we develop interpersonal mindfulness skills, it leads to healthy relationships, which both enable and are supported by *social awareness* and *relationship skills*.

One difference between these two wheels is that the TLS wheel specifically develops stress resilience, which is essential given the ubiquity of chronic stress among youth and the adults around them and the documented impact of chronic stress on the brain and behavior. The other difference is that TLS has a systematic ordering and four-part progression from one competency to the next, starting with stress resilience.

CURRICULUM SCOPE AND SEQUENCE

The full TLS curriculum is four units, each composed of eleven lessons plus one lesson dedicated to reteaching concepts. TLS can be implemented in 20-minute, 30-minute, or 60-minute sessions. In ideal implementation scenarios, three lessons per week are delivered, and a unit is completed in a month. Each lesson focuses on a particular theme and introduces a new posture.

Lesson Structure

We designed TLS to be consistent with best practices in pedagogy and instruction in mind. Each TLS lesson follows a predictable sequence and format that we hope will feel familiar to most teachers and students.

❖ **Student Overview**
The student overview section provides a systematic method for instructors to introduce, explain, and orient students to the purpose and expectations for the day's lesson. This includes a review of the behavioral expectations for TLS. The student overview also includes an activation of background knowledge, in which the lesson theme is introduced, students reflect on a key question regarding the theme, and the theme is connected to the ABC's for the day.

❖ **Acting, Breathing, Centering**
The ABC's (Acting-Breathing-Centering) are the heart of TLS practice. Each ABC lesson provides scripted instructions for how to guide students through the core TLS practice. The script is written intentionally in a way that provides choice whenever possible and invites students to participate at their own pace. The breathing is woven through the script to regulate the nervous system as students explore new concepts and challenges. We have found this type of language helpful when working with youth, and it is of the utmost importance when working with people who have suffered trauma.

Unit 1. Stress Resilience		Unit 2. Self-Awareness	
1.1	Understanding What Stress Is About	2.1	Understanding Self-Awareness
1.2	Recognizing Stress in Your Body	2.2	Building Body Awareness
1.3	Knowing What Stresses You	2.3	Being Aware of Your Body as You Move
1.4	How Stress Affects Your Breath	2.4	Building Awareness of the Breath
1.5	Using Your Breath as a Tool	2.5	The Connection between Breath and Emotion
1.6	How Stress Affects Your Ability to Learn	2.6	Building Awareness of Your Intentions
1.7	Clearing Your Mind, Calming Your Body	2.7	Building Awareness of Thought Patterns
1.8	Feeling Tired vs. Feeling Relaxed	2.8	Thoughts and Feelings Always Change
1.9	How Stress Affects the Choices We Make	2.9	Watching Your Thoughts
1.10	Releasing Stress	2.10	Focusing Inward vs. Focusing Outward
1.11	Long-Term Benefits of Managing	2.11	Choosing Where to Focus Your Mind
1.12	Review and Reteaching	2.12	Review and Reteaching

Unit 3. Emotion Regulation		Unit 4. Healthy Relationships	
3.1	Your Environment Affects Your Thoughts and Feelings	4.1	Your Behavior Affects Your Environment
3.2	You Can Manage Your Thoughts and Feelings	4.2	Understanding Your Habits
3.3	Centering Yourself	4.3	Building Healthy Relationships
3.4	Your Thoughts and Feelings Affect Your Actions	4.4	What Does "Karma" Mean to You?
3.5	Acting vs. Reacting	4.5	Your Role in Creating Your School Culture
3.6	Your Actions Affect Your Brain	4.6	Sharing What You Learn
3.7	Using Tools to Calm Down	4.7	Recognizing That You Are Complete
3.8	Using Tools to Energize	4.8	Connecting with Your Best Self
3.9	Being with Emotions	4.9	Seeing the Good in Yourself and Others
3.10	Practicing Making Choices	4.10	We Are All Connected
3.11	Imagining Possibilities	4.11	Strengthening Yourself to Strengthen Your Community
3.12	Review and Reteaching	4.12	Review and Reteaching

❖ **Wrap-Up**

To conclude the TLS session, students are led through a minute of guided meditation, followed by the closing bell. Connection questions are asked at the end to reinforce lesson themes and monitor student learning and engagement.

Physical Arrangements

TLS has been implemented in a wide variety of settings including classrooms, after-school programs, detention facilities, shelters, and community centers. Although classroom arrangement is flexible, it is important that all students have a clear view of you during group instruction. Arranging the classroom so that students face the front of the room or in a horseshoe shape is optimal. For lessons including forward folds, it will be important to arrange students in a circle or horseshoe so that nobody is facing someone else's back. This is indicated at the beginning of the mindful movement section of those lessons.

It is also helpful to post the agenda somewhere in the room so that students can refer to it. Posting and going over the agenda can help students manage their own focus and attention during TLS sessions. In general, use your best judgment to manage the room so that students feel comfortable and safe enough to practice TLS.

Extension Activities

In addition to the core TLS practices, we have included suggestions for extension activities for each lesson. Through the core TLS practices and extension activities, the TLS curriculum engages various learning styles and modalities.

Required Materials and Instructional Options

We designed TLS for flexible implementation so that it can be used across a wide variety of contexts. We have found that some intervention support materials are necessary to implement TLS, while others are optional supports our instructors have found helpful over the years. Depending on the nature of the context and budgetary or space constraints, reasonable substitutions can be made to support implementation.

Appropriate Material	Function	Substitutions	Requirement
Musical chime or singing bowl	Helps students gain focus	Bell, gong	Yes
Instructor manual	Provides instructor with resources and support	TLS video lessons	Yes
Extension activities workbook	Provides additional activities to deepen lessons learned and apply them to real life		No

GUIDELINES FOR INSTRUCTORS

Adapting TLS for Your Students

In order to lead TLS with students, it is important to practice on your own. Your own mindfulness practice, whatever form it takes, will provide the foundation for sharing TLS authentically and effectively. TLS has been implemented successfully with a variety of students of different ages, abilities, and backgrounds. The specific physical postures are not as important as the focus and breathing employed with them. Thus, students of various physical abilities may adapt the postures as needed and still get the benefits of TLS.

Many of the lessons introduce real-life scenarios in order to support students' understanding and motivation to master skills. To maximize interest, we encourage instructors to utilize examples involving situations that are appropriate to the interests, abilities, and level of understanding of students in the classroom. Each script should be considered an example, and may be modified to fit the unique needs of your students. When adapting the script, however, be sure to maintain the language of invitation and choice, and always remind students of the breath. This is important in order to ensure that your TLS sessions are accessible to students of all backgrounds and experiences, including those dealing with trauma.

As with any intervention, student choice is critical for success. We have found that on average and with time, very few students decline to participate. However, there may be some that would prefer not to participate on a given day or in general. It is important to allow students space and time to determine their comfort level with TLS, and to understand that some students may take longer than others to give it a try or may participate in a way that is different than expected. It is the role of the instructor to maintain a safe space for students who are participating while inviting (not forcing) those who may need more time to decide to engage with the practice. As you become familiar with the practice, adapt the movements to student needs and comfort level—if students are reluctant to practice, start with simple seated exercises and increase movement as they are ready.

Timing

We have found that having a predictable structure for class helps relieve anxiety and create a safer environment for students to participate. However, the background knowledge information contained in the lessons can be communicated to the students at any time during class. If students seem restless at the beginning of class, it might be better to get them moving first and go over the background information in small bits as you do the mindful movement, or at the end of the session when students are more calm and focused.

Maintaining a Safe and Comfortable Space

Repetition and clarity about expectations are important. Review expectations before starting each TLS session if students have difficulties following them. If students have no problems following the expectations, you may choose to only review them periodically.

In order for students to feel comfortable practicing, it is important that you do all of the movements with the students as you instruct. This helps create a sense of community and safety in the room, as everyone focuses on their own experience in parallel practice. Practicing as you instruct also helps you to teach with authenticity and curiosity, drawing on your own moment-to-moment experience.

Be sensitive to students' needs. They may send vocal or subtle messages about unmet needs for safety, sometimes in ways that seem like "acting out." If students feel like others may look at them or make fun of them in TLS, they will not participate fully. Maintaining a safe container not only includes ensuring that all students follow the expectations for behavior, but also can include managing the space between students, asking students to move to where they will be able to focus on themselves more easily, listening and responding to students' concerns, and checking in individually with students whenever possible.

Addressing Barriers to Practice

Students often come into the practice with preconceived notions, including what kind of people meditate or do yoga, how to do TLS correctly, or how the practice is supposed to affect them. These ideas and beliefs can be invisible barriers to participation. Do your best to address these notions before or as they come up. Remind students that TLS is a practice that unites mind, body, and (if appropriate) spirit, and that all cultures have practices to do this. You might even start out asking if students have their own practices to help them bring their body and mind into sync, and honor the diverse practices and traditions in the room.

It is often important to remind students that there is no right or wrong way to feel when doing TLS. It is also not about fixing ourselves or feeling better. The point of the practice is to build awareness of our experience right now, without judging it or ourselves. When asking the closing questions, make sure your words and gestures don't express a preference for students to report feeling better, relaxed, focused, and so on after the practice. Rather, remind students that TLS builds skills through regular practice over time. Assure them that however they are feeling is just fine, and congratulate them for taking the time to notice.

Pacing and Language

Pacing for the mindful movement section is important. Be sure to allow time for students to breathe deeply and notice the sensations in their bodies. This may seem slow to students at first and cause discomfort or acting out. Feel free to point this out and help students refocus through verbal cues, bringing attention to certain sensations and to the breath. The verbal cues offered in the scripts can be helpful. If you come up with other cues that help you in your own practice, feel free to try these out as well. Teaching from your own personal experience can often be more powerful than teaching from a script. However, it is best to keep cues concrete and body-oriented in order to keep students' focus on the present.

You may notice that the language used in the lesson scripts is invitational rather than commanding and provides options whenever possible. This is a mind-body modality, and it is important for students to feel that they are in control of their own bodies. In using this type of language, you allow students to build capacity in sensing and caring for their own bodies and making healthy choices for themselves. If this type of language is different from your normal classroom language, or if you find it challenging to teach in this way, use the examples in the scripts to help you.

For the mindful breathing and guided meditation, it's important to provide concrete cues to help students focus on the present. For students dealing with trauma, silence can be a trigger. Observe student reactions to these sections and provide options for connecting with the body if students appear distressed, zoned out, or uncomfortable. (For example, Sun Breaths p. 80.)

Embedding TLS in Existing Systems

We designed TLS to fit within existing systems that serve young people. We have found that with minor modifications, TLS fits easily within a response-to-intervention (RTI) framework and can be used as a universal, selected, or indicated intervention option.

Monitoring Fidelity of Implementation

Treatment fidelity is the extent to which the intervention was delivered as intended. The TLS instructor manual provides a checklist for each lesson to help instructors monitor whether they have covered each lesson element. It is suggested that, as they go through the lessons, instructors make a note here of any lessons that were not completed or might need review. At the end of each unit is a review lesson, in which the instructor can reteach any material from the unit that was not covered or understood well.

Assessing Student Outcomes and Monitoring Progress

It is important that instructors actively monitor student engagement and learning as well as lesson fidelity on a regular basis. Instructors may choose to check in periodically with students verbally or through questionnaires or other assignments. It is highly recommended to check in with students personally, as much as possible, especially if a student is having difficulty participating.

Instructor Qualifications and Training

TLS has been successfully delivered by a diverse array of practitioners including yoga instructors, teachers, social workers, and psychologists. The curriculum is designed with two options for delivery:

1. In-class TLS (done in the classroom, at desks or standing, normally shorter in duration)

2. Mat-based TLS (done on yoga mats, normally longer in duration)

Mat-based TLS should be implemented by a trained and certified yoga instructor. In-class TLS, the focus of this publication, is shorter and can be implemented by a wider range of people. That being said, the more experience one has practicing yoga or TLS, the better they will be at teaching it.

CURRICULUM LESSON PLANS KEY

Text for Units 1–4 lesson plans include:

1. Overview and lesson plan information

2. Narrative text—scripts for each lesson's section and mindful movement, breathing, or meditation instruction

3. Commentary for instructors' reference

Narrative Scripts

Instructor narratives to students are indented and shown in italics, per the example shown below. When text is not italicized, this indicates a brief lesson plan comment and is not read to students—per the pause shown in the example. This nonitalicized text is for instructor reference and lesson plan commentary—not script that is read to students.

Example:

Begin to notice the rhythm of your own breath. Is it fast or slow? Deep or shallow? Take a few moments to notice the rhythm of your own breath. Pause.

Now take a moment to find your pulse by pressing your fingers against the inside of your wrist, or under your jawbone, or on the left side of your chest.

Text shown between the narratives is intended for instructor reference, and contains lesson plan or topics commentary. This text will not be read to students.

UNIT 1

Stress Resilience

Recent studies show that students experience high levels of stress that often impede their ability to do well in school. Stress touches all aspects of life and can stem from instability at home, poverty, inadequate support systems, traumatic events, high pressures for success, or peer pressure. In this unit, we bring awareness to the body's reactions to stress and then learn and practice ways to manage stress within the body.

We all know what stress feels like, but why do we get it? What is it useful for? The stress response is the body's way of getting you to safety when it senses you are in danger. It creates the conditions in your body for you to run to safety, fight, or freeze until danger passes. This has been very useful for our survival as a species, but nowadays, the stress response often turns on when we are not really in danger. This can cause all kinds of problems.

When the stress response is activated, it deactivates the parts of your brain that handle memory, thinking, making choices, impulse control, and listening. For this reason, stress can affect how well you do in school and the choices you make. In addition, feeling stressed out all the time can have long-term, damaging effects on your heath. Learning ways to manage stress and activate the relaxation response in your body can help mitigate the damaging affects of stress.

Stress management involves knowing what causes you stress, noticing the signs of stress in the body, and using tools to deactivate the stress response when you don't need it. Developing stress management skills now can help you think clearly, make healthy choices in the near-term, and keep you healthier throughout your life.

Objectives

❖ Define stress management
❖ Learn how stress affects body and mind (long- and short-term effects)
❖ Learn foundational skills for stress management
❖ Understand the relaxation response
❖ Build strength and flexibility

LESSON 1.1: UNDERSTANDING WHAT STRESS IS ABOUT

In this lesson, students will be introduced to the TLS program. This lesson uses Mountain Pose as the introductory pose. Experiencing oneself in stillness in Mountain Pose helps build clarity, strength, and stability. Physically, this pose:

❖ Improves posture
❖ Strengthens thighs, knees, and ankles
❖ Supports emotional stability and calm

Lesson objectives are: (a) students will learn what the stress response is and why it is important, and (b) students will practice tools to deactivate the stress response when it is not helpful.

STUDENT OVERVIEW

REVIEW EXPECTATIONS (2 MINUTES)

Review the expectations for TLS sessions, including:

❖ Students clear desks of all distractions including books, papers, food, cell phones, and music.
❖ One-mic rule: one person talks at a time. If students have questions, they can raise a hand or ask at the end of class. Assure students that there will be a few minutes dedicated to questions at the end of each session.
❖ Students focus on their own body and breath. That means not making comments about self or others, not touching others, and not distracting others from their experience.
❖ Students try their best to participate at all times. (However, participation may look different for each student. For some students, it may mean doing only the breathing for as long as they need, until they choose to engage with the movement. Allow students to come to the practice at their own pace, as long as they are not being distracting or disrespect-

ful toward others. Engaging with one's body and mind through TLS is always a choice, and every day is a different experience.)

ACTIVATE BACKGROUND KNOWLEDGE (3 MINUTES)

In response to the class environment each day, you may wish to provide this information to students when you feel it would be best received—that may be at the beginning of class, woven into the mindful movement, or before the silent sitting.

The stress response is our body's way of warning us when there is danger and getting us to safety. It is also known as the fight-or-flight response because our body mobilizes all of its functions to help us fight, flee, or freeze to stay safe. When we feel emotions like anger, fear, and anxiety, those are signs that the stress response is activated. You can feel stress even when you're not really in danger, like when you have a big test or project for school, or when you have problems with your friends or siblings. It can be harmful to us if we feel stress all the time. We need to know how to "deactivate" the stress response when we don't need it.

Activation Question 1.1

Think of a recent time when you felt stressed. How would you rate the level of stress you felt on a scale from 1–10, with 10 being the most stressed and 1 being the most relaxed? Can anyone share an example?

Give students a chance to reflect, and choose a few students to share their responses with the class.

In this lesson, we will learn some tools for deactivating the stress response when we don't need it.

ACTION, BREATHING, CENTERING

OPENING BELL AND FOCUSED BREATHING (2 MINUTES)

We will start our time together today by trying to focus our attention on a sound. I would like to ask you all to listen to the sound of the bell I am going to ring.

Try to keep your attention on the sound of the bell for as long as you can, and when you can't hear it anymore, please raise your hand.

Ring bell or singing bowl.

❖ Allow to vibrate to completion and until all students have raised their hands.

❖ Then ask students to do the same thing, this time closing their eyes or looking down at their desks to focus just on their hearing, and ring the bell again.

❖ Wait until all students have raised their hands.

That was very good. Now I'll lead you in a breathing exercise:
  • *You can keep your eyes closed, or just look down.*
  • *Let all the air out of your lungs.*
  • *Now breathe in, breathe out.*

Lead class in simple breathing, encouraging them to breathe deeply and smoothly.

Continue for 3–4 rounds.

Then tell students that you are going to do the bell exercise one more time.

Ring the bell again, and students raise their hands when they can no longer hear it.

MINDFUL MOVEMENT AND POSE OF THE DAY (6 MINUTES)

Arm Movement with Hands Clasped (Seated)

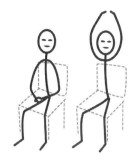

If it feels comfortable, sit up a little bit straighter. Clasp your hands together in front of you. As you breathe in, reach your palms up toward the ceiling as high as it feels comfortable. As you breathe out, watch your hands as they come back down to your lap. As we do this, we'll breathe in for 4 counts and out for 8 counts. Be sure to go at your own pace if I count too slow or too fast for you. Breathe in 1, 2, 3, 4, breathe out 1, 2, 3, 4, 5, 6, 7, 8.

Lead students in 4–5 rounds of rhythmic 4:8 breathing while demonstrating the movement. After counting out loud for a few rounds, invite students to count silently to themselves. Then invite students to relax their arms and go back to breathing normally, letting their hands just rest on their lap or desk.

Robin

For the next movement, feel free to start really small, and experiment with making the movement bigger as you feel comfortable. When you breathe in, draw the shoulders back. When you breathe out, bring the shoulders forward and the chin down.

Guide students while they try a few rounds.

You can keep the movement small, or if you want to get more of a stretch in your back, you can make it bigger. When you breathe in, take the shoulders back and lift the center of your chest. And when you breathe out, round the back, pulling the belly in and letting the head drop forward. Try a few more rounds, noticing what this movement feels like in your body.

Mountain—Pose of the Day

The pose of the day today is Mountain Pose. When we feel stressed, we often feel "swept away" by our feelings and cannot think clearly. Mountain helps us feel our feet firmly on the ground so that we can clear our mind and remember our own strength. To do Mountain Pose, we will stand up.

Pause as students stand up.

Experiment with pointing your feet straight forward, parallel to each other. Does that feel different from how you usually stand?

Show students the difference between casually standing with toes pointed out, and standing with feet parallel and pointed forward.

As you breathe in, imagine there is a quarter sitting on top of your head, and lift it up toward the ceiling. As you breathe out, let your shoulders and arms relax. Breathe in and stand tall, reaching your head toward the ceiling. Breathe out and feel your feet on the floor, wiggling your toes if that helps you feel them. Take 1 more deep breath: standing tall, feeling your feet on the floor and shoulders relaxed.

Mountain Variations

Now close your eyes if it feels okay, or you can look down. If you lean forward slightly, you might feel how your weight shifts into your toes. When you lean back, feel your weight shift to your heels.

Pause, experiment with leaning forward and back.

Now lean to the right side and notice how the weight shifts in the feet. Do the same to the left.

Pause, leaning side to side.

Now let your body sway in a slow circle, noticing how the weight shifts in the feet as you do that.

Pause.

Allow your circles to get smaller and smaller until you settle and find stillness right in the center. That's your center of gravity, where you are strongest. Take a few breaths here, noticing your feet on the floor and the top of your head reaching high.

If you'd like, press your hands together at your chest, and either close your eyes or look down at the place where your hands meet. Can someone lead us in 3 breaths, saying: "Breathe in, breathe out"?

Choose a student to lead the breaths, making sure the student leads them slowly to allow for deep breathing.

Good, thank you (student name). *Now, let's match the breath to movement. Still standing up straight, let's breathe in and raise our arms overhead. Breathe out, and bring your hands to your chest.*

Repeat 2 times.

Trunk Twists

Now you can shake out your arms and take your feet a little farther apart. Make some space between yourself and others, and either let your arms swing or keep your arms bent at chest height as you twist from side to side. Notice the feeling of the air as it brushes past your hands.

Pause.

To keep your knees safe, lift the opposite heel as you twist to the side.

Pause.

If you want to twist more, you can breathe out each time you turn to the side. Demonstrate twisting and breathing out in short, audible spurts each time you twist to the side. Allow students to continue twisting for about 30 more seconds.

Let your twists get smaller and smaller until you are still. Come back to Mountain Pose with your palms together at your chest and take a few breaths, noticing how your body feels.

Have another student lead 3 breaths.

Have the students sit down at their desks with backs straight and feet resting on the floor. Proceed to the Mindful Breathing section.

MINDFUL BREATHING (3 MINUTES)

Lead class in simple breathing, encouraging them to breathe deeply and smoothly.

Begin to notice the rhythm of your own breath. Is it fast or slow? Deep or shallow? Take a few moments to notice the rhythm of your own breath. Pause.

Now take a moment to find your pulse by pressing your fingers against the inside of your wrist, or under your jawbone, or on the left side of your chest. Pause, give students a chance to find their pulse.

Now notice the rhythm of your heartbeat as you breathe. Take a moment to notice if your heartbeat gets faster on the inhale or faster on the exhale. If you have a hard time feeling your heartbeat, don't worry. It's beating in there somewhere, but sometimes it's hard to quiet the mind enough to feel it. Just try focus on your breathing and see what happens.

Allow students to find the answer for themselves. Ask them to share what they find by raising a hand. In people with optimal heart rate variability, the heartbeat gets faster on the inhale and slower on the exhale. This can be increased through mindful breathing practices.

Yes, in many people, the heart beats faster on the inhale. If that's not what you found, don't worry because every body is different. But you might try this experiment again later in the semester, and see if things change.

When we inhale, we give the body more energy, and the heart beats faster.

When we exhale, the body relaxes more, and the heartbeat slows.

That's why the relaxation breath we did in the beginning, where we inhaled for 4 and exhaled for 8, is good for calming down our body.

Let's try the 4-to-8 breath again. If I count too slow or too fast for you, feel free to go with your own rhythm. When you're ready, let all the air out of your lungs.

Pause.

Breathe in 1, 2, 3, 4.

Breathe out 1, 2, 3, 4, 5, 6, 7, 8.

Repeat 2 times.

Now count silently to yourself, breathing in for 4.

Pause.

And out for 8.

Pause.

In deep, out slow.

Pause.

Try to breathe this way for 3 more rounds without losing count.

Pause, allow students to breathe on their own for a few rounds.

Good! You can go back to breathing normally if you'd like.

WRAP-UP

GUIDED MEDITATION AND CLOSING BELL (1 MINUTE)

We're going to end class by sitting silently for 1 minute, just noticing your breathing and how your body feels.

Feel free to close your eyes or look down to help you concentrate only on yourself.

If you like, you can even put your head down and rest it on your arms.

Pause.

Notice your feet resting on the floor, your legs relaxed on the seat.

Notice where your arms and hands are. Maybe you can allow your arms and shoulders to relax a bit more.

Notice how you're breathing.

You might even allow the muscles of your face to relax as you breathe.

Long pause, allow students to sit silently for remainder of the minute.

I will now ring the bell one last time. Listen to the bell and when you can't hear it anymore, please look up at me.

Ring bell and allow it to vibrate to completion.

CONNECTION QUESTIONS (3 MINUTES)

How do you feel?

If you had to rate the level of stress you feel now from 1–10 what would it be? Why?

Ask students if they have any questions about what we did today or about TLS or mindfulness in general, and thank them for their participation.

LESSON 1.2: RECOGNIZING STRESS IN YOUR BODY

In this lesson, students will be introduced to Crescent Moon Pose. Physically, this pose:

❖ Tones and strengthens the abdominal muscles
❖ Stretches the sides of the body

Lesson objectives are (a) students will learn to recognize the physical signs of stress in their bodies, and (b) students will practice noticing body sensations.

STUDENT OVERVIEW

REVIEW EXPECTATIONS (2 MINUTES)

Review the expectations for TLS sessions, including:

❖ Students clear desks of all distractions including books, papers, food, cell phones, and music.
❖ One-mic rule: one person talks at a time. If students have questions, they can raise a hand or ask at the end of class. Assure students that there will be a few minutes dedicated to questions at the end of each session.
❖ Students focus on their own body and breath. That means not making comments about self or others, not touching others, and not distracting others from their experience.
❖ Students try their best to participate at all times. (However, participation may look different for each student. For some students, it may mean doing only the breathing for as long as they need, until they choose to engage with the movement. Allow students to come to the practice at their own pace, as long as they are not being distracting or disrespectful toward others. Engaging with one's body and mind through TLS is always a choice, and every day is a different experience.)

ACTIVATE BACKGROUND KNOWLEDGE (3 MINUTES)

In response to the class environment each day, you may wish to provide this information to students when you feel it would be best received—that may be at the beginning of class, woven into the mindful movement, or before the silent sitting.

> *Once you learn the signs of stress in your body, you can be aware of stress as it starts to arise. Recognizing the signs of stress is the first step in managing stress. Knowing how to manage your stress is important because when the stress response is activated you cannot hear, think, or remember as well. Have you ever gotten nervous during a test and forgotten everything you knew? Have you ever been so mad at someone that you didn't know what to say to them or didn't really hear what they were saying to you? Stress causes the part of your brain that thinks, listens, and remembers to temporarily shut down. But you can learn ways to manage your stress so that you can keep that part of your brain working, even during potentially stressful situations.*

Activation Question 1.2

> *Do you notice any changes in your body when you feel angry, nervous, or stressed? If so, what are they?*

Give students a chance to reflect, and choose a few students to share their responses with the class.

> *In this lesson, we will practice noticing sensations in the body, which will help us to recognize stress when it comes up.*

ACTION, BREATHING, CENTERING

OPENING BELL AND FOCUSED BREATHING (2 MINUTES)

We will start our time together today by trying to focus our attention on a sound. I would like to ask you all to listen to the sound of the bell I am going to ring.

Try to keep your attention on the sound of the bell for as long as you can, and when you can't hear it anymore, please raise your hand.

Ring bell or singing bowl.

* Allow to vibrate to completion and until all students have raised their hands.
* Then ask students to do the same thing, this time closing their eyes or looking down at their desks to focus just on their hearing, and ring the bell again.
* Wait until all students have raised their hands.

  That was very good. Now I'll lead you in a breathing exercise:
  * *You can keep your eyes closed, or just look down.*
  * *Let all the air out of your lungs.*
  * *Now breathe in, breathe out.*

Lead class in simple breathing, encouraging them to breathe deeply and smoothly.

Continue for 3–4 rounds.

Then tell students that you are going to do the bell exercise one more time.

Ring the bell again, and students raise their hands when they can no longer hear it.

MINDFUL MOVEMENT AND POSE OF THE DAY (6 MINUTES)

Mountain

Let's stand up in Mountain Pose. Who remembers how to do Mountain Pose? Have a student describe or demonstrate Mountain Pose.

Review the elements of Mountain Pose:

❖ Feet parallel and about hip-width distance apart
❖ Standing up straight, shoulders relaxing downward

If you'd like, press your hands together at your chest. You can either close your eyes or look down at the place where your hands meet. Can someone lead us in 3 breaths, saying, "breathe in, breathe out"?

Choose a student to lead the breaths, making sure the student leads them slowly to allow for deep breathing.

Good thank you (student's name).

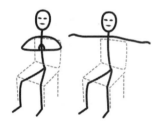

Arm Movements

Make sure you have enough space to reach your arms out to the sides. When we breathe in, we'll take the hands forward, still pressed together, and then apart and out to the sides. When we breathe out, we'll bring the hands back together and then into the chest. Lead students in a couple of rounds, breathing in to reach the hands forward and out, and breathing out to bring them together and in. Encourage students to notice the fingers reaching out wide, and then pressing together as they come back in to the chest.

Good. Now let's add in the breath we did last time, breathing in for 4 counts as we reach wide and breathing out for 8 counts as we bring the arms in.

Lead students by counting a few rounds.

Now as you do it, count silently in your head. In for 4.

Pause.

Out for 8.

Pause.

See if you can do 2 more rounds silently without losing count.

Pause as students continue.

After this round, let your arms relax and hang down. Notice how they feel. Maybe they feel warmer or tingly or like they're more attached to your body. Take a few breaths as you notice.

Shake-Out

The next time we breathe in, we'll tense up all the body, from feet to head. Breathe in, and squeeze all your muscles, starting with your feet, then your ankles, legs, belly, arms, shoulders, and face. Hold it.

Pause.

Breathe out, and relax and release. Let's try it again. Breathe in and squeeze all your muscles: feet, ankles, legs, belly, shoulders, arms, face. Hold it.

Pause.

Breathe out, and relax and release. One more time: Breathe in and squeeze all your muscles, even the little ones. Even the ones deep inside. Hold it.

Pause.

Breathe out, and relax and release. Now let's shake out our arms and legs counting down from 5.

Demonstrate the next movement for the students and allow them to join in:

- Shake your right arm and hand as you say: 5, 4, 3, 2, 1.
- Shake your left arm and hand as you say: 5, 4, 3, 2, 1.
- Shake your right leg, counting down from 5.
- Shake your left leg, counting down from 5.
- Then repeat the whole sequence counting down from 4.

Again counting down from 3, from 2, and 1—the last round will consist of one quick shake per limb. Immediately invite students to be as still as possible, noticing any effects of the shaking. This could include tingling in the hands or legs, or faster breathing or heartbeat.

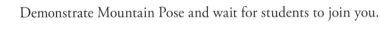

Crescent Moon—Pose of the Day

The pose of the day is called Crescent Moon. Can someone tell me what shape a crescent moon is?

Wait for responses.

Yes! A crescent moon is round and arched. That's the shape our body makes when we do this pose. Crescent Moon stretches and tones the sides of the body. It can help us tune into the sensations we feel in the body and focus on the present moment.

To do Crescent Moon, we start in Mountain Pose.

Demonstrate Mountain Pose and wait for students to join you.

Breathing in, reach your arms up straight and clasp your hands together.

If that doesn't feel good, you can hook your thumbs together with your palms facing forward, or just reach your arms up straight keeping your hands apart.

Encourage students to try it out, even if they do not want to use their arms at all. Meet them where they are.

Each time we breathe in, we stand up tall.
- *When we breathe out, we lean to the right side, just enough to feel a stretch along the side of your body.*
- *Breathe in, stand up tall.*
- *Breathe out lean to the left side.*

Continue to match the movement to your breath. Can someone lead the breath for us? Choose a student to lead the breath.

Try to feel both feet pressing into the floor evenly as you lean to each side.

Allow students to try out 2 rounds per side.

The next time you breathe out, let your arms relax at your sides.

Thank the student for leading the breath.

This time we'll hold the pose for 3 breaths per side. Notice if your body or mind start to feel stressed out or you get the urge to come out of the pose early. See if you can notice any small or big sensations in your body. Use your breath to keep you calm, even if it's uncomfortable, knowing you can come out of the pose at any time if you need to.

Lead students in Crescent Moon to the right and then to the left.
For each side, choose a student to lead the class in 3 breaths. Once you are done, breathe in to stand tall, and breathe out to relax and release

Just stand in Mountain Pose with your arms hanging at your sides. Notice if you feel anything different in your body:
- *Maybe some warmth in your waist or your arms, or*
- *Maybe your heartbeat or breathing is faster than before.*

Close your eyes if you want.

Take a moment to just notice what you feel.

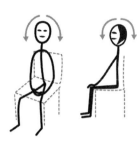

Neck Movements

Please have a seat. Experiment with finding a way to sit comfortably, but with your back straight. We are going to do some movements to release tension in the neck. As you're ready:

- *On an exhale, let your right ear fall toward your right shoulder.*
- *On your next breath in, return your head to center.*
- *On your next breath out, let your left ear fall toward your left shoulder. Repeat this movement 2 more times per side. If this movement seems boring, focus on taking deeper breaths and matching the movement with your breathing.*

Pause while students finish.

Bring your head back to center. This time as you breathe out, look to the right. You can close your eyes or look slightly down. As you breathe in, bring your head back to center, and as you breathe out, turn your head to the left. Repeat this movement 2 more times.

Pause.

Now when you breathe in, lift your chest up and look slightly upward. Be careful not to strain your neck. As you breathe out, tuck your chin and let your head bow forward. Repeat this movement 2 more times with your breath.

When students finish, have them relax and notice how they feel.
Proceed to the Mindful Breathing section.

MINDFUL BREATHING (3 MINUTES)

Lead class in simple breathing, encouraging them to breathe deeply and smoothly.

Notice the rhythm of your breath right now. Your breath will have a different rhythm at different times.

Pause to allow students to notice their breath.

As you notice your breath, let each breath get a little deeper.

Pause.

Close your eyes if it feels okay, or just look down at your desk. Allow your breath to fill up your lungs completely, and then empty them completely.

Pause to let them breathe deeply for a few rounds.

Continue to make full, complete inhales and full, complete exhales. Notice if you are still sitting up straight, or if you forgot about your posture. Sitting with your back straight can help you breathe easier. If you'd like, place a hand on your upper chest. Can you feel your chest move as you breathe?

Pause.

Maybe you can notice your ribs expanding and contracting. Can you feel the ribs in your back move? The ribs go all the way around from the front to the back of the body.

Pause.

Maybe you notice a little bit of movement in your shoulders. Just notice.

Pause.

Now place your hand on your belly if that feels okay. Do you notice your belly moving as you breathe? If you can't feel your belly move, you might try letting the muscles in that area relax a little bit more as you breathe.

Pause.

Now let both hands rest on your lap or on your desk. Without using your hands, can you notice different parts of your body moving as you breathe?

Pause for a longer time.

Whatever you feel is just fine—that's just how you are breathing in this moment.

You've done a great job. Return to breathing normally. Open your eyes and notice how you feel.

WRAP-UP

GUIDED MEDITATION AND CLOSING BELL (1 MINUTE)

We're going to end class by sitting silently for 1 minute, just noticing your breathing and how your body feels.

Feel free to close your eyes or look down to help you concentrate only on yourself.

If you like, you can even put your head down and rest it on your arms.

Pause.

Notice your feet resting on the floor, your legs relaxed on the seat.

Notice where your arms and hands are. Maybe you can allow your arms and shoulders to relax a bit more.

Notice how you're breathing.

You might even allow the muscles of your face to relax as you breathe.

Long pause, allow students to sit silently for remainder of the minute.

I will now ring the bell one last time. Listen to the bell and when you can't hear it anymore, please look up at me.

Ring bell and allow it to vibrate to completion.

CONNECTION QUESTIONS (3 MINUTES)

How do you feel? What is one sensation, or feeling, you felt in your body as we practiced today?

Invite a few students to share their responses, providing examples if needed (i.e. stretch in the side, feeling feet on the floor.)

If you didn't notice any sensations, that's okay too. As we practice TLS we get better and more comfortable with noticing what our body is telling us.

Ask students if they have any questions about what we did today or about TLS or mindfulness in general, and thank them for their participation.

LESSON 1.3: KNOWING WHAT STRESSES YOU

In this lesson, students will be introduced to Forward Warrior (Warrior I) Pose. Physically, this pose:

- ❖ Strengthens and tones the legs and ankles
- ❖ Opens the chest to allow for deeper breathing

Lesson objectives are (a) students will identify the stressors in their lives, and (b) students will practice noticing uncomfortable sensations while remaining calm.

STUDENT OVERVIEW

REVIEW EXPECTATIONS (2 MINUTES)

Review the expectations for TLS sessions, including:

- ❖ Students clear desks of all distractions including books, papers, food, cell phones, and music.
- ❖ One-mic rule: One person talks at a time. If students have questions, they can raise a hand or ask at the end of class. Assure students that there will be a few minutes dedicated to questions at the end of each session.
- ❖ Students focus on their own body and breath. That means not making comments about self or others, not touching others, and not distracting others from their experience.
- ❖ Students try their best to participate at all times. (However, participation may look different for each student. For some students, it may mean doing only the breathing for as long as they need, until they choose to engage with the movement. Allow students to come to the practice at their own pace, as long as they are not being distracting or disrespectful toward others. Engaging with one's body and mind through TLS is always a choice, and every day is a different experience.)

ACTIVATE BACKGROUND KNOWLEDGE (3 MINUTES)

In response to the class environment each day, you may wish to provide this information to students when you feel it would be best received—that may be at the beginning of class, woven into the mindful movement, or before the silent sitting.

> *In addition to knowing what stress feels like in the body, it's helpful to know what events or situations tend to stress you out. Things that cause you stress are called "stressors." Knowing your stressors can help you manage your stress by taking actions to prepare yourself before the stress builds up. Each person is different, and what stresses you out may not bother someone else at all.*
>
> *What are the top 1–2 things in your life that stress you out?*

Give students a chance to reflect, and choose a few students to share their responses with the class.

> *In this lesson, we will explore more challenging poses and notice what we feel in our bodies as we do them. We'll practice noticing uncomfortable sensations while keeping calm, and practice a breathing technique we can use to keep calm when entering into a stressful situation.*

ACTION, BREATHING, CENTERING

OPENING BELL AND FOCUSED BREATHING (2 MINUTES)

We will start our time together today by trying to focus our attention on a sound. I would like to ask you all to listen to the sound of the bell I am going to ring.

Try to keep your attention on the sound of the bell for as long as you can, and when you can't hear it anymore, please raise your hand.

Ring bell or singing bowl.

❖ Allow to vibrate to completion and until all students have raised their hands.

❖ Then ask students to do the same thing, this time closing their eyes or looking down at their desks to focus just on their hearing, and ring the bell again.

❖ Wait until all students have raised their hands.

That was very good. Now I'll lead you in a breathing exercise:
- *You can keep your eyes closed, or just look down.*
- *Let all the air out of your lungs.*
- *Now breathe in, breathe out.*

Lead class in simple breathing, encouraging them to breathe deeply and smoothly.

Continue for 3–4 rounds.

Then tell students that you are going to do the bell exercise one more time.

Ring the bell again, and students raise their hands when they can no longer hear it.

MINDFUL MOVEMENT AND POSE OF THE DAY (6 MINUTES)

Mountain

Today we'll start right away in Mountain Pose. Let's all stand up, please. Notice:
- *Your feet right under your hips,*
- *Your shoulders lined up right above your hips and feet, and*
- *Your head balanced right between your shoulders.*
- *See if you can stand up a little taller.*

When you're ready, press your hands together at your chest, and either close your eyes or look down at the place where your hands meet.

Can someone lead us in 3 breaths?

Choose a student to lead the breaths, making sure the student leads them slowly to allow for deep breathing.

Good, thank you (student's name). Go ahead and release your arms, letting them hang down at your sides.

Arm Movements—Reaching Overhead

When you're ready, the next time you breathe in, raise your arms high above your head. You can also look up at the ceiling if it feels okay on your neck.

As you breathe out smoothly, press your hands together and bring them to your chest.

Help students tune into their bodies by offering verbal cues like,

* ❖ "See if you can notice what muscles work to lift your arms up," or
* ❖ "As you bring your arms down, notice your hands making a straight line through the air."

Let's do this 3 times.

Choose a student to lead the breath as you repeat the movement.

Trunk Twists

Now you can shake out your arms and take your feet a little farther apart. Make sure you have space between yourself and others so you can swing your arms without hitting each other.
* *Let your arms relax and swing, or if you prefer, keep you arms bent at chest height as you twist from side to side.*
* *Lift the opposite heel as you twist to the side so that you don't hurt your knees.* Pause.
* *See if you can feel the air brushing past your hands.* Pause.
* *Notice if you feel a gentle stretch in your back as you twist.*

- *You can twist a little more by breathing out each time you turn to the side.*

Demonstrate twisting and breathing out in short, audible spurts each time you twist to the side.

Now let your twists get smaller and smaller until you are still.

Come back to Mountain Pose with your palms together at your chest and take a few breaths, noticing how your body feels.

Forward Warrior—Pose of the Day

The pose of the day is called Forward Warrior, or Warrior I. Forward Warrior builds strength and flexibility in the lower body. As we build strength, we breathe calmly and learn to be level-headed in times of stress.

Start in Mountain Pose.
- *Take a deep breath and notice your feet on the floor.*
- *As you're ready, bring your right leg a few feet behind you, and press your right heel down on the floor.*
- *Keep your right leg straight as you bend your left leg, bringing the knee directly over the ankle. If your knee goes past your ankle, you can widen your stance by bringing your right foot farther back. Your hips and chest are facing forward.*

Now, let's breathe in and straighten both legs, reaching our arms up like we're going to touch the ceiling. Breathing out, we'll bend the front leg and bring our hands to our chest. Try to keep the back leg straight. Let's try this 2 more times. As you do this, notice if you feel more of a stretch in the legs when you bend or when you straighten.

Choose a student to lead the breaths.

Now if it feels okay, stay in the pose with the front knee bent for 3 more breaths:

- *Keep breathing — that's 3;*
- *Notice if your legs feel warm, or tired, or stretching—2;*
- *1 more breath—1. Great job!*

Come back to Mountain Pose. Take a breath, noticing how you feel.

Repeat the whole Forward Warrior sequence with the left leg back. End in Mountain Pose.

Now we'll take 3 breaths in Mountain Pose, focusing on feeling your feet on the floor and your breath flowing in and out. Who can lead us in 3 breaths?

Have one student lead the class by saying "breathe in, breathe out" 3 times.

Shoulder Movements

We'll do the last movement seated, with your back straight and feet on the floor, if that feels comfortable. Let your hands rest on your thighs. We will do several movements with our shoulders and coordinate them with our breath.

To encourage participation, you can ask the students if they ever feel tension in their shoulders and explain that these movements can help relieve that tension.

On your next inhale, shrug your shoulders up toward your ears like you're saying, "I don't know." On the exhale, let them drop.

Demonstrate.

Imagine bringing tension into that area as you breathe in, and letting it go as your shoulders drop.

Repeat 3 times.

Next, we'll rotate our shoulders in circles. You can choose to make the circles small or big, whatever feels better to you. As you inhale, roll the shoulders up and back. As you exhale, bring the shoulders down and forward.

Repeat 3 times, then reverse the direction and repeat 3 times.

Notice if you feel your shoulders getting warmer. Once you are done, let the shoulders and arms rest and take a deep breath.

Proceed to the Mindful Breathing section.

MINDFUL BREATHING (3 MINUTES)

The relaxation breathing that we've been practicing, where we breathe in for 4 counts and out for 8 counts, is helpful for calming down the nervous system. You can use it anytime you might find yourself in a stressful situation. Nobody around you even has to know you are doing it! Let's practice it now.

Make sure you are sitting comfortably with your back straight. You can close your eyes at any time, or just look down at your desk to help you focus inward. I'm going to start you out:
- *Counting to 4 for the inhale, and*
- *Counting to 8 for the exhale.*

If I count too slow or too fast for you, feel free to go with your own rhythm. Let all the air out of your lungs.

Pause.

- *Breathe in 1, 2, 3, 4.*
- *Breathe out 1, 2, 3, 4, 5, 6, 7, 8.*

Repeat counting 2 more times.

Now count silently to yourself:
- *Breathing in for 4.*

Pause.

- *Breathing out for 8.*

Pause.

Now I'm going to be quiet and let you practice 3 rounds on your own. See if you can keep your mind on the counting and the feeling of the breath. If your mind wanders to other thoughts, bring it back to focus on your breathing as soon as you realize it.

Pause, allow students to breathe on their own for 3 rounds.

Good! You can go back to breathing normally. Notice if it was easy for you to keep your focus on your breath for 3 breaths, or if you got distracted by other thoughts. Sometimes the mind is clear and focused, and sometimes it's fuzzy and jumps around. As you practice noticing how you feel in your mind and your body, you become better at recognizing when you feel stress building up.

WRAP-UP

GUIDED MEDITATION AND CLOSING BELL (1 MINUTE)

We're going to end class by sitting silently for 1 minute, just noticing your breathing and how your body feels.

Feel free to close your eyes or look down to help you concentrate only on yourself.

If you like, you can even put your head down and rest it on your arms.

Pause.

Notice your feet resting on the floor, your legs relaxed on the seat.

Notice where your arms and hands are. Maybe you can allow your arms and shoulders to relax a bit more.

Notice how you're breathing.

You might even allow the muscles of your face to relax as you breathe.

Long pause, allow students to sit silently for remainder of the minute.

I will now ring the bell one last time. Listen to the bell and when you can't hear it anymore, please look up at me.

Ring bell and allow it to vibrate to completion.

CONNECTION QUESTIONS (3 MINUTES)

How do you feel? At the beginning of class we all shared a couple things that cause us stress. Think of one of the things you identified as a stressor. How could you use what you have learned in TLS to help you deal with that stressor? Can anyone share an example?

Ask students if they have any questions about what we did today or about TLS or mindfulness in general, and thank them for their participation.

LESSON 1.4: HOW STRESS AFFECTS YOUR BREATH

In this lesson, students will be introduced to Side Warrior (Warrior II) pose. Physically, this pose:

❖ Releases tension in the hips
❖ Strengthens the legs and ankles
❖ Tones muscles in the arms and back

Lesson objectives are (a) students will learn how stress can affect the breath, and (b) students will practice noticing how they are breathing in challenging and relaxing poses.

STUDENT OVERVIEW

REVIEW EXPECTATIONS (2 MINUTES)

Review the expectations for TLS sessions, including:

❖ Students clear desks of all distractions including books, papers, food, cell phones, and music.
❖ One-mic rule: one person talks at a time. If students have questions, they can raise a hand or ask at the end of class. Assure students that there will be a few minutes dedicated to questions at the end of each session.
❖ Students focus on their own body and breath. That means not making comments about self or others, not touching others, and not distracting others from their experience.
❖ Students try their best to participate at all times. (However, participation may look different for each student. For some students, it may mean doing only the breathing for as long as they need, until they choose to engage with the movement. Allow students to come to the practice at their own pace, as long as they are not being distracting or disrespectful toward others. Engaging with one's body and mind through TLS is always a choice, and every day is a different experience.)

ACTIVATE BACKGROUND KNOWLEDGE (3 MINUTES)

In response to the class environment each day, you may wish to provide this information to students when you feel it would be best received—that may be at the beginning of class, woven into the mindful movement, or before the silent sitting.

Sometimes the way you are breathing can tell you about how you're feeling. When you feel fearful, angry, or anxious, your breathing might get short or even stop for a time. Breathing like this can make you feel more irritable, anxious, depressed, or angry. It can also keep you from getting the oxygen to your brain that you need in order to be able to think clearly and feel good.

Activation Question 1.4

Do you notice a change in your breathing when you are feeling stressed out, angry, or nervous? What do you notice?

Give students a chance to reflect, and choose a few students to share their responses with the class.

Today we'll work on simply noticing our breath and how it changes as we do challenging and relaxing movements.

ACTION, BREATHING, CENTERING

OPENING BELL AND FOCUSED BREATHING (2 MINUTES)

We will start our time together today by trying to focus our attention on a sound. I would like to ask you all to listen to the sound of the bell I am going to ring.

Try to keep your attention on the sound of the bell for as long as you can, and when you can't hear it anymore, please raise your hand.

Ring bell or singing bowl.

- ❖ Allow to vibrate to completion and until all students have raised their hands.
- ❖ Then ask students to do the same thing, this time closing their eyes or looking down at their desks to focus just on their hearing, and ring the bell again.
- ❖ Wait until all students have raised their hands.

  That was very good. Now I'll lead you in a breathing exercise:
  - *You can keep your eyes closed, or just look down.*
  - *Let all the air out of your lungs.*
  - *Now breathe in, breathe out.*

Lead class in simple breathing, encouraging them to breathe deeply and smoothly. Continue for 3–4 rounds.

Then tell students that you are going to do the bell exercise one more time.

Ring the bell again, and students raise their hands when they can no longer hear it.

MINDFUL MOVEMENT AND POSE OF THE DAY (6 MINUTES)

Mountain

Let's all stand up in Mountain Pose.

If needed, review the elements of Mountain Pose:

- ❖ Feet parallel and hip-width distance apart
- ❖ Shoulders relaxed
- ❖ Standing tall

As you breathe in, imagine there is a quarter sitting on top of your head, and lift it up toward the ceiling. As you breathe out, let your shoulders and arms relax. Breathe in and stand tall, reaching your head toward the ceiling. Breathe out and feel your feet on the floor, wiggling your toes if that helps you feel them. Take 1 more deep breath: standing tall, feeling your feet on the floor and shoulders relaxed.

Shoulder Movements (With Hug)

Let's warm up the shoulders and release some tension there. When you're ready, raise your arms straight out to the sides.
- *Breathe in, raise your shoulders up near your ears.*
- *Breathe out, slide your shoulders down away from your ears, reaching your hands wide.*
- *Breathe in shoulders up.*
- *Breathe out, shoulders down and arms wide.*

Now cross your arms in front of you, right on top of left. Cross them as tight as you can, maybe grabbing onto your shoulder blades. Can anyone show us where your shoulder blades are? Grab onto them tight and breathe in, raising your shoulders near your ears. When you breathe out, keep your tight grip and see if you can lower your shoulders down away from your ears a bit. Take another breath, letting your shoulders sink down, and notice if you feel a stretch in the shoulders or upper back.

Pause.

Good, when you're ready release your arms.

Repeat the whole sequence, first with arms out and then crossing the left arm over the right. Then relax the arms and notice how your shoulders feel.

Crescent Moon

Breathing in, reach your arms up straight and clasp your hands together. If that doesn't feel good, you can hook your thumbs together with your palms facing forward, or just reach your arms up straight keeping your hands apart. If you don't feel like lifting your arms right now, you can try it with your hands on your hips.

Each time we breathe in, we reach our hands up and stand tall. When we breathe out, we lean to the right side. Don't lean too far, just enough to feel a stretch. Breathe in, stand up tall. Breathe out lean to the left side. Continue to match the movement to your breath. Can someone lead the breath for us?

Choose a student to lead the breath.

Try to feel both feet pressing into the floor evenly as you lean to each side.

Allow students to try out 2 rounds per side.

The next time you breathe out, let your arms relax at your sides.

Thank the student for leading the breath.

This time we'll hold the pose for 3 breaths per side. Notice if your breath gets faster, or if you start to hold your breath. See if you can keep your breath flowing even if the pose feels stressful to you.

Lead students in Crescent Moon to the right and then to the left. For each side, choose a student to lead the class in 3 breaths. Once the 3 breaths to the right are over:

- Breathe in to come to standing tall
- Breathe out to go to the other side
- Take 3 breaths on the left side
- Then breathe in to stand tall, breathe out to relax and release.

Stand in Mountain Pose with your arms hanging at your sides. Close your eyes if you want. Notice how you are breathing now.

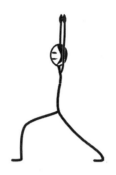

Forward Warrior

Let's come into Forward Warrior, and from there we'll come into the pose of the day, Side Warrior. Like Forward Warrior, Side Warrior builds strength and flexibility in the lower body, and also in the abdominal area. Because we're building strength, the pose might feel difficult. Notice if your breath changes or stops as you do the pose, and try to keep it flowing as best you can.

We'll start in Mountain Pose. Take a deep breath and notice your feet on the floor.

Pause.

As you're ready, bring your right leg straight back and press your right heel down on the floor for Forward Warrior.

Keep your right leg straight as you bend your left leg, bringing the knee directly over the ankle. If your knee goes past your ankle, you can lengthen your stance by bringing your right foot farther back. Your hips and chest are facing forward. Notice any warmth or tiredness in your front leg as you hold the pose. Notice any stretching you feel in your back leg.

(Student name), *can you lead us in 3 breaths here?*

Side Warrior—Pose of the Day

We'll now come into the main pose of the day: Side Warrior. Keeping your legs and feet where they are, turn your chest and hips to face the right. Your arms extend out from your shoulders, left arm forward and right arm back, with the palms facing down. You'll want your right knee to be right above your ankle, so if you need to you can take your legs farther apart. Make sure your knee doesn't lean to the side, but rather bends straight forward.

Try to have your spine straight up and down. Are you still breathing? Now as you're ready, the next time you breathe in, straighten your legs and reach your arms up, palms together. As you breathe out, bend your left leg and bring your arms back out to the sides, palms down. Notice how the legs feel as you bend and straighten the left leg. Let's do this 2 more times with the breath.

Practice with students, connecting the movement with the breathing.

This time stay in Side Warrior with your left leg bent. Let's try to stay here for 3 breaths, focusing your eyes on your left middle finger. Notice if you get the urge to come out of the pose, and if you do, take another deep breath before you decide to hold the pose or come out of it. Who can lead us in 3 breaths?

Repeat the sequence with the left leg back. End with 3 breaths in Mountain Pose.

Instruct students to take a seat. Proceed to the Mindful Breathing section of lesson.

MINDFUL BREATHING (3 MINUTES)

Today we've been talking about how stress affects how we breathe. The amount of breaths you take in a minute is said to reflect about how many thoughts go through your head in a minute. It is important to remember that sometimes the stress we have is not caused by actual events or situations, but by the thoughts we have about those events and situations. Let's do a little experiment to test this. I'm going to count 1 minute, and during the minute, you will count how many breaths you take—breathing in and out equals 1 breath. Once I say "stop," remember your number or write it down somewhere. Are you ready to count your breaths? Ready, go!

Pause for 1 minute.

Stop. Remember how many breaths you took, or write it down. Let's see a show of hands.

- *How many people breathed 0-10 breaths?*
- *11–20? 21–30? 31–40? More than 40?*

Okay, you can put your hands down. Do you think the number of breaths you take per minute corresponds to the number of thoughts going through your head? Have you heard of the phrase, "my mind is racing?" When you stress out you tend to have a lot of thoughts going through your head, your body is tense, and your breathing is short and quick. When you're calm, the thoughts don't come and go as fast, you are able to focus more easily, your muscles are more relaxed, and you breathe more slowly. So the quicker your breaths are, the more stress you might feel. Remember that stress is a big term that could include anger, anxiety, fear, or other emotions that activate the stress response. Try noticing how quick your breath is at different times during the day, and see if it corresponds with how much stress you feel.

No matter how many breaths you took just now, you can always use the breath to calm the mind and body.

So let's take a few breaths together, this time focusing on making each breath last a little longer. You don't have to breathe super deep, just make each breath a little smoother and longer.

Pause.

See if you can take 3 smooth, long breaths, keeping your mind focused on your breathing. Pause.

Good concentration, everyone.

Now that you understand the relationship between your breathing and your thoughts, how could you use your breath to help slow your mind and ease stress?

WRAP-UP

GUIDED MEDITATION AND CLOSING BELL (1 MINUTE)

We're going to end class by sitting silently for 1 minute, just noticing your breathing and how your body feels.

Feel free to close your eyes or look down to help you concentrate only on yourself.

If you like, you can even put your head down and rest it on your arms.

Pause.

Notice your feet resting on the floor, your legs relaxed on the seat.

Notice where your arms and hands are. Maybe you can allow your arms and shoulders to relax a bit more.

Notice how you're breathing.

You might even allow the muscles of your face to relax as you breathe.

Long pause, allow students to sit silently for remainder of the minute.

I will now ring the bell one last time. Listen to the bell and when you can't hear it anymore, please look up at me.

Ring bell and allow it to vibrate to completion.

CONNECTION QUESTIONS (2 MINUTES)

How are you feeling? How are you breathing right now?

Ask students if they have any questions about what we did today or about TLS or mindfulness in general, and thank them for their participation.

LESSON 1.5: USING YOUR BREATH AS A TOOL

In this lesson, students will be introduced to Reverse Plank Pose. Physically, this pose:

❖ Stretches the arms and shoulders and opens up the chest
❖ Tones the thighs and gluteus

Lesson objectives are (a) students will learn how to use their breathing to manage stress, and (b) students will practice using calming breathing techniques.

STUDENT OVERVIEW

REVIEW EXPECTATIONS (2 MINUTES)

Review the expectations for TLS sessions, including:

❖ Students clear desks of all distractions including books, papers, food, cell phones, and music.
❖ One-mic rule: one person talks at a time. If students have questions, they can raise a hand or ask at the end of class. Assure students that there will be a few minutes dedicated to questions at the end of each session.
❖ Students focus on their own body and breath. That means not making comments about self or others, not touching others, and not distracting others from their experience.
❖ Students try their best to participate at all times. (However, participation may look different for each student. For some students, it may mean doing only the breathing for as long as they need, until they choose to engage with the movement. Allow students to come to the practice at their own pace, as long as they are not being distracting or disrespectful toward others. Engaging with one's body and mind through TLS is always a choice, and every day is a different experience.)

ACTIVATE BACKGROUND KNOWLEDGE (3 MINUTES)

In response to the class environment each day, you may wish to provide this information to students when you feel it would be best received—that may be at the beginning of class, woven into the mindful movement, or before the silent sitting.

> *When you're feeling stressed, you can use your breath to help you stay level headed, and even to change your mood. It's important to have tools to calm yourself and clear your mind because the actions you take when you are stressed, angry, or upset affect you and others. If you can use your breath to clear your mind and calm yourself before you act, you are less likely to do something that's harmful to yourself or others. Sometimes we can't change the things that stress us out, but we can use the breath to help us not be so strongly affected by them.*

Activation Question 1.5

> *Have you ever used any of the breathing exercises that you learned in TLS outside of class? Can anyone share an example with us?*

Give students a chance to reflect, and choose a few students to share their responses with the class.

> *Today we'll practice breathing techniques that you can do anytime, without anyone knowing you are doing it, to calm your body and mind.*

ACTION, BREATHING, CENTERING

OPENING BELL AND FOCUSED BREATHING (2 MINUTES)

We will start our time together today by trying to focus our attention on a sound. I would like to ask you all to listen to the sound of the bell I am going to ring.

Try to keep your attention on the sound of the bell for as long as you can, and when you can't hear it anymore, please raise your hand.

Ring bell or singing bowl.

❖ Allow to vibrate to completion and until all students have raised their hands.
❖ Then ask students to do the same thing, this time closing their eyes or looking down at their desks to focus just on their hearing, and ring the bell again.
❖ Wait until all students have raised their hands.

That was very good. Now I'll lead you in a breathing exercise:
- *You can keep your eyes closed, or just look down.*
- *Let all the air out of your lungs.*
- *Now breathe in, breathe out.*

Lead class in simple breathing, encouraging them to breathe deeply and smoothly. Continue for 3–4 rounds.

Then tell students that you are going to do the bell exercise one more time.

Ring the bell again, and students raise their hands when they can no longer hear it.

MINDFUL MOVEMENT AND POSE OF THE DAY (6 MINUTES)

Mountain

Let's all stand up in Mountain Pose.

If needed, review the elements of Mountain Pose:

❖ Feet parallel and hip-width distance apart
❖ Shoulders relaxed
❖ Standing tall

Press your hands together at your chest, and either close your eyes or look down at the place where your hands meet. Can someone lead us in 3 breaths, saying, "breathe in, breathe out"?

Choose a student to lead the breaths, making sure the student leads them slowly to allow for deep breathing.

Standing Backbend as a Movement

For the next pose, we are going to do a standing back bend as a movement. Pay attention to how your back feels, and only go as far as feels comfortable.

- *Inhale, reaching up.*
- *Exhale, bringing your hands to your lower back.*
- *Support your lower back as you inhale, opening up your chest as you lean back a bit.*
- *Exhale, returning to standing.*

We will repeat this movement 3 times. Notice if your breath gets shallow—try to keep it deep and smooth.

Ask a student to lead the movement.

When done, have students stand in Mountain Pose with hands to chest or arms at their sides. Have them take a breath and notice their feet in contact with the floor (wiggling their toes if that helps.)

Side Warrior

Let's come into Side Warrior.

From Mountain Pose, step your left leg way back.
- *Press your left heel to the floor and face your hips and chest to the left.*
- *As you bend your right leg, it's important to make sure your knee bends straight forward over your ankle.*
- *Go ahead and bend and straighten your right leg a few times, noticing how sensations in the legs and hips change as the leg bends.*
- *When you're ready, keep your right leg bent and raise your arms to shoulder height.*
- *If you want, look over the fingers of your right hand.*
- *Notice your spine straight up and down. Looks good!*
- *Now as you breathe in, straighten your legs.*
- *If it feels okay, reach your arms up, palms together.*
- *Breathe out, bend your front leg and bring your arms back out to the sides, palms down.*
- *Let's do this 2 more times with the breath. Breathe in lift, breathe out bend.*

Notice the strength in your legs. Pause.

This time stay in Side Warrior with your right leg bent. Let's try to stay here for 3 breaths. Use your breathing to keep you calm and alert, even if the pose feels difficult. Who can lead us in 3 breaths?

Choose a student to lead the breaths. When they are done, have students come back into Mountain Pose:

- ❖ Bring the left leg forward.
- ❖ Take a few mindful breaths in Mountain before doing the whole Side Warrior sequence with the right leg back.

When you finish, come back to Mountain Pose and have students take 3 breaths with hands pressed together at chest. Have one student lead the breaths.

Reverse Plank—Pose of the Day

Reverse Plank should only be performed if students have a sturdy chair on which to lean. If they have rolling chairs or if chairs are not stable, skip this pose. In this case, you can treat Standing Backbend as a Movement as the pose of the day, as the benefits are similar, and do a Seated Twist (see next) instead of Reverse Plank.

We'll now come into the pose of the day: Reverse Plank.

Reverse Plank opens up the chest area. This allows us to breathe better, getting more oxygen to the brain. This pose also gives us more energy and can help us feel better when we're tired or depressed. To do it you'll have to:
- *Scoot forward to sit right at the edge of your chair.*
- *Grab on to the sides of your chair with both your hands, about 10–12 inches behind you.*
- *Place your feet flat on the floor.*
- *You have two options here, either straighten out your legs and lift your hips off the chair, or keep your legs bent and your hips on your chair.*
- *As you breathe in, press down with your feet and lift your hips off the chair, trying to form a straight line with your legs and chest. If you choose to keep your hips on your chair, lift your chest toward the ceiling, lengthening your arms.*
- *As you breathe out, lower your hips back down.*

Great! Now that you have it, we'll try to hold the pose.

As you're ready, inhale and raise your body. Hold the pose for 3 breaths:
- *Feel your chest rise with your breath—that's 3.*
- *Use your breathing to keep you calm—2.*

• Maybe you feel your arms or shoulders getting tired or stretching . . . 1 more . . . 1. Exhale and slowly lower down. Good job!

Now as you're ready, sit comfortably with your feet on the floor.

Notice how your arms and chest feel after that pose.

Seated Twist

The last pose we'll do today is a Seated Twist to release the muscles in the back.
• Breathing in, sitting up as straight as you can.
• Breathing out, turning to face the right. Take your right hand to the back of your seat and your left hand to your right thigh.
• Try to hold the twist as you breathe deeply.
• Breathing in, see if you can sit up a little straighter in the twist.
• Breathing out, maybe you can twist a little more.
• Breathing in again, notice if your back is straight.
• Breathing out, maybe you can let your shoulders come down away from your ears.
• Take 1 more breath.

Great! As you breathe in, come back to face forward.

You can use the metaphor of a sponge to explain the twist. When you twist a wet sponge, the water comes out. When you put a twisted sponge in the water and let it untwist, it fills with new water. That's what we're doing in our bodies, and it helps us to flush out old fluids and toxins.

Lead students in the seated twist on the other side. You can also have a student say "breathe in, breathe out" as they twist. After students return to face forward, invite them to notice how they are breathing, and notice if they feel they can breathe any deeper or easier after doing the twist.

Proceed to the Mindful Breathing section.

MINDFUL BREATHING (3 MINUTES)

Make sure you are sitting comfortably. Bring your attention to your breath. Pause. *Notice what parts of your body move as you breathe. You may notice your chest moving, your back, your belly, or your shoulders. Just notice.* Pause. *Now place a hand on your belly if that feels comfortable. Try to relax the muscles around your belly and breathe deeper. You might feel your belly push out against your hand as you inhale, and go back in toward your spine as you exhale. This kind of "belly breathing" activates the relaxation response in the body. If you notice that your belly does not move out as you breathe in, it's okay. It may be a sign that you're holding some stress in your body, or you may be used to breathing the other way out of habit. Just try to relax the muscles around your belly and breathe deeply.*

Slowly breathing in to let the belly push out against the hand, breathing out to let the belly come back in. In, out.

Pause.

Now if you had your hand on your belly, take it off and just rest your arms on your desk or your lap. See if you can feel the belly's movement from the inside, without touching it with your hand, as you breathe.

Pause for about 30 seconds.

Good job. Come back to breathing normally and notice how you feel, and any effect the breathing might have had on you.

WRAP-UP

GUIDED MEDITATION AND CLOSING BELL (1 MINUTE)

We're going to end class by sitting silently for 1 minute, just noticing your breathing and how your body feels.

Feel free to close your eyes or look down to help you concentrate only on yourself.

If you like, you can even put your head down and rest it on your arms.

Pause.

Notice your feet resting on the floor, your legs relaxed on the seat.

Notice where your arms and hands are. Maybe you can allow your arms and shoulders to relax a bit more.

Notice how you're breathing.

You might even allow the muscles of your face to relax as you breathe.

Long pause, allow students to sit silently for remainder of the minute.

I will now ring the bell one last time. Listen to the bell and when you can't hear it anymore, please look up at me.

Ring bell and allow it to vibrate to completion.

Connection Questions (3 minutes)

How are you feeling?

Can anyone share an example of when you can use your breath as a tool?

Ask students if they have any questions about what we did today or about TLS or mindfulness in general, and thank them for their participation.

LESSON 1.6: HOW STRESS AFFECTS YOUR ABILITY TO LEARN

In this lesson, students will be introduced to Wide-Legged Crescent Pose. Physically, this pose:

❖ Tones the abdomen and waist
❖ Stretches the intercostal muscles (muscles between the ribs), facilitating deep breathing.

Lesson objectives are (a) students will understand how stress inhibits thinking, hearing, and memory, and (b) students will practice tools they can use in class to focus the mind.

STUDENT OVERVIEW

REVIEW EXPECTATIONS (2 MINUTES)

Review the expectations for TLS sessions, including:

❖ Students clear desks of all distractions including books, papers, food, cell phones, and music.
❖ One-mic rule: one person talks at a time. If students have questions, they can raise a hand or ask at the end of class. Assure students that there will be a few minutes dedicated to questions at the end of each session.
❖ Students focus on their own body and breath. That means not making comments about self or others, not touching others, and not distracting others from their experience.
❖ Students try their best to participate at all times. (However, participation may look different for each student. For some students, it may mean doing only the breathing for as long as they need, until they choose to engage with the movement. Allow students to come to the practice at their own pace, as long as they are not being distracting or disrespectful toward others. Engaging with one's body and mind through TLS is always a choice, and every day is a different experience.)

ACTIVATE BACKGROUND KNOWLEDGE (3 MINUTES)

In response to the class environment each day, you may wish to provide this information to students when you feel it would be best received—that may be at the beginning of class, woven into the mindful movement, or before the silent sitting.

When the stress response is activated, we cannot think, remember, or listen as well. This is because the stress hormones turn "off " the part of the brain that thinks and remembers, called the Prefrontal Cortex, located right here (place hand on forehead). If you try to study, remember things for a test, or listen to your teacher when your stress response is activated, you will have a hard time. Learning to deactivate the stress response can help you do better in school, without putting in extra hours of study time!

Activation Question 1.6

From your own experience, do you think that when you feel stress it affects how you do in school? If so, how?

Remind students that stress is a broad term that includes anxiety, anger, irritation, fear, and so on.

Give students a chance to reflect, and choose a few students to share their responses with the class.

Today we'll practice focusing and clearing the mind of stress by tuning in to sensations in the body and our breathing.

ACTION, BREATHING, CENTERING

OPENING BELL AND FOCUSED BREATHING (2 MINUTES)

We will start our time together today by trying to focus our attention on a sound. I would like to ask you all to listen to the sound of the bell I am going to ring.

Try to keep your attention on the sound of the bell for as long as you can, and when you can't hear it anymore, please raise your hand.

Ring bell or singing bowl.

❖ Allow to vibrate to completion and until all students have raised their hands.
❖ Then ask students to do the same thing, this time closing their eyes or looking down at their desks to focus just on their hearing, and ring the bell again.
❖ Wait until all students have raised their hands.

That was very good. Now I'll lead you in a breathing exercise:
- *You can keep your eyes closed, or just look down.*
- *Let all the air out of your lungs.*
- *Now breathe in, breathe out.*

Lead class in simple breathing, encouraging them to breathe deeply and smoothly.

Continue for 3–4 rounds.

Then tell students that you are going to do the bell exercise one more time.

Ring the bell again, and students raise their hands when they can no longer hear it.

MINDFUL MOVEMENT AND POSE OF THE DAY (6 MINUTES)

Mountain

Let's all stand up in Mountain Pose.

If needed, review the elements of Mountain Pose:

❖ Feet parallel and hip-width distance apart
❖ Shoulders relaxed
❖ Standing tall

Press your hands together at your chest if you'd like, and either close your eyes or look down at the place where your hands meet. Can someone lead us in 3 breaths, saying, "breathe in, breathe out"?

Choose a student to lead the breaths, making sure the student leads them slowly to allow for deep breathing.

Sun Breaths

We'll start with a few Sun Breaths. There are 2 options here:

(1) The first option is to raise your arms out to the sides and up to your ears as you breathe in. As you exhale, bring your arms back down to your sides.

(2) The second option is to do this pose just using your hands: opening up your fingers on the inhale, and closing them into a fist on the exhale.

Demonstrate hand movements.

The cool thing about using your hands is that you can do this with your hands in your lap in class and nobody has to know you're doing mindfulness!

Let's try a few rounds of this, doing whichever option you choose, and matching the movement to the breath.

Inhale, exhale.

You can choose to match your movements and breathing to mine, or follow your own rhythm.

Do 4–5 rounds of Sun Breaths with the students.

Shoulder Movements

Now feel free to let your arms rest at your sides. We are going to do some movements to relax the shoulders. On your next inhale:

- *Shrug your shoulders up toward your ears, like you're saying, "I don't know."*
- *On the exhale, let them drop.*
- *Let's do that 3 more times.*

Imagine bringing tension into that area and letting it go as your shoulders drop.

Pause as you practice shoulder shrugs with students.

For the next movement we will rotate our shoulders in circles: As you inhale, roll the shoulders up and back, and as you exhale bring them down and forward. You can make your circles as big or as small as you want. Even if it feels boring, try not to speed up your movements—keep it slow enough so that you can take deep breaths.

Repeat 3 times. Reverse direction and repeat 3 times.

Wide-Legged Crescent—Pose of the Day

Today's pose is Wide-Legged Crescent Pose. While doing Wide-Legged Crescent, we focus on the sensations, or feelings, in the sides of the body. This can help calm the nervous system and focus the mind on what's happening right now. This movement also

stretches the intercostal muscles between the ribs, allowing us to breathe more deeply.

For this pose, you might choose to bring your feet wider apart, maybe 2–3 feet, so you have more stability. When you breathe in, if it feels okay, take both arms high above your head. When you breathe out take your right hand down to your right thigh and reach your left arm over your head. Lean to the right, but see if you can press your left foot into the floor.

When you breathe in, come back to standing straight up with arms reaching high, if that's comfortable.

If you notice a reluctance to participate, let students know that they can also do the pose with arms down at the sides or with hands on their hips. Meet them where they are at.

When you breathe out lean to the other side. Continue to move with your breath, concentrating on the sensations your feel in your body as you move. Maybe you feel a stretching sensation in your ribs, or in your shoulder, or somewhere else. Can someone lead us by saying, "Breathe in, breathe out," nice and slow?

Repeat movement 3 times on each side. When finished, lower arms to sides.

Trunk Twists

Make sure you have an arm's length of space between yourself and the people around you. Let your arms dangle or bend them at chest height as you gently twist from side to side. Notice the feelings in your arms, shoulders, and back as you do this. You can twist more by lifting the opposite heel as you twist to the side.

Pause.

You can also use your breath for this, breathing out each time you turn to the side.

Demonstrate twisting and breathing out in short, audible spurts each time you twist to the side for about 30 seconds.

Now let your twists get smaller and smaller until you are still. Come back to Mountain Pose with your palms together at your chest and take a few breaths. You might notice your heart beating, or sensations in your arms or shoulders, or your feet in contact with the floor.

Have another student lead 3 breaths.

Robin

Good job! Let's all take a seat. Sit facing the front with your feet on the floor if possible.

Pause.

Robin Pose is another movement you can do in class to help you focus your mind and release stress. If you'd like, you can start really small, so people can barely see the movement. You can make the movement bigger as you feel comfortable. When you breathe in, draw the shoulders back. When you breathe out bring the shoulders forward and the chin down.

Guide students while they try a few rounds.

If you would like to get more of a stretch in the back, when you breathe in take the shoulders back farther and lift the chest, and when you breathe out round the back, pulling the belly in and letting the head drop forward. Try a few more rounds taking full, complete breaths.

Pause.

When you finish the next round, sit still with your spine straight and your feet on the floor. Notice if it's a little easier to breathe deeply than it was when we started doing TLS today.

Proceed to the Mindful Breathing section.

MINDFUL BREATHING (3 MINUTES)

A great way to relax and focus when you are in class is by using the breath. And an added bonus is that nobody knows that you're doing it!

The 4:8 breath can activate the relaxation response in the body and allow the brain to think and remember more clearly. We'll breathe in for 4 counts, and breathe out for 8 counts. Let's do it together. Remember that you can go faster or slower than my counting if you need to.
- *Let all the air out of your lungs.*
- *Take a deep breath in for 4: 1, 2, 3, 4.*
- *Breathe out for 8: 1, 2, 3, 4, 5, 6, 7, 8.*
- *Breathe in 1, 2, 3, 4.*
- *Breathe out 1, 2, 3, 4, 5, 6, 7, 8.*

Repeat counting once more.

Now count to yourself silently, in for 4, out for 8. In deep, out slow.

Pause to let them practice breathing for a few rounds.

As you practice the breath, notice if there are any areas in your body where you feel tension, or muscles working when they don't need to—especially in your shoulders, or your hips, or your face. If you'd like, practice letting some of the tension out as you exhale.

Pause—for about 30 seconds.

After the next round of breathing, you can return to your normal breathing. Notice how your mind feels: maybe you have lots of thoughts, or few. Maybe your mind is clear, or busy, or distracted. Just notice.

WRAP-UP

GUIDED MEDITATION AND CLOSING BELL (1 MINUTE)

We're going to end class by sitting silently for 1 minute, just noticing your breathing and how your body feels.

Feel free to close your eyes or look down to help you concentrate only on yourself.

If you like, you can even put your head down and rest it on your arms.

Pause.

Notice your feet resting on the floor, your legs relaxed on the seat.

Notice where your arms and hands are. Maybe you can allow your arms and shoulders to relax a bit more.

Notice how you're breathing.

You might even allow the muscles of your face to relax as you breathe.

Long pause, allow students to sit silently for remainder of the minute.

I will now ring the bell one last time. Listen to the bell and when you can't hear it anymore, please look up at me.

Ring bell and allow it to vibrate to completion.

CONNECTION QUESTIONS (3 MINUTES)

How are you feeling? Can anyone give an example of how you can use the breathing, centering, or movement of TLS to help you focus in school?

Ask students if they have any questions about what we did today or about TLS or mindfulness in general, and thank them for their participation.

LESSON 1.7: CLEARING YOUR MIND, CALMING YOUR BODY

In this lesson, students will be introduced to Tree Pose. Physically, this pose:

❖ Helps to focus the mind
❖ Improves balance and concentration
❖ Strengthens and firms the legs and abdominal muscles

Lesson objectives are (a) students will learn about the relaxation response and why it is beneficial, and (b) students will practice using breathing techniques to calm themselves while doing challenging poses.

STUDENT OVERVIEW

REVIEW EXPECTATIONS (2 MINUTES)

Review the expectations for TLS sessions, including:

❖ Students clear desks of all distractions including books, papers, food, cell phones, and music.

❖ One-mic rule: one person talks at a time. If students have questions, they can raise a hand or ask at the end of class. Assure students that there will be a few minutes dedicated to questions at the end of each session.

❖ Students focus on their own body and breath. That means not making comments about self or others, not touching others, and not distracting others from their experience.

❖ Students try their best to participate at all times. (However, participation may look different for each student. For some students, it may mean doing only the breathing for as long as they need, until they choose to engage with the movement. Allow students to come to the practice at their own pace, as long as they are not being distracting or disrespectful toward others. Engaging with one's body and mind through TLS is always a choice, and every day is a different experience.)

ACTIVATE BACKGROUND KNOWLEDGE (3 MINUTES)

In response to the class environment each day, you may wish to provide this information to students when you feel it would be best received—that may be at the beginning of class, woven into the mindful movement, or before the silent sitting.

> *The opposite of the stress response in the body is the relaxation response. When the relaxation response is activated, it turns "off" the stress response, allowing us to listen and think clearly. You may think that the relaxation response would make us drowsy and unaware of our surroundings, but it's the opposite: activating the relaxation response makes the mind sharper and more focused, and helps us to be more aware of what's happening right now. Imagine you were playing a sport or performing in a play. Do you think you would probably perform better if you were calm and confident, or stressed and nervous?*

Students might mention that some people perform better under stress.

This is a good time to point out that a little stress can motivate us to work hard, but too much or prolonged stress can keep us from performing at our best, or even harm us.

Activation Question 1.7

> *How does your body feel when you are relaxed?*

Give students a chance to reflect, and choose a few students to share their responses with the class.

> *Taking deep breaths helps to activate the relaxation response. Today we'll practice breathing deeply, even when we're in difficult poses where we have to balance. This helps us practice keeping calm during challenging situations.*

ACTION, BREATHING, CENTERING

OPENING BELL AND FOCUSED BREATHING (2 MINUTES)

We will start our time together today by trying to focus our attention on a sound. I would like to ask you all to listen to the sound of the bell I am going to ring.

Try to keep your attention on the sound of the bell for as long as you can, and when you can't hear it anymore, please raise your hand.

Ring bell or singing bowl.

❖ Allow to vibrate to completion and until all students have raised their hands.
❖ Then ask students to do the same thing, this time closing their eyes or looking down at their desks to focus just on their hearing, and ring the bell again.
❖ Wait until all students have raised their hands.

That was very good. Now I'll lead you in a breathing exercise:
  - *You can keep your eyes closed, or just look down.*
  - *Let all the air out of your lungs.*
  - *Now breathe in, breathe out.*

Lead class in simple breathing, encouraging them to breathe deeply and smoothly.

Continue for 3–4 rounds.

Then tell students that you are going to do the bell exercise one more time.

Ring the bell again, and students raise their hands when they can no longer hear it.

MINDFUL MOVEMENT AND POSE OF THE DAY (6 MINUTES)

Mountain

Let's all stand up in Mountain Pose. As you breathe in, imagine there is a quarter sitting on top of your head, and lift it up toward the ceiling. As you breathe out, let your shoulders and arms relax. Breathe in and stand tall, reaching your head toward the ceiling. Breathe out and feel your feet on the floor, wiggling your toes if that helps you feel them. Take 1 more deep breath: standing tall, feeling your feet on the floor and shoulders relaxed.

Pause to allow students to breathe and focus.

Arm Movements

Make sure you have enough space to reach your arms out to the sides.

When you're ready, the next time you breathe in, take the hands forward, still pressed together, and then apart and out to the sides. Feel your arms and hands work as you reach your fingers wide. When you breathe out, bring the hands back together and then in to the chest.

Lead students in a couple of rounds, breathing in to reach the hands forward and out, and breathing out to bring them together and in.

Good. Now let's add in the relaxation breath:
- *Breathing in for 4 counts—as we reach wide, and*
- *Breathing out for 8 counts—as we bring the arms in.*

Lead students by counting a few rounds.

Now as you do it, count silently in your head.
- *In for 4.* Pause.
- *Out for 8.* Pause.

See if you can do 2 more rounds silently without losing count, noticing your hands and arms moving through the air.

Pause as students continue.

After this round, relax your arms and just notice how they feel.

Shake-Out

Now we'll practice tensing up the body and then releasing tension on the exhale. Sometimes we hold stress in the body so often that we forget what it feels like to relax. This exercise helps us practice releasing tension that we hold. If it feels okay, the next time you breathe in, tense up all your body, from your feet to your head. Squeeze all your muscles, starting with your feet, your ankles, legs, belly, arms, shoulders, and face. Hold it!

Pause.

Breathe out, and relax and release. Try it again. Breathe in and squeeze all your muscles: feet, ankles, legs, belly, shoulders, arms, face . . . hold it!

Pause.

Breathe out, and relax and release. One more time: breathe in and squeeze all your muscles, even the little ones! Even the ones deep inside! Hold it.

Pause.

Breathe out, relax and release. Now let's shake out our arms and legs counting down from 5.

Demonstrate the next movement for the students and have them to join in:

- *Shake your right arm and hand as you say: "5, 4, 3, 2, 1."*
- *Shake your left arm and hand as you say: "5, 4, 3, 2, 1."*
- *Shake your right leg, counting down from 5.*
- *Repeat with your left leg.*

Then repeat the whole sequence counting down from 4. Again, counting down from 3, from 2, and 1—the last round will consist of one quick shake per limb.

Take 3 full breaths in Mountain Pose, noticing any tingling, lightness, or other sensations in your arms, legs, or hands.

Standing Backbend as a Movement

For the next pose, we are going to do a standing back bend as a movement. Pay attention to how your back feels and only go as far as feels comfortable, so you don't hurt yourself.
- *Inhale, reaching up.*
- *Exhale, bringing your hands to your lower back.*
- *Support your lower back as you inhale, opening up your chest and leaning back a bit.*
- *Exhale, returning to standing.*

We will repeat this movement 3 times. Notice if your breath gets shallow—try to keep breathing deeply.

Ask a student to lead the movement. When done, have students stand in Mountain Pose with hands to chest and take a few deep breaths.

Tree—Pose of the Day

The pose of the day is called Tree Pose. Because this is a balancing pose, you have to concentrate on what your body is doing to avoid falling. Concentrating on the sensations in the body is one way to activate the relaxation response. Another way is by breathing deeply—when we take deep breaths in Tree Pose, we learn to calm ourselves in challenging or stressful situations. We'll start in Mountain Pose. Feel your left foot planted firmly on the floor. When you're ready, bring your right foot to your ankle, or to your calf, or to your thigh – but avoid placing it on your knee. Press the sole of the foot into the left leg and point the right knee out to the side.

If it feels okay, press your hands together at your chest. Are you holding your breath? Keep breathing! See if you can stand up a little taller, or breathe a little deeper. If you fall out of the pose, it is no big deal, just focus your eyes on one spot in front of you and try again.

(Student name), can you lead us in 3 breaths?

When you finish 3 breaths, shake out the legs and arms and try the pose on the other side, holding for the same length of time. If you notice students leaning on desks, let them know it's okay to use the desk for help, but encourage them to let go once in awhile to test out their balance. End in Mountain Pose with the palms at the chest and take 3 breaths together.

Dynamic Seated Twist

Good job! Let's all take a seat. Sit facing the front with your feet on the floor if you can.

Pause.

The last pose we'll do today is a Seated Twist. As you breathe in, sit up as straight as you can. As you breathe out, turn to face the right. Take your right hand to the back of your seat and your left hand to your right thigh. Notice any twisting or stretching you feel in your back as you twist. When you breathe in, face front again and feel your hands on your legs, arms relaxed. As you breathe out, twist to the left. Each time you breathe in, face the front and feel yourself centered and sturdy in your seat. Then twist again as you breathe out. Keep going with your own breath.

Allow students to continue for about 3 more rounds on their own. You can also have a student say "breathe in, breathe out" as they twist. After students return to face forward, have them take a deep breath and notice their posture, their feet on the floor, their weight on the seat. Proceed to the Mindful Breathing section.

MINDFUL BREATHING (3 MINUTES)

Make sure you are sitting comfortably. Bring your attention to your breath. Notice if your breath is smooth or uneven; if it's long or short.

Pause.

Try to smooth out your breath and make it last a little longer if that feels good to you.

Pause.

We're going to practice the belly breathing that we did a few sessions ago. Don't worry if breathing this way was hard for you last time, just give it a try like you've never done it before and see what happens this time. If it feels okay, bring a hand to your belly. As you breathe smoothly, notice if you belly is moving. If it's not, try to relax the muscles around your belly. Notice the belly moving outward as you breathe in. Notice it move back in toward your spine as you breathe out. You don't have to make you belly get super big, just notice any small movement that might happen as you breathe. Breathe in and out.

Pause to allow students to breathe for 3–4 rounds.

Now if you'd like, try doing the same breathing but take your hand off your belly. See if you notice the feeling of your belly moving out and in without using your hand. When we breathe in this way, we use a muscle called the diaphragm, located at the bottom of your ribs. This kind of breathing helps you activate the relaxation response in the body. So does paying attention to the little sensations in the body, like we're doing now. Notice any movement you feel in your belly or anywhere else as you breathe.

Pause—for about 30 seconds.

Good job. Come back to breathing normally and notice how you feel. Do you feel any different than before we did the breathing?

WRAP-UP

GUIDED MEDITATION AND CLOSING BELL (1 MINUTE)

We're going to end class by sitting silently for 1 minute, just noticing your breathing and how your body feels.

Feel free to close your eyes or look down to help you concentrate only on yourself.

If you like, you can even put your head down and rest it on your arms.

Pause.

Notice your feet resting on the floor, your legs relaxed on the seat.

Notice where your arms and hands are. Maybe you can allow your arms and shoulders to relax a bit more.

Notice how you're breathing.

You might even allow the muscles of your face to relax as you breathe.

Long pause, allow students to sit silently for remainder of the minute.

I will now ring the bell one last time. Listen to the bell and when you can't hear it anymore, please look up at me.

Ring bell and allow it to vibrate to completion.

CONNECTION QUESTIONS (3 MINUTES)

At the end of our sessions, many of you say that you feel more "relaxed."

- *At what point in the class do you notice that shift?*
- *What does it feel like?*

Ask students if they have any questions about what we did today or about TLS or mindfulness in general, and thank them for their participation.

LESSON 1.8: FEELING TIRED VS. FEELING RELAXED

In this lesson, students will be introduced to Arched Warrior Pose. Physically, this pose:

- ❖ Opens and stretches the chest and intercostal muscles
- ❖ Strengthens the legs
- ❖ Awakens and energizes the body and mind

Lesson objectives are (a) students will recognize the difference between feeling tired and feeling relaxed, and (b) students will practice techniques for relaxing and energizing themselves.

STUDENT OVERVIEW

REVIEW EXPECTATIONS (2 MINUTES)

Review the expectations for TLS sessions, including:

- ❖ Students clear desks of all distractions including books, papers, food, cell phones, and music.
- ❖ One-mic rule: one person talks at a time. If students have questions, they can raise a hand or ask at the end of class. Assure students that there will be a few minutes dedicated to questions at the end of each session.
- ❖ Students focus on their own body and breath. That means not making comments about self or others, not touching others, and not distracting others from their experience.
- ❖ Students try their best to participate at all times. (However, participation may look different for each student. For some students, it may mean doing only the breathing for as long as they need, until they choose to engage with the movement. Allow students to come to the practice at their own pace, as long as they are not being distracting or disrespectful toward others. Engaging with one's body and mind through TLS is always a choice, and every day is a different experience.)

ACTIVATE BACKGROUND KNOWLEDGE (3 MINUTES)

In response to the class environment each day, you may wish to provide this information to students when you feel it would be best received—that may be at the beginning of class, woven into the mindful movement, or before the silent sitting.

Sometimes after doing TLS, you feel more relaxed. Sometimes you feel tired. But they are not the same thing! Just because you feel relaxed doesn't mean you are tired. You can be relaxed and still have energy—for example, when you hang out with people you really like, you tend to feel relaxed and energized. However if you do feel tired after doing TLS, it's perfectly normal, especially if you have been dealing with stress or haven't gotten enough sleep. Practicing makes us more mindful of how we feel and what our bodies need.

Activation Question 1.8

What is the difference between feeling tired and feeling relaxed for you?

Give students a chance to reflect, and choose a few students to share their responses with the class.

Taking a little time to relax the body and mind can help you feel more energetic throughout the day. Today we'll practice some activities to help you relax and refresh your mind and body.

ACTION, BREATHING, CENTERING

OPENING BELL AND FOCUSED BREATHING (2 MINUTES)

We will start our time together today by trying to focus our attention on a sound. I would like to ask you all to listen to the sound of the bell I am going to ring.

Try to keep your attention on the sound of the bell for as long as you can, and when you can't hear it anymore, please raise your hand.

Ring bell or singing bowl.

- ❖ Allow to vibrate to completion and until all students have raised their hands.
- ❖ Then ask students to do the same thing, this time closing their eyes or looking down at their desks to focus just on their hearing, and ring the bell again.
- ❖ Wait until all students have raised their hands.

That was very good. Now I'll lead you in a breathing exercise:
- *You can keep your eyes closed, or just look down.*
- *Let all the air out of your lungs.*
- *Now breathe in, breathe out.*

Lead class in simple breathing, encouraging them to breathe deeply and smoothly.

Continue for 3–4 rounds.

Then tell students that you are going to do the bell exercise one more time.

Ring the bell again, and students raise their hands when they can no longer hear it.

MINDFUL MOVEMENT AND POSE OF THE DAY (6 MINUTES)

Mountain

Let's all stand up in Mountain Pose.

If needed, review the elements of Mountain Pose:

- ❖ Feet parallel and hip-width distance apart
- ❖ Shoulders relaxed
- ❖ Standing tall

Press your hands together at your chest, and either close your eyes or look down at the place where your hands meet. Can someone lead us in 3 breaths, saying, "breathe in, breathe out"?

Choose a student to lead the breaths, making sure the student leads them slowly to allow for deep breathing.

Shoulder Movements

Now you can rest your arms at your sides. We are going to do some movements to release tension from the shoulders. If it feels good to you, try to connect your breath with the movement. We'll make circles with the shoulders: as you inhale roll the shoulders up and back, and as you exhale bring them down and forward. You can make circles big or small, as you'd like.

Repeat "up and back" circles 3 times.

When you're ready, reverse the direction, breathing in as you bring the shoulders back and up, breathing out as you bring them forward and down. Try to go slow enough so you can take deep breaths.

Repeat "up and forward" circles 3 times.

Standing Backbend with Clasp

Next we'll stretch out the shoulders and chest. When you're ready, inhale, reaching your arms up. Exhale, clasping your hands behind your back, or if that's not comfortable, bringing your hands to your lower back. Inhale as you try to straighten your arms, drawing your shoulder blades together and lifting your chest. Exhale and return to standing, releasing your hands and relaxing your shoulders. Let's repeat this movement with the breath 3 times.

Ask a student to lead the breaths.

Good! Shake out your arms and shoulders and return to Mountain Pose.

Arched Warrior—Pose of the Day

Today's pose is Arched Warrior. You might remember that Forward Warrior is a pose of strength and stability. Arched Warrior gives the added benefit of opening the chest, which can give us more energy if we're feeling tired or sad. We'll start in Forward Warrior with the left leg back.

- *Reach the arms up to the ceiling.*
- *Take a few breaths to face your hips and chest toward the front.*
- *Keep your back leg straight if it feels okay, and bend your front knee right over the ankle.*

Keep your breath flowing. If you feel an arch in your lower back, try to straighten it out by drawing the belly in and up, and dropping your tailbone downward.

Pause.

Now if it feels okay, as you breathe in, straighten the front leg and reach up. As you breathe out, bend the front leg and bring the hands together at the chest. Let's do this 2 more times.

(Student name), *can you lead us in 2 more breaths?* Pause.

The next time you breathe in, keep your front leg bent. If it feels okay, lift the center of your chest and reach your arms up and back. Alternatively, you can keep your hands at your chest and lift your chest toward your hands, taking your shoulders back. Keep your breath flowing as you do this. If you feel pain or your breath stops, back off a bit or take a rest.

1 more breath. Good!

Next time you breathe in, lift up and forward to come back to regular Forward Warrior.

Exhale, and bring the left foot forward to Mountain Pose.

Let's take 3 breaths here with the hands at the chest.

Look down at your hands or close your eyes. Notice if you can feel your heart beating. How are you breathing?

Choose a student to lead 3 breaths. Once they are done, repeat the Forward Warrior/Arched Warrior sequence with the right leg back. End in Mountain again with 3 focused breaths.

Shoulder Movements with Hug

For the last movement, we'll stretch the shoulders in the opposite way.
- *Inhaling, reach your arms out to the sides.*
- *Exhale, give yourself a big tight hug, grabbing your shoulder blades with your hands if you reach.*
- *Hold on tight as you take a big breath in. You might notice your shoulders rise toward your ears.*
- *Then breathe out and see if you can move your shoulders down away from your ears a little bit.*

Keep relaxing your shoulders down as you breathe. Feel your ribs expand and contract. You might notice a stretch in your shoulders or back here. Maybe give yourself a little massage with your fingers where they touch your body.

After a few breaths, release the arms. Lead students through the movement once more, this time with the opposite arm on top. When done, instruct students to relax their arms and notice how they feel, especially in the areas of the shoulders and chest.

Invite students to have a seat and proceed to the Mindful Breathing section.

MINDFUL BREATHING (3 MINUTES)

Notice the rhythm of your breath right now. Your breath will have a different rhythm at different times.

Pause to allow students to notice their breath.

As you notice your breath, let each breath get a little deeper.

Pause.

Close your eyes if it feels okay, or just look down at your desk. Allow your breath to fill up your lungs completely, and then empty them completely.

Pause to let them breathe deeply for a few rounds.

Now as you inhale—if it feels okay—tense up your body. Tense up your legs and arms, your belly, your chest. When you exhale, release all the tension, relaxing your muscles. Do that again, tensing up as you inhale.

Pause.

And relaxing as you exhale. You might even imagine you are blowing out tension and thoughts as you exhale. Do this 2 more times:
- *Inhale tense, exhale relax.*
- *Inhale tense, exhale let it all go.*

Pause.

Now come back to breathing normally. Notice what parts of your body feel relaxed, and any areas that may still feel tense. There's no right way to be, just notice.

WRAP-UP

GUIDED MEDITATION AND CLOSING BELL (1 MINUTE)

We're going to end class by sitting silently for 1 minute, just noticing your breathing and how your body feels.

Feel free to close your eyes or look down to help you concentrate only on yourself.

If you like, you can even put your head down and rest it on your arms.

Pause.

Notice your feet resting on the floor, your legs relaxed on the seat.

Notice where your arms and hands are. Maybe you can allow your arms and shoulders to relax a bit more.

Notice how you're breathing.

You might even allow the muscles of your face to relax as you breathe.

Long pause, allow students to sit silently for remainder of the minute.

I will now ring the bell one last time. Listen to the bell, and when you can't hear it anymore, please look up at me.

Ring bell and allow it to vibrate to completion.

CONNECTION QUESTIONS (3 MINUTES)

Now that we have talked about being tired versus being relaxed, did anyone feel more tired at any point during the practice? More relaxed? More energized? During what part of the practice did you notice that?

Ask students if they have any questions about what we did today or about TLS or mindfulness in general, and thank them for their participation.

LESSON 1.9: HOW STRESS AFFECTS THE CHOICES WE MAKE

In this lesson, students will be introduced to Star Gazer Pose. Physically, this pose:

❖ Stretches hips and intercostal muscles
❖ Tones the abdominals and waist
❖ Strengthens the legs

Lesson objectives are (a) students will understand the difference between acting and reacting, and (b) students will practice pausing before they act.

STUDENT OVERVIEW

REVIEW EXPECTATIONS (2 MINUTES)

Review the expectations for TLS sessions, including:

❖ Students clear desks of all distractions including books, papers, food, cell phones, and music.
❖ One-mic rule: one person talks at a time. If students have questions, they can raise a hand or ask at the end of class. Assure students that there will be a few minutes dedicated to questions at the end of each session.
❖ Students focus on their own body and breath. That means not making comments about self or others, not touching others, and not distracting others from their experience.
❖ Students try their best to participate at all times. (However, participation may look different for each student. For some students, it may mean doing only the breathing for as long as they need, until they choose to engage with the movement. Allow students to come to the practice at their own pace, as long as they are not being distracting or disrespectful toward others. Engaging with one's body and mind through TLS is always a choice, and every day is a different experience.)

ACTIVATE BACKGROUND KNOWLEDGE (3 MINUTES)

In response to the class environment each day, you may wish to provide this information to students when you feel it would be best received—that may be at the beginning of class, woven into the mindful movement, or before the silent sitting.

Learning to calm yourself before taking action or making a decision is an important skill. When you feel stressed, the part of the brain that thinks temporarily turns "off." That's why it's important not to make big decisions when you feel stressed!

If you feel angry, frustrated, anxious, or stressed out, you are more likely to make a bad choice, or to react without thinking through your options.

Has anyone here ever reacted out of anger or fear and then gotten in trouble?

Has anyone ever stopped yourself from reacting when you're angry or stressed, and as a result made a better decision?

Activation Question 1.9

What is a decision that you have had to make recently?

Give students a chance to reflect, and choose a few students to share their responses with the class. Remind students that even seemingly small decisions like what they eat, whether to do their homework or not, and whether to come to school or not are choices that they make that affect their lives.

The pose of the day today is a little more challenging. As we do the pose, we will practice noticing sensations in the body while breathing calmly. If you get the urge to come out of the pose, practice taking a deep breath to calm yourself and then choose how to act. You may be able to stay in the pose longer, or you may decide that it's not good for you and you need to come out of it. Either way, you practice staying calm and making a choice that's good for you.

ACTION, BREATHING, CENTERING

OPENING BELL AND FOCUSED BREATHING (2 MINUTES)

We will start our time together today by trying to focus our attention on a sound. I would like to ask you all to listen to the sound of the bell I am going to ring.

Try to keep your attention on the sound of the bell for as long as you can, and when you can't hear it anymore, please raise your hand.

Ring bell or singing bowl.

* Allow to vibrate to completion and until all students have raised their hands.
* Then ask students to do the same thing, this time closing their eyes or looking down at their desks to focus just on their hearing, and ring the bell again.
* Wait until all students have raised their hands.

   That was very good. Now I'll lead you in a breathing exercise:
   * *You can keep your eyes closed, or just look down.*
   * *Let all the air out of your lungs.*
   * *Now breathe in, breathe out.*

Lead class in simple breathing, encouraging them to breathe deeply and smoothly.

Continue for 3–4 rounds.

Then tell students that you are going to do the bell exercise one more time.

Ring the bell again, and students raise their hands when they can no longer hear it.

MINDFUL MOVEMENT AND POSE OF THE DAY (6 MINUTES)

Mountain

Let's all stand up in Mountain Pose.

Have a student describe or demonstrate Mountain Pose. Review the elements:

❖ Feet parallel and hip-width distance apart
❖ Shoulders relaxed
❖ Chest lifted

If you'd like, press your hands together at your chest, and either close your eyes or look down at the place where your hands meet. Can someone lead us in 3 breaths, saying, "breathe in, breathe out"?

Choose a student to lead the breaths, making sure the student leads them slowly to allow for deep breathing.

Good, thank you (student name). *Go ahead and release your arms, letting them hang down at your sides.*

Sun Breaths

We'll start with a few Sun Breaths. There are 2 options here:

(1) The first option is to raise your arms out to the sides and up to your ears as you breathe in. As you exhale, bring your arms back down to your sides.

(2) The second option is to do this pose just using your hands: opening up your fingers on the inhale, and closing them into a fist on the exhale.

Demonstrate hand movements.

The cool thing about using your hands is that you can do this with your hands in your lap in class and nobody has to know you're doing mindfulness!

- *Let's try a few rounds of this, doing whichever option you choose, and matching the movement to the breath.*
- *Inhale, exhale.*
- *You can choose to match your movements to mine, or follow your own rhythm.*

Do 4–5 rounds of Sun Breaths with the students.

Wide-Legged Crescent

If it feels comfortable, take your feet wider apart. When you breathe in, take both arms high above your head. When you breathe out, take your right hand down to your right thigh and reach your left arm over your head. Do you feel a stretch in your left side? If having the arms up doesn't work for you, you can do the pose with your arms down or hands on your waist.

When you breathe in, come back to standing straight up, maybe reaching your arms high. When you breathe out, lean to the other side.

Continue to move with your breath, concentrating on the sensations your feel in your body as you move. Maybe you feel a stretching sensation in your ribs, or in your hips, or somewhere else. See if you can feel both pressing evenly into the floor as you move.

Can someone lead us by saying, "Breathe in, breathe out," nice and slow?

Repeat movement 3 times on each side. When finished, lower arms to sides.

Trunk Twists

Make sure you have an arm's length of space between yourself and the people around you. Let your arms dangle as you gently twist from side to side. (If there is not enough space for this, give students the option to keep the arms bent at chest height.)

Notice the feelings in your arms, shoulders, or back as you do this. You can twist more by lifting the opposite heel as you twist to the side.

Pause.

You can also use your breath for this, breathing out each time you turn to the side.

Demonstrate twisting and breathing out in short, audible spurts each time you twist to the side, for about 30 seconds.

Now let your twists get smaller and smaller until you are still. We'll come back to Mountain Pose with our palms together and take a few breaths. Notice how your body and breath feel after doing the twists.

Have another student lead 3 breaths.

Star Gazer—Pose of the Day

The pose of the day is called Star Gazer. This pose strengthens the legs and the abs, and helps us breathe more deeply. To do it, we first have to come into Side Warrior.

From Mountain Pose, take your left leg back. Press your left heel to the floor and face your hips and chest to the left. As you're ready, start to bend your right leg so that your knee is right above your ankle. Notice any stretching that happens as you bend your knee. When you find a good angle for bending your knee, keep it bent and raise your arms to shoulder height.

If you'd like, look over the fingers of your right hand. Notice how strong your legs are. You might feel them getting warmer. Let's try to stay here for 3 breaths. Who can lead us in the breaths?

Hold Side Warrior as student leads 3 breaths.

Now to come into Star Gazer, raise your right arm up toward the ceiling, and rest your left hand gently on your straight back leg, either above or below the knee. Try to keep your right leg bent. It helps to draw the belly in toward the spine as you exhale in Star Gazer—that way you use your abdominal strength to hold you up rather than straining your back.

You might feel a stretch somewhere along your right side here. If you notice the urge to come out of the pose, take a deep breath to calm yourself before you take action. You might find that it's okay to stay in the pose for another breath or 2, or you might decide to take a rest. We'll hold for 3 breaths.
- *(Slowly) 3—breathing in and out.*
- *2—almost there!*
- *And 1.*

Excellent. When you breathe in come back up to Side Warrior. As you breathe out, bring the left leg forward for Mountain Pose.

Choose a student to lead 3 mindful breaths in Mountain Pose.

Did anyone notice the urge to come out of the pose early? Did you do it? Did anyone manage to take deep breaths to calm yourself rather than following the urge? Let's try it on the other side. Remember, you can always choose to come out of a pose early if you feel you need to. The important thing is that you do so mindfully, rather than reacting to your impulses without pausing to think. Taking deep breaths can help you pause and think more clearly.

Lead students through the Side Warrior and Star Gazer sequence with the right leg back. When you finish, come back to Mountain Pose and have students take 3 breaths with the hands pressed together at the chest. Have one student lead the breaths.

When students finish, have them take a seat. Proceed to the Mindful Breathing section.

MINDFUL BREATHING (3 MINUTES)

Try to sit comfortably with your back straight. You can close your eyes at any time, or just look down at your desk to help you focus inward. We're going to practice a familiar breathing technique that can help you clear your mind and release stress.

We'll breathe in for 4 counts and breathe out for 8. If I count too slow or too fast for you, feel free to go with your own rhythm.

Let all the air out of your lungs, breathing out.

Pause.

- *Breathe in: 1, 2, 3, 4.*
- *Breathe out: 1, 2, 3, 4, 5, 6, 7, 8.*

Repeat counting 2 more times.

Now count silently to yourself:
- *Breathing in for 4.* Pause.
- *Breathing out for 8.* Pause.

Now I'm going to be quiet and let you practice 3 rounds on your own. See if you can keep your mind on the counting and the feeling of the breath. If your mind wanders to other thoughts, bring it back to focus on your breathing as soon as you realize it.

Pause, allow students to breathe on their own for 3 rounds.

Good. You can go back to breathing normally if you'd like, or practice 4:8 breathing for a little longer. Depending on your state of mind, it sometimes takes longer for you to focus your mind and calm yourself down. Try not to judge yourself if it's hard for you to focus, just give yourself some more time and keep focusing back on your breathing.

WRAP-UP

GUIDED MEDITATION AND CLOSING BELL (1 MINUTE)

We're going to end class by sitting silently for 1 minute, just noticing your breathing and how your body feels.

Feel free to close your eyes or look down to help you concentrate only on yourself.

If you like, you can even put your head down and rest it on your arms.

Pause.

Notice your feet resting on the floor, your legs relaxed on the seat.

Notice where your arms and hands are. Maybe you can allow your arms and shoulders to relax a bit more.

Notice how you're breathing.

You might even allow the muscles of your face to relax as you breathe.

Long pause, allow students to sit silently for remainder of the minute.

I will now ring the bell one last time. Listen to the bell and when you can't hear it anymore, please look up at me.

Ring bell and allow it to vibrate to completion.

CONNECTION QUESTIONS (3 MINUTES)

How do you feel? Why is it important to think before you act? What are some ways this can impact your life?

Ask students if they have any questions about what we did today or about TLS or mindfulness in general, and thank them for their participation.

LESSON 1.10: RELEASING STRESS

In this lesson, students will be introduced to Tall Tree Pose. Physically, this pose:

❖ Helps to focus the mind
❖ Improves balance and concentration
❖ Strengthens and firms the legs and abdominal muscles

Lesson objectives are (a) students will learn about the importance of letting go of stress, and (b) students will practice using tools to release stress.

STUDENT OVERVIEW

REVIEW EXPECTATIONS (2 MINUTES)

Review the expectations for TLS sessions, including:

❖ Students clear desks of all distractions including books, papers, food, cell phones, and music.
❖ One-mic rule: one person talks at a time. If students have questions, they can raise a hand or ask at the end of class. Assure students that there will be a few minutes dedicated to questions at the end of each session.
❖ Students focus on their own body and breath. That means not making comments about self or others, not touching others, and not distracting others from their experience.
❖ Students try their best to participate at all times. (However, participation may look different for each student. For some students, it may mean doing only the breathing for as long as they need, until they choose to engage with the movement. Allow students to come to the practice at their own pace, as long as they are not being distracting or disrespectful toward others. Engaging with one's body and mind through TLS is always a choice, and every day is a different experience.)

ACTIVATE BACKGROUND KNOWLEDGE (3 MINUTES)

In response to the class environment each day, you may wish to provide this information to students when you feel it would be best received—that may be at the beginning of class, woven into the mindful movement, or before the silent sitting.

We have all seen someone lose their cool over something that seems small. But oftentimes that person is really expressing emotions that they have been holding inside. Finding ways to release your stress and pent up emotions a little at a time can help you feel better physically, mentally, and emotionally. Learning to release stress and anger in a healthy way can also help you avoid situations where you are unable to control your reactions.

Activation Question 1.10

What are some healthy ways to release stress?

Give students a chance to reflect, and choose a few students to share their responses with the class.

Today we'll discuss and practice ways to use TLS as a tool for releasing stress.

ACTION, BREATHING, CENTERING

OPENING BELL AND FOCUSED BREATHING (2 MINUTES)

We will start our time together today by trying to focus our attention on a sound. I would like to ask you all to listen to the sound of the bell I am going to ring.

Try to keep your attention on the sound of the bell for as long as you can, and when you can't hear it anymore, please raise your hand.

Ring bell or singing bowl.

❖ Allow to vibrate to completion and until all students have raised their hands.

❖ Then ask students to do the same thing, this time closing their eyes or looking down at their desks to focus just on their hearing, and ring the bell again.

❖ Wait until all students have raised their hands.

> *That was very good. Now I'll lead you in a breathing exercise:*
> - *You can keep your eyes closed, or just look down.*
> - *Let all the air out of your lungs.*
> - *Now breathe in, breathe out.*

Lead class in simple breathing, encouraging them to breathe deeply and smoothly.

Continue for 3–4 rounds.

Then tell students that you are going to do the bell exercise one more time.

Ring the bell again, and students raise their hands when they can no longer hear it.

MINDFUL MOVEMENT AND POSE OF THE DAY (6 MINUTES)

Mountain

Let's all stand up in Mountain Pose.

As you breathe in, lift the top of your head up toward the ceiling. As you breathe out, let your shoulders and arms relax. Breathe in and stand tall, reaching your head toward the ceiling. Breathe out and feel your feet on the floor, wiggling your toes if that helps you feel them. Take 1 more deep breath: standing tall, feeling your feet on the floor and shoulders relaxed.

Pause to allow students to breathe and focus.

Arm Movements

We'll start this movement with the hands pressed together at the chest. When we breathe in, we'll take the hands forward, still pressed together, and then apart and out to the sides. You may need to adjust your arm height so that you all have room to reach out. Feel your fingers reaching wide. When we breathe, out we'll bring the hands back together and then into the chest.

Lead students in a couple of rounds, breathing in to reach the hands forward and out, and breathing out to bring them together and in.

Good. Now let's add in the breath we did last time:
- *Breathing in for 4 counts—as we reach wide, and*
- *Breathing out for 8 counts—as we bring the arms in.*

Lead students by counting a few rounds out loud.

Now as you do it, count silently in your head.
- *In for 4.* Pause.
- *Out for 8.* Pause.

Good, one more time.

Now relax your arms at your sides. Notice if they got a little tired.

Standing Backbend as a Movement

For the next pose, we are going to do a standing back bend as a movement. Pay attention to how your back feels and only go as far as feels comfortable, so you don't get hurt.
- *Inhale, reaching up.*
- *Exhale, bringing your hands to your lower back.*
- *Support your lower back as you inhale, opening up your chest and maybe leaning back a bit.*
- *Exhale, returning to standing.*

We will repeat this movement 3 times. Notice if your breath gets shallow—try to keep breathing deeply.

Ask a student to lead the movement and breathing. When done, have students stand in Mountain Pose with hands to chest. Have them take a breath and feel their feet on the floor.

Shake-Out

The next time you breathe in, if it feels okay, tense up all your body, from your feet to your head. Squeeze all your muscles, starting with your feet, your ankles, legs, belly, arms, shoulders, and face. Hold it!

Pause.

Breathe out, and relax and release. Try it again. Breathe in and squeeze all your muscles: feet, ankles, legs, belly, shoulders, arms, face . . . hold it!

Pause.

Breathe out, and relax and release. One more time: breathe in and squeeze all your muscles, even the little ones! Even the ones deep inside! Hold it.

Pause.

Breathe out, relax and release. Now let's shake out our arms and legs counting down from 5.

Demonstrate the next movement for the students and allow them to join in:

- Shake your right arm and hand as you say: "5, 4, 3, 2, 1."
- Shake your left arm and hand as you say: "5, 4, 3, 2, 1."
- Shake your right leg, counting down from 5.
- Repeat with your left leg.

Then repeat the whole sequence counting down from 4. Again, counting down from 3, from 2, and 1—the last round will consist of one quick shake per limb.

Then invite students to stand still in Mountain Pose, noticing their breathing and noticing any tingling, lightness, or other sensations they might feel in their arms, legs, or hands.

Tall Tree—Pose of the Day

The pose today is called Tall Tree. It's a more challenging version of Tree Pose. To balance in Tall Tree, you have to focus your mind and release any stressful or distracting thoughts. Remember to keep breathing to relax your body and help you balance.

We'll start in Mountain Pose.

Feel your left foot planted firmly on the floor. When you're ready, bring your right foot to your ankle, or to your calf, or to your thigh, avoiding the knee. Remember, it might help you balance if you focus your eyes on one spot in front of you. You might also experiment with standing up a little straighter to help you balance.

If you'd like, bring your hands to your chest. Take a few breaths here.

Pause.

Feel free to stay in Tree Pose, or if you feel ready, raise your arms up toward the ceiling. Take a few breaths and see if you can find your balance here. If this is still easy for you, try looking up at the ceiling as you balance.

(Student name), can you lead us in 3 breaths?

If students have a hard time balancing, have them take a deep breath and try to clear their minds of other thoughts. It's also good to remind them that it doesn't matter whether they can balance well today or not. It's more important that they keep trying to do the pose and don't take it too seriously.

When you finish 3 breaths, shake out the legs and arms and try the pose on the other side. End in Mountain Pose with the palms at the chest and take 3 breaths together.

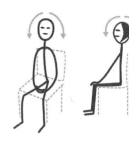

Neck Movements

Please have a seat. See if you can find a way to sit comfortably, but with your back straight. We are going to do some movements to release tension in the neck. As you're ready:

- *On you next exhale, let you right ear fall toward your right shoulder.*
- *On your next breath in, return your head to center.*
- *On your next breath out, let your left ear fall toward your left shoulder. Repeat this movement 2 more times per side. Be gentle with your neck as you move to the rhythm of your own breath.*

Pause while students finish, or invite one student to lead the breath.

When you're ready, bring your head back to center. As you breathe out, look to the right. You can close your eyes or look slightly down. As you breathe in, bring your head back to center. As you breathe out, turn your head to the left. Repeat this movement 2 more times. Pause.

Now when you breathe in, lift your chest up and look slightly upward. Be careful not to strain your neck. As you breathe out, tuck your chin and let your head bow forward. Repeat this movement 2 more times with your breath.

When students finish, invite them to relax, and notice how their shoulders and neck feel. Proceed to the Mindful Breathing section.

MINDFUL BREATHING (3 MINUTES)

Make sure you are sitting comfortably with your back straight. You can close your eyes at any time, or just look down at your desk to help you focus inward. Find the rhythm of your breath.

Pause between each sentence:

Notice if your breath is long or short.

Fast or slow.

Smooth or uneven.

Notice if your breath starts to get deeper as you pay attention to it.

Pause.

Now notice how your body feels.

Notice the weight of your body on the chair. Notice your hands resting on your lap or desk.

See if you can feel the sensation of your clothes touching your skin.

As you inhale, notice how your body feels on the inside. In particular, notice if you feel any tension or muscles "holding on" anywhere in your body. It might be in your shoulders, face, hips, or elsewhere. If it feels good to you, each time you exhale imagine breathing out some of the tension. Inhale notice how your body feels. Exhale release any stress you feel. Inhale notice, exhale release.

Pause and let students breathe a few rounds.

Now notice your thoughts. If you are thinking about things that cause you stress or anxiety, use each exhale to release those thoughts. You can imagine those thoughts were like a weight sitting on your chest, and with each breath out imagine that pressure leaving you so your body feels a little lighter. Practicing letting go mentally and physically.

Pause and let students breathe a few more rounds.

Good! You can go back to breathing normally. Notice how your body feels. Notice how your mind feels—some examples might be busy, clear, cloudy, relaxed, moving slow, moving fast, and so on.

WRAP-UP

SILENT SITTING AND CLOSING BELL (1 MINUTE)

We're going to end class by sitting silently for 1 minute, just noticing your breathing and how your body feels.

Feel free to close your eyes or look down to help you concentrate only on yourself.

If you like, you can even put your head down and rest it on your arms.

Pause.

If students were following along well during the Mindful Breathing, you might choose to be silent for the remainder of the minute and allow them to continue the meditation on their own. However if there is still a good deal of distraction in the room, you might choose to guide them with your words:

Notice your feet resting on the floor, your legs relaxed on the seat.

Notice where your arms and hands are. Maybe you can allow your arms and shoulders to relax a bit more.

Notice how you're breathing.

You might even allow the muscles of your face to relax as you breathe.

Long pause, allow students to sit silently for remainder of the minute.

I will now ring the bell one last time. Listen to the bell and when you can't hear it anymore, please look up at me.

Ring bell and allow it to vibrate to completion.

CONNECTION QUESTIONS (3 MINUTES)

Do you feel like you've released any stress? If so, what did we do today that seemed to help the most?

Ask students if they have any questions about what we did today or about TLS or mindfulness in general, and thank them for their participation.

LESSON 1.11: LONG-TERM BENEFITS OF MANAGING STRESS

In this lesson, students will be introduced to Flamingo Pose. Physically, this pose:

❖ Stretches the hips and legs, releasing tension in the back
❖ Helps calm and focus the mind
❖ Improves balance

Lesson objectives are (a) students will learn some of the health risks associated with chronic stress and why it is important to release stress, and (b) students will practice clearing the mind of stressful thoughts through balancing and deep breathing.

STUDENT OVERVIEW

REVIEW EXPECTATIONS (2 MINUTES)

Review the expectations for TLS sessions, including:

❖ Students clear desks of all distractions including books, papers, food, cell phones, and music.
❖ One-mic rule: one person talks at a time. If students have questions, they can raise a hand or ask at the end of class. Assure students that there will be a few minutes dedicated to questions at the end of each session.
❖ Students focus on their own body and breath. That means not making comments about self or others, not touching others, and not distracting others from their experience.
❖ Students try their best to participate at all times. (However, participation may look different for each student. For some students, it may mean doing only the breathing for as long as they need, until they choose to engage with the movement. Allow students to come to the practice at their own pace, as long as they are not being distracting or disrespectful

toward others. Engaging with one's body and mind through TLS is always a choice, and every day is a different experience.)

ACTIVATE BACKGROUND KNOWLEDGE (3 MINUTES)

In response to the class environment each day, you may wish to provide this information to students when you feel it would be best received—that may be at the beginning of class, woven into the mindful movement, or before the silent sitting.

Having your stress response activated all the time can be harmful. Stress is linked to major health problems such as heart attacks, stroke, chronic pain, high blood pressure, obesity, immune system problems, and digestive disorders. It also contributes to anxiety and depression and can negatively affect our relationships. You may think it's dumb to relax your body if you're just going to come back to the same stressful situation afterward, but taking time to release your stress can keep your mind and body healthy in the long run.

Activation Question 1.11

Can you think of an adult in your life that often seems stressed out? If so, what effect do you think stress has on this person physically and mentally?

Give students a chance to reflect, and choose a few students to share their responses with the class.

Today we're going to give the mind a break from stress by doing balancing poses. To keep from falling, you have to focus your whole attention on what's happening right now—there's no room for worrying about the future or dwelling on the past. That's why balancing is a great way to clear the mind of stress.

ACTION, BREATHING, CENTERING

OPENING BELL AND FOCUSED BREATHING (2 MINUTES)

We will start our time together today by trying to focus our attention on a sound. I would like to ask you all to listen to the sound of the bell I am going to ring.

Try to keep your attention on the sound of the bell for as long as you can, and when you can't hear it anymore, please raise your hand.

Ring bell or singing bowl.

❖ Allow to vibrate to completion and until all students have raised their hands.

❖ Then ask students to do the same thing, this time closing their eyes or looking down at their desks to focus just on their hearing, and ring the bell again.

❖ Wait until all students have raised their hands.

That was very good. Now I'll lead you in a breathing exercise:
- *You can keep your eyes closed, or just look down.*
- *Let all the air out of your lungs.*
- *Now breathe in, breathe out.*

Lead class in simple breathing, encouraging them to breathe deeply and smoothly.

Continue for 3–4 rounds.

Then tell students that you are going to do the bell exercise one more time.

Ring the bell again, and students raise their hands when they can no longer hear it.

MINDFUL MOVEMENT AND POSE OF THE DAY (6 MINUTES)

Mountain

Let's all stand up in Mountain Pose.

Have a student describe or demonstrate Mountain Pose. Review the elements:

❖ Feet parallel and hip-width distance apart
❖ Shoulders relaxed
❖ Standing tall

If you'd like, press your hands together at your chest, and either close your eyes or look down at the place where your hands meet. Can someone lead us in 3 breaths, saying, "breathe in, breathe out"?

Choose a student to lead the breaths, making sure the student leads them slowly to allow for deep breathing.

Shoulder Movements

Go ahead and release your arms to your sides. We are going to do some movements to relax the shoulders:
* *On your next inhale, shrug your shoulders up toward your ears, and*
* *On the exhale let them drop.*
* *Let's do that 3 more times.*

Imagine bringing tension into that area and letting it go as your shoulders drop. For the next movement, we'll rotate our shoulders in small circles:
* *As you inhale, rolling the shoulders up and back, and*
* *As you exhale, bringing them down and forward.*

Try to keep your breath and movement slow, and notice what you feel in your shoulders as they move. For example, you might feel clicking, warmth, or stretching sensations.

Repeat 3 times.

Reverse direction and repeat 3 times.

Release your shoulders and notice if they feel warmer, or looser, or anything else.

Flamingo—Pose of the Day

The pose today is called Flamingo. As a balancing pose, Flamingo helps us to focus on what's happening right now—because if we think about other things, we might lose our balance!

Flamingo Pose also shows us that breathing calmly is more effective than tensing up when we want to accomplish something difficult.

Start standing in Mountain Pose.
- *Breathe in and stand a little taller.*
- *Breathe out and bend your right leg up toward your chest. You can grab your shin with your hands or hold your leg under your thigh.*
- *Inhale, place both feet firmly on the floor again and stand tall.*
- *Exhale and switch legs, raising the left leg.*
- *Inhale, place your left foot down and feel both feet on the floor.*

Keep going with your breath. Experiment with keeping your back straight and tall as you do the movement.

Choose a student to lead the breath and repeat 2 more times on each side.

To help with balance, look at a spot that's not moving, like a spot on the floor or the wall in front of you. It can also help to draw the belly in toward the spine as you breathe out and balance.

Now that we're warmed up, we're going to hold the pose for 3 or 4 breaths, and then go straight into Forward Warrior.
- *Inhale, stand up tall.*
- *Exhale, raise the right leg.*

Try to breathe calmly as you balance. If you notice that you're holding your breath, see if it helps you to balance better if you breathe deep, smooth breaths.

(Student's name) can you say, "breathe in, breathe out 3 times?"

If students slump in the pose, encourage them to try standing up a little straighter.

When the 3 breaths are almost done, instruct students to keep their leg up. Bring the right leg straight back to Forward Warrior. Try to make the transition without touching the foot to the floor in between poses.

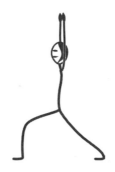

Forward Warrior

Keep your right leg straight as you bend your left leg, bringing the left knee right over the ankle. If your knee goes past your ankle, you can lengthen your stance by bringing your right foot farther back. Notice your right heel pressing onto the floor behind you. Your hips and chest are facing forward here.

Now, when you breathe in, straighten both legs and look up toward the ceiling, reaching the arms up and apart. When you breathe out, bend your front leg and bring your hands to your chest. If it feels okay, keep the back leg straight. Let's try this 2 more times.

Choose a student to lead the breaths, going slow enough to encourage students to take deep inhales. Deep inhales combined with lifting the arms high and wide, which lifts the chest, can be an invigorating movement for students if they are feeling tired.

Now we'll just take 2 more breaths to be still in Forward Warrior with the front knee bent. Try to breathe deeply and notice any sensations you feel in the pose, such as warmth, fatigue, stretching, or something else. Maybe you can let the shoulders relax a bit. We are building up our ability to control our reactions here!

Great job! Come back to Mountain Pose. Shake out your legs.

Ask students if anyone noticed if it was easier to balance if they tense up the body and hold the breath, or if they relax and breathe deeply.

> *You might notice that it's easier to balance when you are relaxed and supple, rather than when you are rigid and tight.*

Repeat the whole sequence on the left side, starting with Flamingo and holding it for 3 breaths, then transitioning directly to Forward Warrior. When you finish the sequence have students shake out their legs and arms, and then take 3 breaths in Mountain Pose with hands to chest.

Proceed to the Mindful Breathing section.

MINDFUL BREATHING (3 MINUTES)

Make sure you are sitting comfortably. Bring your attention to your breath. Try to inhale fully and exhale all the air out.

Pause.

We're going to do a progressive relaxation, tensing up our muscles as we inhale, and releasing them as we exhale. This helps us to release stress from the body's muscles and tissues. The progressive relaxation can free up the muscles and make the body feel more peaceful.

I'll lead you through it, and you can follow along as you feel comfortable:
- *Take a big breath in, and tense up your feet and legs.*
- *Make the muscles tight and hold them, and if it feels okay, hold your breath. Hold it.*
- *Breathe out and relax your legs and feet.*

Do this one more time: breathe in and tighten the muscles from your toes up through your thighs. Hold it. Breathe out and release the muscles, letting your legs be heavy on your seat.

Pause.

Now focus on your hands, arms, and shoulders:

- *Breathe in and tighten all the muscles, from your fingers up your arms to your shoulders. You might make fists, or splay your fingers wide. Hold it.*
- *Breathe out and relax your hands, arms, and shoulders.*
- *One more time, breathe in and tense up hands, arms, and shoulders.*
- *Breathe out and release, letting your arms rest on the desk or your lap.*

Pause.

Now focus on your chest and belly:

- *Breathe in, and tighten the muscles in your belly and chest. Hold it.*
- *Now breathe out and release.*
- *Once more, breathe in and hold your breath, tightening up your belly and chest.*
- *Squeeze the muscles. Breathe out and release your belly and chest.*

Pause.

Now focus on your neck and face:

- *Breathe in, and tighten the muscles in your face, like you just bit into a sour lemon. Maybe you can tense up your neck too.*
- *Now breathe out and relax the neck and face.*
- *Last time, breathe in. Tighten the muscles in the neck and the face. Hold it.*
- *Now breathe out and let your face and neck and whole body relax.*

Go back to breathing normally. Take a moment to notice how your body feels.

WRAP-UP

GUIDED MEDITATION AND CLOSING BELL (1 MINUTE)

We're going to end class by sitting silently for 1 minute, just noticing your breathing and how your body feels.

Feel free to close your eyes or look down to help you concentrate only on yourself.

If you like, you can even put your head down and rest it on your arms.

Pause.

Notice your feet resting on the floor, your legs relaxed on the seat.

Notice where your arms and hands are. Maybe you can allow your arms and shoulders to relax a bit more.

Notice how you're breathing.

Allow yourself to breathe in deeply and out completely.

Long pause, allow students to sit silently for remainder of the minute.

I will now ring the bell one last time. Listen to the bell and when you can't hear it anymore, please look up at me.

Ring bell and allow it to vibrate to completion.

CONNECTION QUESTIONS (3 MINUTES)

How do you feel? What are some healthy habits you can start or continue that will help you to manage stress?

Ask students if they have any questions about what we did today or about TLS or mindfulness in general, and thank them for their participation.

LESSON 1.12: REVIEW AND RETEACHING

The purpose of this lesson is to review and reteach any essential skills before moving on to Unit 2. Although this lesson is optional, we encourage instructors to review their fidelity checklists and instructor notes, and formulate a lesson plan based on what they think students would benefit from most. If content was covered equally well, instructors may want to attempt to reteach lessons during which students did not appear well-engaged and attempt new strategies to motivate and engage students. Or instructors may choose to review a lesson during which a high percentage of students were absent. After reviewing your notes, make a plan for what you intend to reteach and why.

UNIT 1 REVIEW FORM

UNIT 1. Lesson	% Implementation	% Students absent	Overall engagement
1.1: Understanding What Stress Is About			
1.2: Recognizing Stress in Your Body			
1.3: Knowing What Stresses You			
1.4: How Stress Affects Your Breath			
1.5: Using Your Breath as a Tool			
1.6: How Stress Affects Your Ability to Learn			
1.7: Clearing Your Mind, Calming Your Body			
1.8: Feeling Tired vs. Feeling Relaxed			
1.9: How Stress Affects the Choices We Make			
1.10: Releasing Stress			
1.11: Long-Term Benefits of Managing Stress			

_____ I choose to reteach lesson(s) because _____.

_____ All students have mastered skills. No reteaching is necessary.

UNIT 2

Self-Awareness

Self-awareness is the capacity to notice yourself, including your thoughts, emotions, and behaviors. In order to manage stress, you first must become aware of its presence; thus, self-awareness is an important element of stress management. In this unit, we build awareness of our bodies, breath, emotions, and thought patterns, and learn how they are all connected. We also learn tools for focusing the mind and managing stressful emotions.

How many of us are aware of what we are doing, as we are doing it, all the time? So often we spend our time thinking about other things, not really aware of the movements of our body, how we are breathing, or how we feel. Building awareness of what you are doing, thinking, and feeling in the present moment is a powerful skill that affects all aspects of your life.

Being aware of your body and its signals can help you stay healthy and safe. Being aware of your breath can help you to manage your emotions. Being aware of your thought patterns can help you understand yourself better and keep a positive outlook. Having greater awareness of all of these aspects of yourself can help you build self-confidence, self-control, and emotional balance. By developing self-awareness, you can enhance your focus and clarity of mind, your ability to reach your goals, and your overall well-being.

Objectives

❖ Define self-awareness and how it relates to stress management
❖ Develop awareness of physical sensations, feelings, and thoughts
❖ Build understanding that thoughts and feeling come and go
❖ Learn centering practices that promote self-awareness
❖ Understand the difference between action and reaction
❖ Increase focus, attention, and balance

LESSON 2.1: UNDERSTANDING SELF-AWARENESS

In this lesson, students will be introduced to the Standing Backbend Pose. Physically, this pose:

- ❖ Energizes and invigorates; helps counteract feelings of depression or lethargy
- ❖ Helps to maintain flexibility in the upper back.
- ❖ Opens the chest to facilitate deeper breathing.

Lesson objectives are (a) students will explore what it means to be self-aware, and (b) students will practice noticing body sensations and feelings.

STUDENT OVERVIEW

REVIEW EXPECTATIONS (2 MINUTES)

Review the expectations for TLS sessions, including:

- ❖ Students clear desks of all distractions including books, papers, food, cell phones, and music.
- ❖ One-mic rule: one person talks at a time. If students have questions, they can raise a hand or ask at the end of class. Assure students that there will be a few minutes dedicated to questions at the end of each session.
- ❖ Students focus on their own body and breath. That means not making comments about self or others, not touching others, and not distracting others from their experience.
- ❖ Students try their best to participate at all times. (However, participation may look different for each student. For some students, it may mean doing only the breathing for as long as they need, until they choose to engage with the movement. Allow students to come to the practice at their own pace, as long as they are not being distracting or disrespectful toward others. Engaging with one's body and mind through TLS is always a choice, and every day is a different experience.)

ACTIVATE BACKGROUND KNOWLEDGE (3 MINUTES)

In response to the class environment each day, you may wish to provide this information to students when you feel it would be best received—that may be at the beginning of class, woven into the mindful movement, or before the silent sitting.

> *Self-awareness is the ability to notice your own body, thoughts, feelings, and actions. If you want to manage your emotions, increase your self-control, or change bad habits, being aware of yourself is the first step. In school you usually learn to focus on what your teachers tell you or have you read, or you focus on your friends. But you seldom are taught to focus inside, and build awareness of yourself.*

Activation Question 2.1

Why do you think having self-awareness is important?

Give students a chance to reflect, and choose a few students to share their responses with the class.

> *While we do TLS today, we'll stop once in a while to notice how we feel, to build self-awareness.*

ACTION, BREATHING, CENTERING

OPENING BELL AND FOCUSED BREATHING (2 MINUTES)

We will start our time together today by trying to focus our attention on a sound. I would like to ask you all to listen to the sound of the bell I am going to ring.

Try to keep your attention on the sound of the bell for as long as you can, and when you can't hear it anymore, please raise your hand.

Ring bell or singing bowl.

❖ Allow to vibrate to completion and until all students have raised their hands.

❖ Then ask students to do the same thing, this time closing their eyes or looking down at their desks to focus just on their hearing, and ring the bell again.

❖ Wait until all students have raised their hands.

> *That was very good. Now I'll lead you in a breathing exercise:*
> * *You can keep your eyes closed, or just look down.*
> * *Let all the air out of your lungs.*
> * *Now breathe in, breathe out.*

Lead class in simple breathing, encouraging them to breathe deeply and smoothly.

Continue for 3–4 rounds.

Then tell students that you are going to do the bell exercise one more time.

Ring the bell again, and students raise their hands when they can no longer hear it.

MINDFUL MOVEMENT AND POSE OF THE DAY (6 MINUTES)

> *Part of self-awareness is being able to notice how you feel. Take a moment to notice how you're feeling right now: if you have a lot of energy and you want to get moving, or if you feel low-energy and feel like sitting still.*
>
> * *If you feel high-energy, raise a "thumbs-up" in the air. Keep it raised so I can see.*
> * *If you feel low-energy, raise a "thumbs-down" in the air.*

If there are more thumbs-ups than thumbs-downs, do Option A: Standing Shoulder Movements.

If there were more thumbs-downs, do Option B: Seated Robin Pose.

Then proceed with the rest of the Mindful Movement. Modifying the sequence according to how students are feeling models the behavior of listening to signals from the body and making healthy choices for oneself.

Option A—Standing Shoulder Movements

Okay, looks like most people want to get moving! Let's stand up in Mountain Pose, but keeping your knees slightly bent.

You can do this movement with your hands clasped together behind your back, or with you hands resting on the front of your thighs.
- *When you breathe in, draw your shoulders back, lifting your upper chest toward the ceiling.*
- *When you breathe out, let your shoulders round forward.*

Continue to the rhythm of your own breath:
- *Inhale shoulders back,*
- *Exhale shoulders forward.*

We're warming up the shoulders and back here—you might even notice them getting warmer or looser.

Allow students to repeat 3 more times. Then proceed to Mountain Pose.

Option B—Seated Robin Pose

Okay let's start sitting down with a small movement. You can make it bigger as you feel comfortable.

As you're ready, on an inhale, draw the shoulders back.

Pause.

When you exhale, bring the shoulders forward and the chin down.

Guide students while they try a few rounds.

If you would like a boost of energy, try taking bigger inhales. If you want more of a stretch here, when you breathe in take the shoulders back and lift the center of your chest, maybe looking up. And when you breathe out round the back, pulling the belly in and letting the head drop forward.

We're warming up the shoulders and back here—maybe you notice them getting warmer or more flexible.

Try a few more rounds at your own pace, taking deep breaths.

Pause while students repeat about 3 times.

Good. Let's all stand up in Mountain Pose.

Mountain

Find a comfortable way to stand with your feet hip-width distance apart. If it feels comfortable, press your hands together at your chest, and either close your eyes or look down at the place where your hands meet.

- *As you breathe in, feel the center of your chest lift gently upward.*
- *As you breathe out, feel your feet planted firmly on the floor. You can wiggle your toes if that helps you feel your feet.*
- *Can someone lead us in 3 breaths, saying, "breathe in, breathe out"?*

Choose a student to lead the breaths, making sure the student leads them slowly to allow for deep breathing.

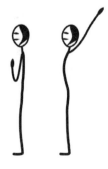

Standing Backbend—Pose of the Day

The pose of the day is Standing Backbend. In backward bending poses, it's important to be aware of how your body feels and only go as far as is comfortable for you. Doing standing backbend as a movement has been helping prepare us to hold the pose a little bit longer. This pose teaches us to pay attention to what our body tells us, so we don't get hurt. Chest opening and backward bending movements like this one can also help us shift our mood when we are feeling lethargic or depressed.

Now place your hands together at your chest.

- *As you breathe in, feel your upper chest rise up toward your thumbs.*
- *As you breathe out pull your belly in a little and bring your shoulders back.*

Keep pulling your belly in with each exhale so that your back doesn't have to do all the work. Continue to breathe and lift your upper chest toward your hands. Now either keep your hands at your chest, or if you'd like, raise your arms high above your head and slightly back. See if you can hold this pose for 3 deep breaths.

If you feel any crunching in your lower back, come out of the bend a little and pull the belly in, so that you feel the bend more in your upper back.

- *2 more breaths.*
- *Last one.*
- *Breathe in and lift yourself out of the backbend, standing tall.*
- *Breathe out, hands to the chest.*

Is your heart beating any faster? How are you breathing? What is your energy level like right now?

Trunk Twists

Now you can shake out your arms and bring your feet a little farther apart. We'll start to twist the upper body from side to side. Either let your arms relax and swing as you twist, or bend your arms at chest height. Feel the air brush past your hands.

Pause to allow students to feel the twists.

Now let your twists get smaller and smaller until you are still.

Come back to Mountain Pose with your palms together at your chest and take a few breaths, noticing how your body feels.

Have another student lead 3 breaths.

Tree

For our final pose we'll try balancing in Tree.

In order to balance, we have to be aware of what's going on in our bodies. If you pick one spot that isn't moving to focus your eyes on, it keeps you from getting distracted and helps you focus inward. Feel your left foot planted firmly on the floor. When you're ready, bring your right foot to your ankle, or to your calf, or to your thigh, avoiding your knee. Keep breathing. If you'd like, bring your hands to your chest.

Notice if you can stand up a little straighter here.

Have another student lead 3 breaths.

When finished, lead students through Tree Pose on the other side. Encourage students to notice their chest lifted and the standing foot planted firmly on the ground. End in Mountain Pose with 3 breaths.

Proceed to the Mindful Breathing section.

MINDFUL BREATHING (3 MINUTES)

Sit in a way where you can be relaxed with your back straight. Notice the rhythm of your breath right now. Your breath will have a different rhythm at different times, depending on your mood.

Pause to allow students to notice their breath.

As you notice your breath, let each breath get a little deeper.

Pause.

Close your eyes if it feels okay, or just look down at your desk. Allow your breath to fill up your lungs completely, and then empty them completely.

Pause to let them breathe deeply for a few rounds.

Continue to make full, complete inhales and full, complete exhales. Notice if you are still sitting up straight, or if you forgot about your posture. If you'd like, place a hand on your upper chest. Can you feel your chest move as you breathe?

Pause for about 30 seconds.

Now, place your hand on your belly if that feels okay. Do you notice your belly moving as you breathe? Try to relax the muscles around your belly and breathe deeply to allow it to expand as you breathe in.

Pause for about 30 seconds.

Now let both hands rest on your lap or on your desk. Without using your hands, can you notice different parts of your body moving as you breathe?

Pause.

Maybe you feel your belly or chest moving. Maybe you can even notice some movement in your shoulders. Maybe even the ribs in your back move—the ribs go all the way around from the front to the back. There's no right answer, just notice anything in your body that is moving as you breathe.

Pause.

Whatever you feel is just fine—that's just how you are breathing in this moment.

Thanks for taking this time to focus on yourself and build your self-awareness!. Return to breathing normally, and notice how you feel.

WRAP-UP

GUIDED MEDITATION AND CLOSING BELL (1 MINUTE)

We're going to end class by sitting silently for 1 minute.

Feel free to close your eyes or look down to help you concentrate only on yourself.

If you like, you can even put your head down and rest it on your arms.

Pause.

Notice your feet resting on the floor, your legs relaxed on the seat.

Notice where your arms and hands are. Maybe you can allow your arms and shoulders to relax a bit more.

Notice how you're breathing.

You might even allow the muscles of your face to relax as you breathe.

Long pause, allow students to sit silently for remainder of the minute.

I will now ring the bell one last time. Listen to the bell and when you can't hear it anymore, please look up at me.

Ring bell and allow it to vibrate to completion.

CONNECTION QUESTIONS (3 MINUTES)

How are you feeling?

What do you think is the difference between being self-aware and self-conscious?

Ask students if they have any questions about what we did today or about TLS or mindfulness in general, and thank them for their participation.

LESSON 2.2: BUILDING BODY AWARENESS

In this lesson, students will be introduced to Half Sun Salutations. Physically, this pose:

- ❖ Calms the mind and invigorates the body
- ❖ Helps maintain elasticity in the spine
- ❖ Stretches the hamstrings

Lesson objectives are (a) students will learn the importance of being aware of signals from the body, and (b) students will practice body awareness by noticing body sensations and spatial orientation.

STUDENT OVERVIEW

REVIEW EXPECTATIONS (2 MINUTES)

Review the expectations for TLS sessions, including:

- ❖ Students clear desks of all distractions including books, papers, food, cell phones, and music.
- ❖ One-mic rule: one person talks at a time. If students have questions, they can raise a hand or ask at the end of class. Assure students that there will be a few minutes dedicated to questions at the end of each session.
- ❖ Students focus on their own body and breath. That means not making comments about self or others, not touching others, and not distracting others from their experience.
- ❖ Students try their best to participate at all times. (However, participation may look different for each student. For some students, it may mean doing only the breathing for as long as they need, until they choose to engage with the movement. Allow students to come to the practice at their own pace, as long as they are not being distracting or disrespectful toward others. Engaging with one's body and mind through TLS is always a choice, and every day is a different experience.)

ACTIVATE BACKGROUND KNOWLEDGE (3 MINUTES)

In response to the class environment each day, you may wish to provide this information to students when you feel it would be best received—that may be at the beginning of class, woven into the mindful movement, or before the silent sitting.

> *One aspect of self-awareness is being aware of how the body feels. The body has its own intelligence. It can tell you when you've had enough to eat, when you are stretching too far, or when a situation is no longer safe. If you cannot listen to and recognize the cues your body is giving, you are more likely to do things that are potentially harmful to yourself. That could be as simple as overdoing it when playing sports or as serious as using substances that you know can have a negative impact on your life.*

Activation Question 2.2

> *Can you think of a time when you were not able to listen to what your body was telling you, and it caused you discomfort or harm?*

Give students a chance to reflect, and choose a few students to share their responses with the class. If helpful, provide the example of eating popcorn at the movies, and being so absorbed in the movie that you don't pay attention to your body and eat too much popcorn, making you feel sick afterward. Other examples might include forgetting to eat; not resting an injury; not sleeping enough and being cranky to the next day; or being pressured into doing things that don't feel safe.

> *Today, we will be doing poses and breathing exercises that help us build body awareness and improve our ability to listen to our bodies.*

ACTION, BREATHING, CENTERING

OPENING BELL AND FOCUSED BREATHING (2 MINUTES)

We will start our time together today by trying to focus our attention on a sound. I would like to ask you all to listen to the sound of the bell I am going to ring.

Try to keep your attention on the sound of the bell for as long as you can, and when you can't hear it anymore, please raise your hand.

Ring bell or singing bowl.

❖ Allow to vibrate to completion and until all students have raised their hands.

❖ Then ask students to do the same thing, this time closing their eyes or looking down at their desks to focus just on their hearing, and ring the bell again.

❖ Wait until all students have raised their hands.

That was very good. Now I'll lead you in a breathing exercise:
- *You can keep your eyes closed, or just look down.*
- *Let all the air out of your lungs.*
- *Now breathe in, breathe out.*

Lead class in simple breathing, encouraging them to breathe deeply and smoothly.

Continue for 3–4 rounds.

Then tell students that you are going to do the bell exercise one more time.

Ring the bell again, and students raise their hands when they can no longer hear it.

MINDFUL MOVEMENT AND POSE OF THE DAY (6 MINUTES)

The pose of the day today includes forward folds. so it is best not to have students standing behind one another. You may wish to position students in a circle around the room before beginning the Mindful Movement section.

Mountain

Let's all stand up in Mountain Pose.

If needed, review the elements of Mountain Pose:
- ❖ Feet parallel and hip-width distance apart
- ❖ Shoulders relaxed
- ❖ Standing tall

If it feels comfortable, press your hands together at your chest, and either close your eyes or look down at the place where your hands meet. Can someone lead us in 3 breaths, saying, "breathe in, breathe out"?

Choose a student to lead the breaths, making sure the student leads them slowly to allow for deep breathing.

Flamingo

Breathe in and stand a little taller. Breathe out and bend your right leg up toward your chest. You can grab your shin with your hands or hold your leg under your thigh. Does anybody remember the name of this pose?

Yes, Flamingo! Keep breathing as you try to balance.

Choose a student to lead the class in 3 deep breaths.

Notice if you're hunched over, and see how it feels to straighten your back a little. Good.

- *On an inhale, place both feet firmly on the floor and stand tall.*

- *Exhale and raise the left leg in the same way.*
- *Standing tall, breathing deeply.*

Pause.

Let's take 3 breaths on this side. (Student's name) can you say, "breathe in, breathe out" 3 times?

On your next inhale, place your left foot down and feel both feet on the floor.

Arched Warrior

On the next exhale, we'll lift up the right leg one more time.
- *Inhale.*
- *Exhale and take it straight behind you for Forward Warrior.*

If it feels okay, press your back heel to the ground with the back leg straight, and bend the front leg. Still taking deep breaths. If you feel an arch in your lower back, try to straighten it out by lifting your belly and bringing your tailbone forward.

Pause.

The next time you breathe in, if it feels alright to you, lift the center of the chest, take the arms slightly back. Keep your breath moving as you do this. If you feel your lower back crunching, lift up a bit more with your chest and belly. The arch should be just in your upper back. 2 more breaths. Try to keep breathing deeply, even if it's harder here. 1 more breath.

Pause.

Breathe in, and come back to regular Forward Warrior. Breathe out, come back to Mountain.

Repeat the sequence on the left side:

❖ Lifting the left leg into Flamingo, then back to Forward Warrior.

❖ Hold Arched Warrior for about 3 breaths.

❖ Have students come back to Forward Warrior as they breathe in, and Mountain as they breathe out.

Choose a student to lead 3 breaths in Mountain Pose.

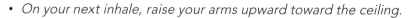

Half Sun Salutation—Pose of the Day

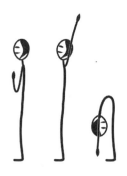

The pose of the day is called Half Sun Salutation. The Sun Salutation is a series of poses that connect the breath to the movement. As you concentrate on moving with your breath, you build awareness of your body and learn to be more conscious of your actions.

The Sun Salutation starts in Mountain Pose with the hands together at the chest.

- *On your next inhale, raise your arms upward toward the ceiling.*
- *If it feels okay, you can reach your arms back slightly for a mini-backbend in the upper back.*
- *On the exhale, fold forward. You can fold forward a lot, feeling a stretch in the back of the legs. Or if you feel more comfortable you can just fold forward a little, letting your arms and neck relax and your upper back round. Keep your knees bent a little or a lot, whatever feels best to you.*

Take a breath here and notice where you feel a stretch. Find the place where you feel a stretch but it's not too much.

Pause.

When you inhale, experiment with flattening out your back like a tabletop. Place your hands on the fronts of your legs. Notice your back muscles working to flatten your back. See if you can bring your shoulders away from your ears to keep your neck long and straight. Breathe. Next time you exhale, relax and fold forward again.

Inhale, come back to standing, reaching the arms straight up. Exhale, hands to the front of the chest, Mountain Pose. You just did 1 round of Half Sun Salutation.

We are going to repeat that series 3 times, but with only 1 breath per movement. Try to keep your movement connected to your breath—don't start moving until your breath starts. Ready? On your next inhale, raise your arms up and maybe a little back.

Slowly, to allow for deep breathing:

Exhale, fold forward. Inhale, flat back. Exhale, fold forward. Inhale, reach your arms straight up. Exhale, hands to chest.

Repeat 2 more times. When you finish, instruct students to stay in Mountain Pose and notice how they are breathing; notice if their heart is beating faster; notice how their body feels. Have one student lead everyone in 3 breaths in Mountain Pose.

Invite students to take a seat. Proceed to the Mindful Breathing section.

MINDFUL BREATHING (3 MINUTES)

Sit as comfortably as you can with your back straight. Notice the rhythm of your breath. Try to make your breath smooth and just notice it moving in and out.

Pause.

As you breathe, notice if you belly is moving. If you'd like, place a hand on your belly to feel it.

Pause.

You might notice the belly expanding outward a little as you breathe in. Bring it gently back in toward your spine as you breathe out. Breathe in and out. If your belly isn't moving with your breath, that's okay. Just try to relax some of the muscles in your abdomen and focus on taking deep breaths.

Pause to allow students to breathe for 3–4 rounds.

> *Now if your hand is on your belly, take it off.*
> - *See if you can feel your belly moving out and in without using your hand, just feeling it from the inside.*
> - *Breathing all the way down to your belly helps you activate the relaxation response in the body. So does paying attention to the little sensations in the body, like we're doing now. It also helps us build awareness of the body, so that we can notice the important signals that it gives us.*
> - *Notice any movement you feel in your belly or anywhere else as you breathe.*

Pause to allow students to breathe 3–4 rounds.

> *Good job. When you're ready, you can go back to normal breathing, if you would like.*

WRAP-UP

GUIDED MEDITATION AND CLOSING BELL (1 MINUTE)

We're going to end class by sitting silently for 1 minute, just noticing your breathing and how your body feels.

Feel free to close your eyes or look down to help you concentrate only on yourself.

If you like, you can even put your head down and rest it on your arms.

Pause.

Notice your feet resting on the floor, your legs relaxed on the seat.

Notice where your arms and hands are. Maybe you can allow your arms and shoulders to relax a bit more.

Notice how you're breathing.

You might even allow the muscles of your face to relax as you breathe.

Long pause, allow students to sit silently for remainder of the minute.

I will now ring the bell one last time. Listen to the bell and when you can't hear it anymore, please look up at me.

Ring bell and allow it to vibrate to completion.

CONNECTION QUESTIONS (3 MINUTES)

Today we worked on building body awareness. What is one thing that you were aware of in your body during TLS today?

Examples could include breathing, heartbeat getting faster, or feeling feet on the floor.

Ask students if they have any questions about what we did today or about TLS or mindfulness in general, and thank them for their participation.

LESSON 2.3: BEING AWARE OF YOUR BODY AS YOU MOVE

In this lesson, students will be introduced to Lunge Pose. Physically, this pose:

- ❖ Stretches the hip flexors
- ❖ Strengthens the legs
- ❖ Improves balance and focus

Lesson objectives are (a) students will learn the importance of being aware of their bodies as they go about their daily activities and interact with others, and (b) students will practice being aware of their bodies as they move.

STUDENT OVERVIEW

REVIEW EXPECTATIONS (2 MINUTES)

Review the expectations for TLS sessions, including:

- ❖ Students clear desks of all distractions including books, papers, food, cell phones, and music.
- ❖ One-mic rule: one person talks at a time. If students have questions, they can raise a hand or ask at the end of class. Assure students that there will be a few minutes dedicated to questions at the end of each session.
- ❖ Students focus on their own body and breath. That means not making comments about self or others, not touching others, and not distracting others from their experience.
- ❖ Students try their best to participate at all times. (However, participation may look different for each student. For some students, it may mean doing only the breathing for as long as they need, until they choose to engage with the movement. Allow students to come to the practice at their own pace, as long as they are not being distracting or disrespectful toward others. Engaging with one's body and mind through TLS is always a choice, and every day is a different experience.)

ACTIVATE BACKGROUND KNOWLEDGE (3 MINUTES)

In response to the class environment each day, you may wish to provide this information to students when you feel it would be best received—that may be at the beginning of class, woven into the mindful movement, or before the silent sitting.

As you interact with people and go about your life day to day, it is helpful to be aware of yourself. The sensations in your body can be clues about what you need (like food, water, or rest) and how others make you feel. These clues can help you in your friendships and other relationships, and help you build healthy habits. Besides, your body is always in the present, but your mind is often focused on the past or the future. Being aware of your body as you go through your day can help you focus on the here and now, and spend less time stuck in the past or worrying about the future.

Activation Question 2.3

As you go through your day, you do lots of movements, from brushing your teeth to walking down the street. In general, do you think that you move with awareness, or do you tend to do most things on autopilot, without being aware of your body?

Give students a chance to reflect, and choose a few students to share their responses with the class.

Today we will do some mindfulness exercises that help us build body awareness and improve our ability to listen to our bodies.

ACTION, BREATHING, CENTERING

OPENING BELL AND FOCUSED BREATHING (2 MINUTES)

We will start our time together today by trying to focus our attention on a sound. I would like to ask you all to listen to the sound of the bell I am going to ring.

Try to keep your attention on the sound of the bell for as long as you can, and when you can't hear it anymore, please raise your hand.

Ring bell or singing bowl.

❖ Allow to vibrate to completion and until all students have raised their hands.
❖ Then ask students to do the same thing, this time closing their eyes or looking down at their desks to focus just on their hearing, and ring the bell again.
❖ Wait until all students have raised their hands.

That was very good. Now I'll lead you in a breathing exercise:
• *You can keep your eyes closed, or just look down.*
• *Let all the air out of your lungs.*
• *Now breathe in, breathe out.*

Lead class in simple breathing, encouraging them to breathe deeply and smoothly.

Continue for 3–4 rounds.

Then tell students that you are going to do the bell exercise one more time.

Ring the bell again, and students raise their hands when they can no longer hear it.

MINDFUL MOVEMENT AND POSE OF THE DAY (6 MINUTES)

Mountain

Today we'll start right away in Mountain Pose.

Pause as students stand up.

As you breathe in, lift the top of your head up toward the ceiling. As you breathe out, let your shoulders and arms relax. Breathe in and stand tall, reaching your head toward the ceiling. Breathe out and feel your feet on the floor, wiggling your toes if that helps you feel them. Take 1 more deep breath: standing tall, feeling your feet on the floor and shoulders relaxed. Great, go ahead and release your arms, letting them hang down at your sides.

Arm Movements—Reaching Overhead

When you're ready, the next time you breathe in raise your arms high above your head. You can also look up at the ceiling if it feels okay on your neck. As you breathe out smoothly, press your hands together and bring them to your chest.

Help students tune into their bodies by offering verbal cues like,
- *"Notice what muscles work to lift your arms up," or*
- *"As you bring your arms down, notice your hands making a straight line through the air."*

Now, let's add in some rhythmic breathing. Breathe in to a count of 4 as you reach your arms up. Breathe out to a count of 8 as you bring your hands to your chest.

Count for a few rounds and then invite students to do 2–3 more rounds counting silently to themselves. Then shake our your arms and rest them at your sides.

Crescent Moon

Breathing in, reach your arms up straight and clasp your hands together. If that doesn't feel good, you can hook your thumbs together with your palms facing forward, or just reach your arms up straight keeping your hands apart. If you don't feel like raising your arms right now, you can put your hands on your hips. Try out the movement in whatever way feels okay. Maybe that will change as we keep moving.

Each time we breathe in, we reach our hands up higher or stand taller. When we breathe out, we lean a little to the right side. Breathe in, stand up tall. Breathe out lean to the left side. Continue to match the movement to your breath. Notice exactly where you feel the stretch as you lean to each side.

Pause.

Try to feel both feet pressing into the floor evenly as you lean to each side.

Choose a student to lead the breath as they do 2 more rounds to the right and left.

The next time you breathe out, let your arms relax at your sides.

Thank the student for leading the breath. Instruct students to bring hands together at the chest, and notice if the chest is moving as they breathe. Invite them to notice if the breath is slowing down. Maybe they can notice their own heart beating.

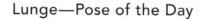

Lunge—Pose of the Day

The pose of the day is Lunge Pose.

Lunge stretches the hip flexors, which can tighten and cause us back pain, especially if we sit in a chair all day. Pay attention to what

you feel as you move in and out of Lunge to keep your body safe and build awareness of your body.

Lunge is a lot like Forward Warrior, but with the back heel lifted up toward the ceiling. Let's start with the left leg back, and right leg forward.

If you'd like more of a stretch, place your legs farther apart. The front leg is bent with the knee right above the ankle. If the knee goes farther forward than the ankle, scoot your front foot forward or your back foot back.

Try to straighten the back leg if it feels okay. That might make you feel more of a stretch.

Pause.

Breathe in, and if it feels okay raise your arms up toward your ears.

Now let's check out the difference between bending and straightening the arms.

- *Everyone bend your arms like they're tired and hold them up.*

How does that feel? Do they feel heavy?

- *Now straighten your arms and reach toward the ceiling.*

How does that feel?

You might notice that reaching your arms straight keeps your energy flowing and makes them feel lighter, while letting your arms bend can weigh you down. You can choose which one you do. Are your legs starting to feel tired? See if you can hold the pose for just 2 more breaths. Breathe deeply to calm yourself.

Choose a student to lead 2 breaths. Then try the other side. Try to have students hold the pose for the same amount of time on both sides. Then come back to Mountain Pose for 3 breaths.

Seated Twist

Good job! Let's all take a seat. Sit facing the front, and place your feet on the floor if that feels comfortable.

Pause.

The last pose we'll do today is a Seated Twist. As you breathe in, sit up as straight as you can. As you breathe out, turn to face the right. You can take your right hand to the back of your seat and your left hand to your right thigh to help you twist.

- *When you breathe in, face front again and feel your arms relaxed, hands on your legs.*
- *As you breathe out, twist to the left.*
- *Each time you breathe in, face the front and feel yourself centered and sturdy in your seat.*
- *Each time you twist, notice where you feel it in your body.*
- *See if you can make the twist start at your pelvis and go gently up your spine to your neck.*
- *Keep going with your own breath: inhale twist, exhale face forward.*
- *Draw your belly muscles toward your spine as you move to help protect your lower back.*

Allow students to continue for about 3 more rounds on their own. You can also have a student say "breathe in, breathe out" as they twist. After students return to face forward, have them take a deep breath and notice how their shoulders or backs feel after twisting.

Proceed to the Mindful Breathing section.

MINDFUL BREATHING (3 MINUTES)

Find a way to sit comfortably with your back straight. You can close your eyes at any time, or just look down at your desk to help you focus inward.

At the beginning of this session, we did movement along with the 4:8 breathing. Remember that breathing out for twice as long as we breathe in helps us to calm ourselves and focus. Now we're going to do the same breathing, but without moving our arms. If you paid attention to your body and breath as we did the yoga movements, you might notice that now it's easier for you to focus your attention on your body, even while you're being still. Try to keep your attention on how your body feels as we breathe in for 4 and out for 8.

For example, you might feel some parts of your body move as you breathe, or you might feel your feet touching the floor or your weight on the seat. Or you might notice the air flowing past the nostrils.

If I count too slow or too fast for you, feel free to go with your own rhythm.

Pause.

Breathe in 1, 2, 3, 4. Breathe out 1, 2, 3, 4, 5, 6, 7, 8.

Repeat counting.

Now count silently to yourself:
- *Breathing in for 4.* Pause.
- *Breathing out for 8.* Pause.
- *In for 4.* Pause.
- *Out for 8.* Pause.

Now I'm going to be quiet and let you practice 3 rounds on your own. See if you can keep your mind on your body and the feeling of the breath. If your mind wanders to other thoughts, just bring it back and try again.

Pause, allow students to breathe on their own for 3 rounds.

Good! You can go back to breathing normally.

WRAP-UP

GUIDED MEDITATION AND CLOSING BELL (1 MINUTE)

We're going to end class by sitting silently for 1 minute, just noticing your breathing and how your body feels.

Feel free to close your eyes or look down to help you concentrate only on yourself.

If you like, you can even put your head down and rest it on your arms.

Pause.

Notice your feet resting on the floor, your legs relaxed on the seat.

Notice where your arms and hands are. Maybe you can allow your arms and shoulders to relax a bit more.

Notice how you're breathing.

You might even allow the muscles of your face to relax as you breathe.

Long pause, allow students to sit silently for remainder of the minute.

I will now ring the bell one last time. Listen to the bell and when you can't hear it anymore, please look up at me.

Ring bell and allow it to vibrate to completion.

CONNECTION QUESTIONS (3 MINUTES)

How are you all feeling? Can anyone give an example of an activity or situation in your life where it is important that you move or act with awareness?

Ask students if they have any questions about what we did today or about TLS or mindfulness in general, and thank them for their participation.

LESSON 2.4: BUILDING AWARENESS OF THE BREATH

In this lesson, students will be introduced to Chair Pose. Physically, this pose:

❖ Strengthens and tones the legs and abdominals
❖ Stretches the ankles and calves

Lesson objectives are (a) students will learn the importance of being aware of their breathing, and (b) students will practice becoming aware of their breathing.

STUDENT OVERVIEW

REVIEW EXPECTATIONS (2 MINUTES)

Review the expectations for TLS sessions, including:

❖ Students clear desks of all distractions including books, papers, food, cell phones, and music.
❖ One-mic rule: one person talks at a time. If students have questions, they can raise a hand or ask at the end of class. Assure students that there will be a few minutes dedicated to questions at the end of each session.
❖ Students focus on their own body and breath. That means not making comments about self or others, not touching others, and not distracting others from their experience.
❖ Students try their best to participate at all times. (However, participation may look different for each student. For some students, it may mean doing only the breathing for as long as they need, until they choose to engage with the movement. Allow students to come to the practice at their own pace, as long as they are not being distracting or disrespectful toward others. Engaging with one's body and mind through TLS is always a choice, and every day is a different experience.)

ACTIVATE BACKGROUND KNOWLEDGE (3 MINUTES)

In response to the class environment each day, you may wish to provide this information to students when you feel it would be best received—that may be at the beginning of class, woven into the mindful movement, or before the silent sitting.

Activation Question 2.4

Throughout the day are you aware of your breathing? How is your breathing when you are angry? Anxious? Calm?

Give students a chance to reflect on each question, and choose a few students to share their responses with the class.

Awareness of the breath is another type of self-awareness.

Sometimes when you are in a stressful situation—like an argument, or you are very worried—you might hold your breath or take really short breaths without realizing it. This can make you feel even more stressed, and even deprive the brain of oxygen. If you are aware of your breath when this happens, you can change your breathing to help you stay calm and think clearly.

From time to time during our session today, I'll ask you to notice how you are breathing, so that you can practice building awareness of your breath.

ACTION, BREATHING, CENTERING

OPENING BELL AND FOCUSED BREATHING (2 MINUTES)

We will start our time together today by trying to focus our attention on a sound. I would like to ask you all to listen to the sound of the bell I am going to ring.

Try to keep your attention on the sound of the bell for as long as you can, and when you can't hear it anymore, please raise your hand.

Ring bell or singing bowl.

❖ Allow to vibrate to completion and until all students have raised their hands.

❖ Then ask students to do the same thing, this time closing their eyes or looking down at their desks to focus just on their hearing, and ring the bell again.

❖ Wait until all students have raised their hands.

That was very good. Now I'll lead you in a breathing exercise:
- *You can keep your eyes closed, or just look down.*
- *Let all the air out of your lungs.*
- *Now breathe in, breathe out.*

Lead class in simple breathing, encouraging them to breathe deeply and smoothly.

Continue for 3–4 rounds.

Then tell students that you are going to do the bell exercise one more time.

Ring the bell again, and students raise their hands when they can no longer hear it.

MINDFUL MOVEMENT AND POSE OF THE DAY (6 MINUTES)

Mountain

Let's all stand up in Mountain Pose.

If needed, review the elements of Mountain Pose:

❖ Feet parallel and hip-width distance apart
❖ Shoulders relaxed
❖ Standing tall

If it feels comfortable, press your hands together at your chest, and

either close your eyes or look down at the place where your hands meet.

Can someone lead us in 3 breaths, saying, "breathe in, breathe out"?

Choose a student to lead the breaths, making sure the student leads them slowly to allow for deep breathing.

Standing Backbend with Clasp

Let's warm up our backs.
- *We'll inhale to reach up, exhale to clasp your hands behind your back, or bring your hands to your lower back if you prefer.*
- *Inhale as you draw your shoulder blades together and lift your chest.*

If your hands are clasped, try to straighten your arms.
- *Exhale and return to standing, releasing your hands and relaxing your shoulders.*

Let's repeat this movement with the breath 3 times.

Ask a student to lead the breaths.

Good! Shake out your arms and shoulders and return to Mountain Pose.

Notice if it feels like you have a little more room to breathe now.

Lunge

Now let's review Lunge Pose, the one we learned last time.
- *Take a deep breath in, and as you breathe out take your right leg back, with the right heel up off the floor.*
- *See how it feels to keep your right leg straight and bend your left leg.*

You might feel a stretch in the front of your right thigh.
- *Breathe in, and if it feels okay, reach high overhead with your arms.*
- *Breathe out, sinking your hips down.*

Now we'll move with the breath:
- *Inhale, keeping the arms up and straightening the legs*
- *Exhale, bending the front leg and taking the hands to the chest.*

Notice if your breaths are deep or shallow—try to keep them slow and deep if you can.

- *Inhale, up*
- *Exhale, bend*

In: reaching up, straight legs.

Out: bend just the front leg. Good!
- *When you're ready, bring your right foot forward to Mountain Pose.*
- *Let your arms rest at your sides, and notice your breath going in and out.*

Repeat with the left leg back. End in Mountain Pose with 3 mindful breaths.

Chair—Pose of the Day

Today's main pose of the day is called Chair Pose, because it looks like you're sitting on an invisible chair. Chair builds stability and strength in the legs. Watch out that you don't hold your breath! You can use your breath to count the time and keep yourself relaxed in Chair.

Now, we're only going to do this one time, so give it your best shot. Start by placing the feet together. You have a choice here: Either (1) reach your arms straight over your head, or (2) place your hands together at your chest.

Breathe in, lifting up your chest; breathe out, bending your legs as if you were sitting down on a chair behind you. Notice if this gets difficult—if you notice your breath change, try to keep breathing smoothly. Let's see if we can hold it for 3 more breaths—maybe you can even sink down lower with each breath.

Choose a student to lead the breaths.

Breathe in to straighten your legs. Breathe out, let your arms relax. How do your legs feel?

Shake-Out

Let's shake out our arms and legs.
- Shake your right arm and hand as you say "5, 4, 3, 2, 1."
- Shake your left arm and hand as you say: "5, 4, 3, 2, 1."
- Shake your right leg, counting down from 5.
- Repeat with your left leg.
- Then repeat the whole sequence counting down from 4.

Repeat counting down from 3, from 2, and 1—the last round will consist of one quick shake per limb. Then have students come back to Mountain Pose with their hands at their chest. Invite them to notice how they are breathing, and if their breath slows down as they stay in Mountain for several breaths.

Neck Movements

Please have a seat. Find a way that you can sit comfortably with your back straight. We are going to do some movements to release tension in the neck.
- *As you exhale, let your right ear fall toward your right shoulder, just until you feel a stretch.*
- *On your next breath in, return your head to center.*
- *On your next breath out, let your left ear fall toward your left shoulder, noticing if you feel a stretch or other sensation in your neck or shoulder.*

Repeat this movement 2 more times. Be gentle with your neck as you move to the rhythm of your own breath.

Pause while students finish.

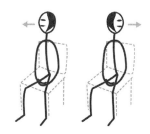

Bring your head back to center.
- *As you breathe out, look to the right. You can either close your eyes, or look down slightly.*
- *As you breathe in, bring your head back to center.*
- *As you breathe out, turn your head to the left.*

Repeat this movement 2 more times. Notice if you get bored and try to speed up your breath to make the movement go faster. See if you can give your breath time to be deep and long, even if the movement feels slow to you.

Pause.

Come back to center. Now when you breathe in, lift your chest up and look slightly upward. Be careful not to strain your neck. As you breathe out, tuck your chin and let your head bow forward. Repeat this movement 2 more times with your breath, noticing any sensations in the back of your neck.

Pause.

Now just sitting still for a moment, notice your breath going in and out.

Proceed to Mindful Breathing section of lesson.

MINDFUL BREATHING (3 MINUTES)

Make sure you are still sitting comfortably with your back straight. We're going to notice what parts of the body move as we breathe.
- *If it feels okay, place one hand on your belly.*
- *Notice if your belly is moving as you breathe. If not, try to relax the muscles around your belly as you take deep breaths.*

- *You may notice the belly moving out as you breathe in, like it's getting bigger, and moving back in toward your spine as you breathe out.*

You don't have to try to make your belly get big, just notice any small movement that might happen as you breathe.

Pause.

Now place your hands on your ribs on both sides. Notice your ribs moving out to the sides as you breathe in, and back in as you breathe out. Again, don't try to make big movements, just notice whatever movement happens.

Pause.

Now, if you'd like, place a hand on your chest. Notice how your chest moves as you breathe. You might feel it lift away from your heart as you breathe in, and fall back in toward your heart as you breathe out. Just notice how the chest moves as you take long, smooth breaths.

Pause.

Good. Now you can just relax your hands down to your lap or desk. Rather than concentrating on a specific part of the body as you breathe, just notice whatever is moving. Does one part move more than the others? Does one part move first, followed by the others, or do they all move together? Take a moment to just notice the movements connected with your breath.

Longer pause.

Good concentration, everybody.

WRAP-UP

GUIDED MEDITATION AND CLOSING BELL (1 MINUTE)

We're going to end class by sitting silently for 1 minute, just noticing your breathing and how your body feels.

Feel free to close your eyes or look down to help you concentrate only on yourself.

If you like, you can even put your head down and rest it on your arms.

Pause.

Notice your feet resting on the floor, your legs relaxed on the seat.

Notice where your arms and hands are. Maybe you can allow your arms and shoulders to relax a bit more.

Notice how you're breathing.

You might even allow the muscles of your face to relax as you breathe.

Long pause, allow students to sit silently for remainder of the minute.

I will now ring the bell one last time. Listen to the bell and when you can't hear it anymore, please look up at me.

Ring bell and allow it to vibrate to completion.

CONNECTION QUESTIONS (2 MINUTES)

How are you feeling? Did anyone notice that your breathing got short or stopped during some of the exercises we did? What were you doing when your breath changed?

Students often hold their breath when trying to balance, but this creates tension in the body and makes it harder to balance. We can best balance—and better deal with other challenges—if we keep breathing to maintain our calm and focus.

Ask students if they have any questions about what we did today or about TLS or mindfulness in general, and thank them for their participation.

LESSON 2.5: THE CONNECTION BETWEEN BREATH AND EMOTION

In this lesson, students will be introduced to Twisting Chair Pose. Physically, this pose:

* Maintains flexibility of the spine and intercostal muscles
* Strengthens and tones the legs
* Helps rid the body of toxins

Lesson objectives are (a) students will become more aware of how their emotions affect their breathing, and vice-versa, and (b) students will practice noticing their breathing and their emotions.

STUDENT OVERVIEW

REVIEW EXPECTATIONS (2 MINUTES)

Review the expectations for TLS sessions, including:

* Students clear desks of all distractions including books, papers, food, cell phones, and music.
* One-mic rule: one person talks at a time. If students have questions, they can raise a hand or ask at the end of class. Assure students that there will be a few minutes dedicated to questions at the end of each session.
* Students focus on their own body and breath. That means not making comments about self or others, not touching others, and not distracting others from their experience.
* Students try their best to participate at all times. (However, participation may look different for each student. For some students, it may mean doing only the breathing for as long as they need, until they choose to engage with the movement. Allow students to come to the practice at their own pace, as long as they are not being distracting or disrespectful

toward others. Engaging with one's body and mind through TLS is always a choice, and every day is a different experience.)

ACTIVATE BACKGROUND KNOWLEDGE (3 MINUTES)

In response to the class environment each day, you may wish to provide this information to students when you feel it would be best received—that may be at the beginning of class, woven into the mindful movement, or before the silent sitting.

> *In the last lesson, we talked about being aware of our breathing. The way we are breathing can tell us a lot about our emotions if we take a moment to notice. Has anyone ever noticed your breath get quicker or shallower when you are feeling stressed, angry, or anxious? Has anyone ever noticed yourself taking a deep sigh when you are relaxing?*

> *Just as our emotions affect the way we breathe, we can also change the way we breathe in order to affect our emotions and mood. Scientists have found that just changing the way you are breathing can affect your mood by 40 percent! By breathing deeper when you notice frustration, anxiety, or anger, you can signal to your nervous system to relax. This can help you calm your body, think more clearly, and act with more awareness.*

Activation Question 2.5

> *In your own life, can you think of an example of when you might use your breath to manage your emotions? How might that change the outcome of the situation?*

Give students a chance to reflect, and choose a few students to share their responses with the class.

> *You might find the pose of the day today a bit challenging. See if*

you can use your breathing to keep you calm and focused on your body as you try it out.

ACTION, BREATHING, CENTERING

OPENING BELL AND FOCUSED BREATHING (2 MINUTES)

We will start our time together today by trying to focus our attention on a sound. I would like to ask you all to listen to the sound of the bell I am going to ring.

Try to keep your attention on the sound of the bell for as long as you can, and when you can't hear it anymore, please raise your hand.

Ring bell or singing bowl.

❖ Allow to vibrate to completion and until all students have raised their hands.

❖ Then ask students to do the same thing, this time closing their eyes or looking down at their desks to focus just on their hearing, and ring the bell again.

❖ Wait until all students have raised their hands.

> *That was very good. Now I'll lead you in a breathing exercise:*
> * *You can keep your eyes closed, or just look down.*
> * *Let all the air out of your lungs.*
> * *Now breathe in, breathe out.*

Lead class in simple breathing, encouraging them to breathe deeply and smoothly.

Continue for 3–4 rounds.

Then tell students that you are going to do the bell exercise one more time.

Ring the bell again, and students raise their hands when they can no longer hear it.

MINDFUL MOVEMENT AND POSE OF THE DAY (6 MINUTES)

Mountain

Let's all stand up in Mountain Pose. Mountain pose is a great thing to do when you feel yourself swept away by worries, anger, or other emotions and need to ground yourself. You can do it anywhere and anytime, and people don't even have to know you are doing TLS.

If needed, review the elements of Mountain Pose:

❖ Feet parallel and hip-width distance apart
❖ Shoulders relaxed
❖ Standing tall

Each time you breathe in, see if you can reach the top of your head toward the ceiling. Each time you breathe out, feel where your feet are touching the floor, wiggling your toes if that helps. Breathing in, allowing your chest to lift; breathing out, letting your arms hang down from your shoulders and feeling your feet on the floor.

Choose a student to lead 3 more breaths, making sure the student leads them slowly to allow for deep breathing.

Wrist-Cross Crescent

Cross your right wrist over your left in front of you. Feel the backs of your hands pressing together.
- *As you're ready, on a breath in, lift your arms above your head.*
- *Breathe out, lean to the left, just enough so you feel a stretch somewhere on your right side.*
- *Breathe in, lift your arms up straight.*
- *Breathe out, lean to the left again. Try to keep both feet pressing evenly into the floor.*
- *Breathe in, come up straight.*
- *Last one: breathe out lean, breathe in come up.*

Now bring your arms forward and cross them more, more, more—until your arms are crossed above the elbows. Give yourself a big hug, grabbing onto your shoulder blades with your hands. Take a big breath in, feel your ribs expand as you breathe. Breathe out, and see if you can keep your grip on your shoulder blades, as you lower your shoulders down away from your ears.

Take 1 more breath here, and see if you feel a stretch in the upper back or shoulders. Good! Shake out your arms if you'd like. Let's do the other side.

Lead class in the same movements on the other side: left wrist crosses over right, lean to the right, then cross more until you are giving yourself a hug. Once you are done, have students shake out their arms.

Flamingo

We're going to do Flamingo moving with the breath.
- *Breathe in and stand tall, reaching the top of your head toward the ceiling.*
- *When you exhale, bend your right leg and grab your shin with your hands, maybe raising your knee up toward your chest. If you can't reach your shin, you can grab under your thigh.*
- *Inhale, place both feet firmly on the floor and stand tall.*
- *Exhale, and raise the left leg in the same way.*
- *Inhale, place your left foot down and feel both feet on the floor.*

Continue the movement with the breathing.

Notice what happens to your breath if you feel like you're going to lose your balance. As best you can, keep breathing deeply and connecting the movement with the breathing.

Choose a student to lead the breath and repeat 2 more times on each side.

To help with balance, look at a spot that's not moving, like a spot on the floor or the wall in front of you. It can also help to draw the belly in toward the spine as you breathe out.

End in Mountain Pose and have students notice if they are breathing deeply or shallowly.

Chair

Let's review Chair Pose. Remember, if the pose feels challenging, you can focus on taking deep breaths to help you keep time and give you patience.

- *Place your feet together.*
- *Reach your arms straight over your head and clasp your hands together, if that feels okay.*
- *Breathe in reach up higher with your arms, and as you breathe out bend your legs.*

Pretend you are sitting down on a chair behind you. You might feel your legs start to get warm. Notice how you are breathing. We'll just hold it for 3 breaths.

Choose a student to say the breaths.

Breathe in to straighten your legs. Breathe out let your arms relax. Very good.

Twisting Chair—Pose of the Day

Today's main pose of the day: Twisting Chair.

Twisting Chair is a challenging pose—it can make you feel like you're tied up in knots! Before you try it, you might make an intention to try to keep breathing as deeply as the pose allows you, in order to keep your mind focused and calm. This way you'll practice keeping your cool in challenging situations, and be less likely to get frustrated trying to do the pose "perfectly."

We start the pose in Chair. We'll first twist to look to the right. There are a few ways to twist here.

- *The first way is to extend your arms and hook your left arm on the outside of your right leg, extending your right arm straight up toward the ceiling. If this is too much, you can bring your right hand to your hip.*
- *Another option is to press your hands together at your chest, and hook your left elbow on the outside of your right thigh.*

Whichever one you choose, use your left arm pushing against your right leg to help you twist. Can someone lead us in 3 breaths?

Choose a student to lead breaths.

Good, inhale to come out of the twist and straighten your legs. Was that hard or easy?

Did anyone notice they forgot to breathe? How did you feel when you were trying the pose?

Remind students that all answers are okay. What's important is to practice self-awareness by trying to notice.

Let's try the other side.

Lead students in Twisted Chair to the left. Hold for 3 breaths. Then come out of the twist and straighten the legs.

Trunk Twists

Now you can shake out your arms and bring your feet a little farther apart. If you have room, let your arms just relax and swing as you twist from side to side. If you don't, you can keep your arms bent at chest height. Lift up your opposite heel as you twist to the side to protect your knees. You might try breathing out each time you turn to the side.

Demonstrate twisting and breathing out in short, audible spurts each time you twist to the side.

Now let your twists get smaller and smaller until you are still.

Come back to Mountain Pose with your palms together at your chest and take a few breaths, noticing how your body feels.

Invite another student to lead 3 breaths in Mountain Pose.

Have students take a seat. Proceed to the Mindful Breathing section.

MINDFUL BREATHING (3 MINUTES)

Find a way to sit comfortably with your back straight. You can close your eyes at any time, or just look down at your desk to help you focus inward. Find the rhythm of your breathing. Notice how the breath feels as it comes in and goes out.

Pause.

Notice the moment when the inhale turns into an exhale. Notice the moment when the exhale turns into an inhale.

Pause.

Now if it feels okay, each time you get to the top of the inhale, pause for just a second or two. Then let the breath out. When you get to the bottom of your exhale, pause for a second or two. So you're noticing how it feels to be full of air for a moment, then following the breath all the way out. Notice how it feels to be empty and still for a moment, and then watch the breath as it comes back in.

Pause.

See if you can do this breathing on your own for a few more rounds.

Pause.

You can go back to breathing normally for a bit. Here's a little trick for using your breath to manage your emotions:

- *Pausing after the inhale can give you a little boost of energy.*
- *Pausing after the exhale can calm you down.*
- *If you've been feeling sad or low-energy, try only pausing when you're full of breath, to give you more energy.*
- *If you've been feeling anxious, stressed, or angry, try pausing only when you are empty of breath, to calm you.*
- *If you haven't been feeling either of these, keep pausing on both the inhale and the exhale, to help you stay balanced.*

Choose which one you want to do and try it for a few rounds now. You can take a break at any time if you need to. If you have any questions, just raise a hand.

Pause and let students try the breathing on their own.

Good job! Please go back to breathing normally and notice how you feel.

WRAP-UP

GUIDED MEDITATION AND CLOSING BELL (1 MINUTE)

We're going to end class by sitting silently for 1 minute, just noticing your breathing and how your body feels.

Feel free to close your eyes or look down to help you concentrate only on yourself.

If you like, you can even put your head down and rest it on your arms.

Pause.

Notice your feet resting on the floor, your legs relaxed on the seat.

Notice where your arms and hands are. Maybe you can allow your arms and shoulders to relax a bit more.

Notice how you're breathing.

You might even allow the muscles of your face to relax as you breathe.

Long pause, allow students to sit silently for remainder of the minute.

I will now ring the bell one last time. Listen to the bell and when you can't hear it anymore, please look up at me.

Ring bell and allow it to vibrate to completion.

CONNECTION QUESTIONS (3 MINUTES)

How are you all feeling right now? Which breathing technique did you choose to do during the Mindful Breathing? How did it feel?

Ask students if they have any questions about what we did today or about TLS or mindfulness in general, and thank them for their participation.

LESSON 2.6: BUILDING AWARENESS OF YOUR INTENTIONS

In this lesson, students will be introduced to Bird Pose. Physically, this pose:

❖ Strengthens and firms the legs and abdominal muscles
❖ Increases stability of the hips and ankles
❖ Improves balance

Lesson objectives are (a) students will learn what an intention is and why intentions are important, and (b) students will have an opportunity to set intentions for their TLS practice.

STUDENT OVERVIEW

REVIEW EXPECTATIONS (2 MINUTES)

Review the expectations for TLS sessions, including:

❖ Students clear desks of all distractions including books, papers, food, cell phones, and music.
❖ One-mic rule: one person talks at a time. If students have questions, they can raise a hand or ask at the end of class. Assure students that there will be a few minutes dedicated to questions at the end of each session.
❖ Students focus on their own body and breath. That means not making comments about self or others, not touching others, and not distracting others from their experience.
❖ Students try their best to participate at all times. (However, participation may look different for each student. For some students, it may mean doing only the breathing for as long as they need, until they choose to engage with the movement. Allow students to come to the practice at their own pace, as long as they are not being distracting or disrespectful toward others. Engaging with one's body and mind through TLS is always a choice, and every day is a different experience.)

ACTIVATE BACKGROUND KNOWLEDGE (3 MINUTES)

In response to the class environment each day, you may wish to provide this information to students when you feel it would be best received—that may be at the beginning of class, woven into the mindful movement, or before the silent sitting.

> *An intention is an attitude or aim that you consciously choose to work toward. Setting an intention can help you reach your goals little by little, by reminding you of the attitudes and actions you need to achieve them. For example, if your goal is to graduate, you might set an intention to go to class every day, even if your friends skip. If your goal is to be a better sister or brother, you might make an intention to have patience even when your siblings are irritating you.*

> *Setting an intention can help us not to get carried away by negativity in our environment. It can also help us keep our focus when we know we are going into a difficult conversation or conflict. By setting intentions, we can move closer to our goals, day by day. Our TLS practice can support this by helping us be more aware of our intentions and actions, as well as the thoughts and emotions behind them.*

Activation Question 2.6

> *What is a goal that you have, and what's an intention you can set to help you reach that goal?*

Give students a chance to reflect, and choose a few students to share their responses with the class.

> *People often set an intention in order to get the most out of their mindfulness practice. For example, I will refocus on my breath as many times as I need to; I will be patient with myself; I will be accepting of myself no matter how I show up today. If you want, set an intention for your practice now.*

ACTION, BREATHING, CENTERING

OPENING BELL AND FOCUSED BREATHING (2 MINUTES)

We will start our time together today by trying to focus our attention on a sound. I would like to ask you all to listen to the sound of the bell I am going to ring.

Try to keep your attention on the sound of the bell for as long as you can, and when you can't hear it anymore, please raise your hand.

Ring bell or singing bowl.

❖ Allow to vibrate to completion and until all students have raised their hands.

❖ Then ask students to do the same thing, this time closing their eyes or looking down at their desks to focus just on their hearing, and ring the bell again.

❖ Wait until all students have raised their hands.

That was very good. Now I'll lead you in a breathing exercise:
- *You can keep your eyes closed, or just look down.*
- *Let all the air out of your lungs.*
- *Now breathe in, breathe out.*

Lead class in simple breathing, encouraging them to breathe deeply and smoothly.

Continue for 3–4 rounds.

Then tell students that you are going to do the bell exercise one more time.

Ring the bell again, and students raise their hands when they can no longer hear it.

MINDFUL MOVEMENT AND POSE OF THE DAY (6 MINUTES)

Mountain

Let's all stand up in Mountain Pose.

If needed, review the elements of Mountain Pose:

❖ Feet parallel and hip-width distance apart
❖ Shoulders relaxed
❖ Standing tall

If you'd like, press your hands together at your chest, and either close your eyes or look down at the place where your hands meet. Can someone lead us in 3 breaths, saying, "breathe in, breathe out"?

Choose a student to lead the breaths, making sure the student leads them slowly to allow for deep breathing.

Arm Movements

The next time you breathe in, take the hands forward, still pressed together, and then apart and out to the sides, reaching as wide as you can with the fingers. When you breathe out, bring the hands slowly back together and then in to the chest.

Lead students in a couple of rounds, breathing in to reach the hands forward and out, and breathing out to bring them together and in. Encourage students to move slowly to build awareness of their bodies as they move.

Good. Now let's add in some rhythm, breathing in for 4 counts as we reach wide and breathing out for 8 counts as we bring the arms in. Feel free to go at your own speed if I count too fast or too slow for you. Try to move with the intention of matching your movement as much as possible to your breathing.

Lead students by counting a few rounds.

Now count silently in your head.

- *In for 4.* Pause.
- *Out for 8.* Pause.

See if you can do 2 more rounds silently without losing count.

Pause as students continue.

After this round, return to breathing normally. Let your arms relax, and notice how your shoulders feel.

Forward Warrior

Next we'll do Forward Warrior. Who remembers how to do Forward Warrior?

Ask a student to model the pose.

Bring your right leg straight back and press your right heel down on the floor. Try to keep your right leg straight as you bend your left leg, bringing the left knee right over the ankle. If your knee goes past your ankle, you can widen your stance by bringing your right foot farther back. In this pose, our hips and chest face forward as much as feels comfortable.

Now, when we breathe in, we'll straighten both legs and reach our arms up toward the ceiling. When we breathe out, we'll bend the front leg and bring the hands to the chest. Do you notice the sensations in your legs change as you bend and straighten them? Try to keep the back leg straight. Let's try this 2 more times, moving slowly with the breath.

Choose a student to lead the breaths. After the second exhale, stay in the pose with the front knee bent for 2 more breaths, encouraging students to use deep breaths to keep themselves calm and build patience.

Bird—Pose of the Day

We're going to go straight into the main pose of the day, Bird Pose. Extend your arms out to the sides to help you balance. If you made an intention for your practice today, see if you can use it to work through this more challenging pose.

As you're ready, lean forward and start to lift your right leg off the floor. You can lift it just a few inches or higher if you feel comfortable. If you lose your balance, smooth out your breath to calm yourself before you try it again. Keep your breath flowing as you try the pose. Remember, it helps you balance if you look at a spot in front of you that's not moving, and if you pull your belly in gently as you breathe. Remember your intention for your practice today!

Choose a student to lead the breaths. Come out of the pose by lowering the right leg into Forward Warrior, then bringing it forward to Mountain Pose.

Was anyone able to remember their intention with everything else that was going on? When things get challenging or stressful, that's often when we forget about our intentions! But with practice we get better at managing stress and remembering. Let's try it again on the other side.

Lead students through the Forward Warrior series, and then into Bird with the left leg lifted. When finished, bring everyone back to Mountain Pose and have one student lead 3 breaths.

Shoulder Movements

By now you will probably know your students and what helps them to focus. You may choose to do the shoulder movements seated or standing up, whichever helps your students to keep their attention focused.

Let your arms relax at your sides. We are going to do some movements to release tension from the shoulders. On your next inhale, shrug your shoulders up toward your ears, and on the exhale, let them drop. Let's do that 3 more times. You might notice the muscles tensing up to raise the shoulders and letting go to drop them.

For the next movement, we'll rotate our shoulders in circles:
- *As you inhale, roll the shoulders up and back.*
- *As you exhale, bring them down and forward.*
- *You can make your circles small or big, whatever feels more comfortable to you.*
- *Notice any stretching or clicking or warmth you feel in your shoulders as you move and breathe.*

Repeat 3 times. Remind students to keep the movement slow so that they can breathe deeply. Reverse direction and repeat 3 times.

If they are not seated already, have students take a seat. Proceed to the Mindful Breathing section.

MINDFUL BREATHING (3 MINUTES)

Find a way to sit comfortably with your back straight. You can close your eyes at any time, or just look down at your desk to help you focus inward. We're going to practice a meditation, and the whole point of the meditation is to just observe all the details you can about your breathing. Notice if you have the tendency to judge how you should be feeling or how you should be breathing, and try to just observe without judging yourself.

Now, try to keep this intention or your own intention for your practice in the back of your mind as you bring your attention to your breathing. Notice how long it takes for your breath to come in and to go out.

Slowly, with pauses to allow students time to notice each quality.

Notice the rhythm of your own breath right now:
- *Is it fast or slow? Is it deep or shallow?*

Pause.

- *Allow your breath the time to be as deep as feels comfortable.*

Pause.

- *Notice if your breath is smooth or choppy. Is it colder as it comes in and warmer as it goes out?*

Pause.

- *Maybe you can feel your chest and ribs moving with your breath.*

Pause.

- *Maybe you can feel your belly moving with your breath, too.*

Pause.

- *Maybe you can even feel your shoulders and back moving with your breath, as your ribs reach all the way around you to your back.*

Take a moment to notice the qualities of each breath that comes in and goes out, as if you didn't want to miss even one little detail.

Pause to allow students to breathe for 3–4 rounds.

Good job. Come back to breathing normally and notice how you feel.

If you take a moment to notice how you are breathing during the day, you might notice that sometimes your breath is really shallow, only moving into the upper part of your chest. Breathing like that can make you feel more anxious, stressed, or unfocused.

Breathing deeper, all the way down to your belly, can help you clear your mind and release stress.

As you go through the rest of your day today, try noticing how you're breathing, once in a while. Experiment with deepening the breath and notice how it makes you feel. Experiencing stress and difficult emotions can make it hard to focus on your intentions. Using your breath to help manage your emotions is a great way to support yourself in reaching your goals!

WRAP-UP

GUIDED MEDITATION AND CLOSING BELL (1 MINUTE)

We're going to end class by sitting silently for 1 minute, just noticing your breathing and how your body feels.

Feel free to close your eyes or look down to help you concentrate only on yourself.

If you like, you can even put your head down and rest it on your arms.

Pause.

Notice your feet resting on the floor, your legs relaxed on the seat.

Notice where your arms and hands are. Maybe you can allow your arms and shoulders to relax a bit more.

Notice how you're breathing.

You might even allow the muscles of your face to relax as you breathe.

Long pause, allow students to sit silently for remainder of the minute.

I will now ring the bell one last time. Listen to the bell and when you can't hear it anymore, please look up at me.

Ring bell and allow it to vibrate to completion.

CONNECTION QUESTIONS (3 MINUTES)

How is everyone feeling? Can anyone share which intention you chose for your practice, and why? What situations in real life might benefit from you choosing that intention?

Ask students if they have any questions about what we did today or about TLS or mindfulness in general, and thank them for their participation.

LESSON 2.7: BUILDING AWARENESS OF THOUGHT PATTERNS

In this lesson, students will be introduced to Extended Flamingo Pose. Physically, this pose:

❖ Stretches the hips and legs, releasing tension in the back
❖ Improves balance

Lesson objectives are (a) students will notice one or two thought patterns, or stories that they tell themselves (about self or others), and (b) students will practice noticing their thoughts and bringing their attention back to their body sensations and breath.

STUDENT OVERVIEW

REVIEW EXPECTATIONS (2 MINUTES)

Review the expectations for TLS sessions, including:

❖ Students clear desks of all distractions including books, papers, food, cell phones, and music.
❖ One-mic rule: one person talks at a time. If students have questions, they can raise a hand or ask at the end of class. Assure students that there will be a few minutes dedicated to questions at the end of each session.
❖ Students focus on their own body and breath. That means not making comments about self or others, not touching others, and not distracting others from their experience.
❖ Students try their best to participate at all times. (However, participation may look different for each student. For some students, it may mean doing only the breathing for as long as they need, until they choose to engage with the movement. Allow students to come to the practice at their own pace, as long as they are not being distracting or disrespectful toward others. Engaging with one's body and mind through TLS is always a choice, and every day is a different experience.)

ACTIVATE BACKGROUND KNOWLEDGE (3 MINUTES)

In response to the class environment each day, you may wish to provide this information to students when you feel it would be best received—that may be at the beginning of class, woven into the mindful movement, or before the silent sitting.

Thought patterns are habits of thinking in a certain way or making certain assumptions or judgments. They're like stories we tell ourselves. We tell ourselves a lot of stories about ourselves and about the world around us. Some common stories are, "I'm not good enough," "People like me can't do that," "People like them are rude/smart/etc." Often we forget we even tell ourselves these stories, but deep inside we believe them. If we don't recognize these stories for what they are, they can affect our behavior, without us realizing it.

Activation Question 2.7

Do you think that people's beliefs about themselves or others affect their actions? Can you give an example?

Give students a chance to reflect, and choose a few students to share their responses with the class.

Today we'll continue to focus on our movements and our breathing. If you notice that you start thinking, try to be aware of your thoughts, and then bring your focus back to your breathing.

ACTION, BREATHING, CENTERING

OPENING BELL AND FOCUSED BREATHING (2 MINUTES)

We will start our time together today by trying to focus our attention on a sound. I would like to ask you all to listen to the sound of the bell I am going to ring.

Try to keep your attention on the sound of the bell for as long as you can, and when you can't hear it anymore, please raise your hand.

Ring bell or singing bowl.

❖ Allow to vibrate to completion and until all students have raised their hands.

❖ Then ask students to do the same thing, this time closing their eyes or looking down at their desks to focus just on their hearing, and ring the bell again.

❖ Wait until all students have raised their hands.

That was very good. Now I'll lead you in a breathing exercise:
- *You can keep your eyes closed, or just look down.*
- *Let all the air out of your lungs.*
- *Now breathe in, breathe out.*

Lead class in simple breathing, encouraging them to breathe deeply and smoothly.

Continue for 3–4 rounds.

Then tell students that you are going to do the bell exercise one more time.

Ring the bell again, and students raise their hands when they can no longer hear it.

MINDFUL MOVEMENT AND POSE OF THE DAY (6 MINUTES)

Mountain

Let's all stand up in Mountain Pose.

Pause as students stand.

As you breathe in, lift the top of your head up toward the ceiling. As you breathe out, let your shoulders and arms relax. Breathe in and stand tall, reaching your head toward the ceiling. Breathe out and feel your feet on the floor, wiggling your toes if that helps you feel them. Take 1 more deep breath: standing tall, feeling your feet on the floor, and shoulders relaxed. Great, go ahead and release your arms, letting them hang down at your sides.

Standing Backbend as a Movement

For the next pose, we are going to do a standing back bend as a movement. Pay attention to how your back feels and only go as far as feels comfortable, so you don't get hurt.
- *Inhale, reaching up.*
- *Exhale, bringing your hands to your lower back.*
- *Support your lower back as you inhale, opening up your chest as you lean back a bit.*
- *Exhale, returning to standing.*

We will repeat this movement 3 times. Notice if your breath gets shallow—try to keep breathing deeply.

Ask a student to lead the movement. When done, have students stand in Mountain Pose with hands to chest. Have a student lead 3 breaths.

Notice if you can easily keep your mind focused on your breath, or if it is wandering. Either one is fine, because that's your experience right now. The point is to notice.

Flamingo

Breathe in and stand tall, reaching the top of your head toward the ceiling.
- *On the exhale, we'll bend the right leg into Flamingo Pose, grabbing your shin or under your thigh.*
- *Inhale, we'll place both feet firmly on the floor and stand tall.*
- *Exhale, we'll raise the left leg in the same way.*
- *Inhale, placing your left foot down and feeling both feet on the floor.*

As you continue doing this, try to keep the movement connected to your breath and make your movements and your breath smooth.

To help with balance, look at a spot that's not moving, like a spot on the floor or the wall in front of you. It can also help to draw the belly in toward the spine as you breathe out to balance.

Lead students in repeating the movement 2 more times on each side. Finish in Mountain Pose.

Extended Flamingo—Pose of the Day

Today's main pose of the day is Extended Flamingo.

Extended Flamingo is another challenging pose. You might notice yourself say "I can't," and give up before you start. But everyone can try it! Just do your best, keep breathing, and notice how the pose is for you today.
- *Now, the next time you lift up the right leg into Flamingo Pose, take a breath to find your balance.*
- *When you're ready, grab under your thigh, and try to extend the leg straight out in front of you. Just go as far as you can go and hold it for 3 breaths.*

Notice if you find yourself thinking about how you should be doing the pose rather than how it feels to do the pose. Notice if you're judging yourself.
- *The important thing isn't how you look, but noticing your breathing and how your body feels For example, you might feel something in your legs, back, or shoulders.*
- *Good, 2 more breaths.* **Slowly:** *Breathe in, and out. Breathe in, and out. Good job!*
- *Let your leg bend more and bring it back down to the floor. Shake it out, and come back to Mountain Pose before we try it on the other side.*

Take 3 breaths in Mountain Pose noticing how your legs feel. Then repeat Extended Flamingo with the left leg lifted.

Remind students to notice where their mind is, and that it's easier to balance if the mind focuses on the breath and the body. Have a student lead 3 breaths to hold the pose. End in Mountain Pose.

Side Warrior

Next, we'll do Side Warrior. When you're ready, take your left leg back. Press your left heel to the floor and face your hips and chest to the left. Experiment with bending your right leg more or less, and see how that affects how the pose feels. Make sure your knee doesn't lean to the side, but rather bends straight forward over your ankle. Once you find a good amount of bend for the front leg, raise your arms to shoulder height and look over the fingers of your right hand. Try to maintain your upper body straight up and down. Take a breath. Where is your mind? Is it focused on your body, on your breath, or elsewhere?

Star Gazer

From Side Warrior, we'll come into Star Gazer. Raise your right arm up toward the ceiling, and rest your left hand gently on your straight back leg, either above or below the knee. Try to do this without straightening your right leg. You might feel a stretch somewhere along your right side here. Notice where your mind is. Try to focus it on your breath, your arm reaching high, and your feet touching the floor, as we hold for 3 breaths.

Choose a student to lead the breaths.

When you breathe in, come back up to Side Warrior Pose. As you breathe out, bring the left leg forward to Mountain Pose.

Choose a student to lead 3 mindful breaths in Mountain Pose. Lead students through the Side Warrior and Star Gazer sequence with the right leg back. When you finish, come back to Mountain Pose and have students take 3 breaths with the hands pressed together at the chest.

Trunk Twists

Now you can shake out your arms and bring your feet a little farther apart. We'll start to twist the upper body from side to side. Let your arms swing as you twist, or bend them at chest height. Lift up the opposite heel as you twist to the side to protect your knees. Can you feel the air brush past your hands or arms?

Pause to allow students to feel the twists.

Now let your twists get smaller and smaller until you are still. Come back to Mountain Pose with your palms together at your chest and take a few breaths, noticing how your body feels.

Have another student lead 3 breaths.

Instruct students to take a seat. Proceed to the Mindful Breathing section.

MINDFUL BREATHING (3 MINUTES)

Come to sit comfortably with your back straight. You can close your eyes at any time, or just look down at your desk to help you focus inward.

Does anybody remember the experiment we did a few weeks ago, where we counted the number of breaths we breathed in 1 minute? Often the faster you breathe, the more thoughts you have swirling around in your head. It's hard to notice your thoughts when they're racing! So we're going to practice slowing the breath down so that we can slow down our thoughts enough to notice them. I'll lead you in breathing in for 4 counts and out for 8 counts. However, if you feel like the counting doesn't work for you today, feel free to just breathe in deeply and breathe out slowly to your own rhythm.

Start by exhaling to let all the air out of your lungs.

Pause.

- *Breathe in 1, 2, 3, 4.*
- *Breathe out 1, 2, 3, 4, 5, 6, 7, 8.*
- *Breathe in 1, 2, 3, 4.*
- *Breathe out 1, 2, 3, 4, 5, 6, 7, 8.*
- *Now count silently to yourself, breathing in for 4*

Pause.

- *And out for 8.*

Pause.

- *In deeply and out slowly.*

Pause.

Now I'm going to be quiet and let you practice 4 or 5 rounds on your own.

If thoughts come up, just notice what they are and come back to your breathing. Try not to get carried away by your thoughts.

Pause, allow students to breathe on their own for 4–5 rounds.

Good! Now if you have noticed any negative thoughts come up today, about yourself or others, take a moment to notice what they are. Imagine breathing out those negative thoughts on your exhale.

Pause to allow students to breathe a few times.

Taking this opportunity to practice choosing which thoughts you focus on, and which ones you let go of. Breathing in deeply, and breathing out any negative thoughts.

Pause.

Good. Go ahead and go back to breathing normally if you'd like.

WRAP-UP

GUIDED MEDITATION AND CLOSING BELL (1 MINUTE)

We're going to end class by sitting silently for 1 minute, just noticing your breathing and how your body feels.

Feel free to close your eyes or look down to help you concentrate only on yourself.

If you like, you can even put your head down and rest it on your arms.

Pause.

Notice your feet resting on the floor, your legs relaxed on the seat.

Notice where your arms and hands are. Maybe you can allow your arms and shoulders to relax a bit more.

Notice how you're breathing.

You might even allow the muscles of your face to relax as you breathe.

Long pause, allow students to sit silently for remainder of the minute.

I will now ring the bell one last time. Listen to the bell and when you can't hear it anymore, please look up at me.

Ring bell and allow it to vibrate to completion.

CONNECTION QUESTIONS (3 MINUTES)

How is everyone feeling? Do you think it would be useful to be able to notice and breathe out negative thoughts that you have during the day? Why or why not?

Ask students if they have any questions about what we did today or about TLS or mindfulness in general, and thank them for their participation.

LESSON 2.8: THOUGHTS AND FEELINGS ALWAYS CHANGE

In this lesson, students will be introduced to Cow Face Pose. Physically, this pose:

❖ Increases mobility in the shoulders
❖ Stretches the upper arms

Lesson objectives are (a) students will recognize the temporary nature of thoughts and feelings, and (b) students will practice noticing thoughts and feelings, then bringing their attention back to their body and breath.

STUDENT OVERVIEW

REVIEW EXPECTATIONS (2 MINUTES)

Review the expectations for TLS sessions, including:

❖ Students clear desks of all distractions including books, papers, food, cell phones, and music.
❖ One-mic rule: one person talks at a time. If students have questions, they can raise a hand or ask at the end of class. Assure students that there will be a few minutes dedicated to questions at the end of each session.
❖ Students focus on their own body and breath. That means not making comments about self or others, not touching others, and not distracting others from their experience.
❖ Students try their best to participate at all times. (However, participation may look different for each student. For some students, it may mean doing only the breathing for as long as they need, until they choose to engage with the movement. Allow students to come to the practice at their own pace, as long as they are not being distracting or disrespectful toward others. Engaging with one's body and mind through TLS is always a choice, and every day is a different experience.)

ACTIVATE BACKGROUND KNOWLEDGE (3 MINUTES)

In response to the class environment each day, you may wish to provide this information to students when you feel it would be best received—that may be at the beginning of class, woven into the mindful movement, or before the silent sitting.

> *Your thoughts and feelings are always changing. It's important to know this because when you're feeling angry or sad, you know that you won't always feel that way. It will eventually change. And when you're really happy, you won't try to make it last forever, because that's impossible. Everything changes. Has anyone ever felt really down or sad at one time, and felt like things would always be that way? But no matter how strong your feelings are, later something shifts and you realize that your feelings have changed. That's the nature of our emotions—they give us information, but they are not who we are.*

Activation Question 2.8

> *Think of the last time you were excited (alternatively: worried or sad). How long did that feeling last?*

Give students a chance to reflect, and choose a few students to share their responses with the class.

> *While we're practicing today, whenever you notice thoughts or feelings come up, just notice them. You'll notice that sooner or later they go away, and new thoughts or feelings come up.*

ACTION, BREATHING, CENTERING

OPENING BELL AND FOCUSED BREATHING (2 MINUTES)

We will start our time together today by trying to focus our attention on a sound. I would like to ask you all to listen to the sound of the bell I am going to ring.

Try to keep your attention on the sound of the bell for as long as you can, and when you can't hear it anymore, please raise your hand.

Ring bell or singing bowl.

❖ Allow to vibrate to completion and until all students have raised their hands.
❖ Then ask students to do the same thing, this time closing their eyes or looking down at their desks to focus just on their hearing, and ring the bell again.
❖ Wait until all students have raised their hands.

That was very good. Now I'll lead you in a breathing exercise:
- *You can keep your eyes closed, or just look down.*
- *Let all the air out of your lungs.*
- *Now breathe in, breathe out.*

Lead class in simple breathing, encouraging them to breathe deeply and smoothly.

Continue for 3–4 rounds.

Then tell students that you are going to do the bell exercise one more time.

Ring the bell again, and students raise their hands when they can no longer hear it.

MINDFUL MOVEMENT AND POSE OF THE DAY (6 MINUTES)

Seated Twist

We'll start by doing a spinal twist.
- *Breathing in, sit up as straight as you can.*
- *Breathing out, turn to face the right. Stop when you feel a gentle twist or stretch in your back, or hip, or shoulders.*
- *To help you twist, you can take your right hand to the back of your seat and your left hand to your right thigh.*
- *See if you can hold the twist and breathe as deep as this pose allows.*
- *Breathing in, see if you can sit up a little straighter in the twist.*
- *Breathing out, maybe you can twist a little more.*
- *In: chest lifts.*
- *Out: shoulders come down away from your ears.*
- *1 more breath.* Pause. *Great!*
- *As you breathe in, come back to face forward.*

You can use the metaphor of a sponge to explain the twist. When you twist a wet sponge, the water comes out. When you put a twisted sponge in the water and let it untwist, it fills with new water. That's what we're doing in our bodies, and it helps us to flush out old fluids and toxins.

Lead students in the seated twist on the other side. You can also have a student say "breathe in, breathe out" as they twist. After students return to face forward, invite them to notice how they are breathing, and notice if they feel they can breathe any deeper or easier after doing the twist.

Mountain

Let's all stand up in Mountain Pose.

If needed, review the elements of Mountain Pose:

❖ Feet parallel and hip-width distance apart
❖ Shoulders relaxed
❖ Standing tall

Press your hands together at your chest if you'd like, and either close your eyes, or look down at the place where your hands meet. Can someone lead us in 3 breaths, saying, "breathe in, breathe out"?

Choose a student to lead the breaths, making sure the student leads them slowly to allow for deep breathing.

Standing Backbend with Clasp

Let's warm up our backs in a different direction now.
* *Inhale and reach up. Exhale and clasp your hands behind your back, or if it feels more comfortable, bring your hands to your lower back.*
* *Inhale as you draw your shoulder blades together and lift your chest. If your hands are clasped, try to straighten your arms.*
* *Exhale and return to standing, releasing your hands and relaxing your shoulders.*
* *Let's repeat this movement with the breath 3 times. Notice where you feel a stretch as you do it.*

Ask a student to lead the 3 breaths.

Good! Shake out your arms and shoulders and return to Mountain Pose. Notice what your energy level and mood are like now. It may or may not be different than when we were sitting.

Cow Face—Pose of the Day

The main pose of the day is called Cow Face. Cow Face Pose stretches the shoulders and arms and releases tension in that area. Notice how the feeling of the pose changes as you relax your shoulders and breathe deeply. Cow Face Pose was given its name because when it is done sitting on the ground with the legs crossed, the person looks like a cow's face.

We start Cow Face Pose by standing in Mountain Pose.
- *Reach your right arm straight overhead, with your palm facing forward.*
- *Bend the right arm and try to rest the right palm on your back. The right elbow should point straight up, right next to the head.*
- *You can use your left hand pressing on your right upper arm to help you stretch the right triceps.*

Relax your shoulders and take a deep breath. You can either stay here, or reach your left arm out to the side and point the thumb down toward the floor. Swoop your left arm down and bend the elbow to slide the hand up along the back. Can you touch your hands together? If so, try to clasp your fingers together. If not, you can grab your shirt with your hands. Or you might choose to bring the left hand back to the right upper arm to help you stretch. Whatever option you choose, hold it for 3 breaths. Try to relax the shoulders downward as you hold.

Choose a student to lead the breaths. Then have students relax the arms and shake them out.

Repeat Cow Face Pose on the other side. After shaking out the arms, end with 3 breaths in Mountain Pose with palms pressed together at the chest.

Notice if your shoulders or back feel looser after the poses we just did. Or maybe your mood loosened up or shifted. If not, that's ok, we are just practicing noticing changes in our experience.

Tall Tree

We'll finish with a balancing pose, Tall Tree.
- *We'll start in Mountain Pose. Feel your left foot planted firmly on the floor.*
- *When you're ready, bring your right foot to your ankle, or to your calf, or to your thigh, avoiding your knee.*

Remember, it might help you balance if you focus your eyes on one spot in front of you. You might also experiment with standing up a little straighter to help you balance.
- *If you'd like, bring your hands to your chest. Take a few breaths here.*

Pause.
- *Feel free to stay in Tree Pose, or if you feel ready, raise your arms up toward the ceiling. Take a few breaths and see if you can find your balance here. If this is still easy for you, try looking up at the ceiling as you balance.*

Choose a student to lead 3 breaths. If students have a hard time balancing, have them take a deep breath and try to clear their minds of other thoughts. Remind them that some days it's easier to balance than others.

When you finish taking 3 breaths, shake out the legs and arms and try the pose on the other side. End in Mountain Pose with the palms at the chest and take 3 breaths together. Ask students to notice how they are breathing, and if they can, tune into their energy level and mood.

Instruct students to take a seat. Proceed to the Mindful Breathing section.

MINDFUL BREATHING (3 MINUTES)

Please sit comfortably with your back straight. Notice the rhythm of your breath. Notice it moving in and out.

Pause.

Is your breath fast or slow? Deep or shallow? Smooth or uneven? Just notice, without necessarily changing your breath.

Pause.

Now if it feels okay, allow your breath to get deeper.
- *As you breathe, notice if your belly is moving.*
- *Bring one hand to your belly if you'd like.*
- *If it's not moving, no problem. Try to relax the muscles around your belly and breathe deeply.*

Pause.

See if you can notice the belly pushing out a little as you breathe in, and moving back in toward your spine as you breathe out.

Pause.

Just notice any movement, small or big, that might happen as you breathe. Breathe in and out.

Pause to allow students to breathe for 3–4 rounds.

Now if you'd like, take your hand off your belly. See if you can feel your belly moving out and in without using your hand, just feeling it from the inside.

Pause.

Notice if your posture has changed—try to maintain a straight-backed, relaxed posture. Notice any movement you feel in your belly or anywhere else in your body as you breathe.

Pause to allow students to breathe 3–4 rounds.

Now if your hand is on your belly, take it off. See if you can feel your belly moving out and in without using your hand, just feeling it from the inside.

Pause to allow students to breathe 3–4 rounds.

Good job. Come back to breathing normally.

Pause.

Just notice, are you breathing differently now than when we first sat down? How are you feeling? If you've noticed any shifts in your breathing, the thoughts going through your head, or your mood, just be aware of that. If you don't notice any change, that's also good information to be aware of.

WRAP-UP

GUIDED MEDITATION AND CLOSING BELL (1 MINUTE)

We're going to end class by sitting silently for 1 minute, just noticing your breathing and how your body feels.

Feel free to close your eyes or look down to help you concentrate only on yourself.

If you like, you can even put your head down and rest it on your arms.

Pause.

Notice your feet resting on the floor, your legs relaxed on the seat.

Notice where your arms and hands are. Maybe you can allow your arms and shoulders to relax a bit more.

Notice how you're breathing.

You might even allow the muscles of your face to relax as you breathe.

Long pause, allow students to sit silently for remainder of the minute.

I will now ring the bell one last time. Listen to the bell and when you can't hear it anymore, please look up at me.

Ring bell and allow it to vibrate to completion.

CONNECTION QUESTIONS (3 MINUTES)

How is everyone feeling?

In the short time we practiced TLS today, did you observe any of your thoughts or feelings changing?

Ask students if they have any questions about what we did today or about TLS or mindfulness in general, and thank them for their participation.

LESSON 2.9: WATCHING YOUR THOUGHTS

In this lesson, students will be introduced to Tree Pose with the eyes closed. Physically, this pose:

❖ Helps to focus the mind
❖ Improves balance and concentration
❖ Strengthens and firms the legs and abdominal muscles

Lesson objectives are (a) students will learn how to use their breath as a focus point so that they can notice thoughts come and go without being swept away by them, and (b) students will practice refocusing their attention on the breath.

STUDENT OVERVIEW

REVIEW EXPECTATIONS (2 MINUTES)

Review the expectations for TLS sessions, including:

❖ Students clear desks of all distractions including books, papers, food, cell phones, and music.
❖ One-mic rule: one person talks at a time. If students have questions, they can raise a hand or ask at the end of class. Assure students that there will be a few minutes dedicated to questions at the end of each session.
❖ Students focus on their own body and breath. That means not making comments about self or others, not touching others, and not distracting others from their experience.
❖ Students try their best to participate at all times. (However, participation may look different for each student. For some students, it may mean doing only the breathing for as long as they need, until they choose to engage with the movement. Allow students to come to the practice at their own pace, as long as they are not being distracting or disrespectful toward others. Engaging with one's body and mind through TLS is always a choice, and every day is a different experience.)

ACTIVATE BACKGROUND KNOWLEDGE (3 MINUTES)

In response to the class environment each day, you may wish to provide this information to students when you feel it would be best received—that may be at the beginning of class, woven into the mindful movement, or before the silent sitting.

> *Earlier we talked about the stories we tell ourselves in our minds— about how good or bad we are, about what we can or can't do, or about other people. When we notice these stories, we can step back from them and decide if we want to believe them or not. If we are aware of them, the stories no longer have so much power over our actions. Noticing our thoughts gives us the power to change them if we want. You can notice your stories, or thought patterns, by watching your thoughts come and go. Watching your thoughts is different from "thinking"—when you watch your thoughts, you try not to get carried away by any one thought or fear or fantasy. Your focus remains on your breath as you watch your thoughts, so you can observe them as they come and go.*

Activation Question 2.9

> *Can you think of any beliefs you had about yourself in the past? Do you think these beliefs were helpful or harmful to you?*

Give students a chance to reflect, and choose a few students to share their responses with the class.

> *Today while we practice yoga, you might notice yourself thinking about something else. As soon as you notice your mind is not on what you're doing, bring your attention back to your breath. Do this as many times as you notice your mind wander. As you practice doing this, you'll get better at noticing your thought patterns.*

ACTION, BREATHING, CENTERING

OPENING BELL AND FOCUSED BREATHING (2 MINUTES)

We will start our time together today by trying to focus our attention on a sound. I would like to ask you all to listen to the sound of the bell I am going to ring.

Try to keep your attention on the sound of the bell for as long as you can, and when you can't hear it anymore, please raise your hand.

Ring bell or singing bowl.

❖ Allow to vibrate to completion and until all students have raised their hands.
❖ Then ask students to do the same thing, this time closing their eyes or looking down at their desks to focus just on their hearing, and ring the bell again.
❖ Wait until all students have raised their hands.

> *That was very good. Now I'll lead you in a breathing exercise:*
> * *You can keep your eyes closed, or just look down.*
> * *Let all the air out of your lungs.*
> * *Now breathe in, breathe out.*

Lead class in simple breathing, encouraging them to breathe deeply and smoothly.

Continue for 3–4 rounds.

Then tell students that you are going to do the bell exercise one more time.

Ring the bell again, and students raise their hands when they can no longer hear it.

MINDFUL MOVEMENT AND POSE OF THE DAY (6 MINUTES)

Mountain

Let's all stand up in Mountain Pose.

Press your hands together at your chest, and either close your eyes or look down at the place where your hands meet. As you breathe in, lift the top of your head up toward the ceiling. As you breathe out, let your shoulders and arms relax. Breathe in and stand tall, reaching your head toward the ceiling. Breathe out and feel your feet on the floor, wiggling your toes if that helps you feel them. Take 1 more deep breath: standing tall, feeling your feet on the floor and shoulders relaxed.

Pause to allow students to breathe and focus.

Shoulder Movements

Let your arms relax at your sides. Let's warm up our shoulders. You can start by rotating your shoulders in small circles. As your circles get bigger, you can connect your breath with your movement: inhale the shoulders up and back, exhale them down and forward. Notice if you try to breathe faster to make the movement go faster—try to give your breath enough time to be deep. Slowing down the breath can help us slow down our thoughts, so that we can notice what they are. You might notice some stretching, clicking, or warmth in your shoulders as you move and breathe.

Repeat 3 times. Reverse direction and repeat 3 times.

Side Warrior

Make sure you have space behind you, because we're going to take a big step back for Side Warrior.

- *Start in Mountain Pose and take your left leg back.*
- *Press your left heel to the floor and face your hips and chest to the left.*

Notice how it feels to bend your right leg as you keep your left leg straight—does that increase the stretch you feel?

- *Make sure your right knee is bent straight forward, right above your ankle. If it feels okay, raise your arms to shoulder height and look over the fingers of your right hand. Feel the strength in your arms and legs.*

Now as we breathe in, we'll straighten our legs and reach our arms up, palms together. As we breathe out, we'll bend our front leg and bring our arms back out to the sides, palms down.

Demonstrate 1 round of breath.

This time we'll switch legs by facing the opposite direction.

- *Inhale, straighten your legs and reach your arms up.*
- *Swivel your feet so that your left foot faces the back and the right foot faces the side.*
- *Exhale and bend your left leg to do Side Warrior facing the back.*

Take a breath, checking to make sure your right leg is straight and your heel is pressing into the floor. If it feels okay, your arms are out wide, and you're looking over your left fingers.

Pause.

On the next inhale straighten your leg and reach up. Switch the feet. Exhale bend the right leg. Side Warrior.

If students lose their focus here, you might wish to bring them back to Mountain Pose for 3 breaths before moving on.

Star Gazer

Now we'll add Star Gazer.
- *Raise your right arm up toward the ceiling, as high as feels comfortable to you.*
- *You can rest your left hand gently on your straight back leg, either above or below the knee. Notice if your right leg is still bent, or if you forgot about it and straightened it.*
- *Keep breathing—you might feel a stretch in your right side here.*

The next time you breathe out, come back to Side Warrior.
- *Breathe in, straighten your legs, reach up, and switch your feet to the back.*
- *Breathe out, Side Warrior facing the back.*
- *Breathe in, lift the left arm for Star Gazer.*
- *Breathe out, Side Warrior.*
- *Breathe in, straighten you legs, reach up, and switch your feet to face the front.*
- *Breathe out, Side Warrior with the right leg bent.*

Lead students in 2 more rounds of this sequence.

Try to keep your breath and your movements slow, so you can be aware of your body as you move. Connecting movement to breath helps us to slow down our thoughts and focus the mind.

When you finish 2 rounds to the front and back, bring the left leg forward to Mountain Pose. Have a student lead 3 breaths with the hands together at the chest.

Tree with Eyes Closed—Pose of the Day

The main pose of the day is Tree Pose with your eyes closed. This is a difficult balancing pose! As you try closing your eyes, notice what thoughts come up, for example:

- *"You're gonna fall," or*
- *"Wow, I'm doing it!"*

This pose also reminds us that sometimes you learn a lot by just trying something—it doesn't matter if you can do it perfectly or not.

Make sure your left foot is planted firmly on the floor.

- *Bring your right foot to your ankle, or to your calf, or to your thigh, avoiding your knee.*
- *Press the sole of the right foot into the left leg and point the right knee out to the side.*
- *If you'd like, bring your hands to your chest. Take a few breaths here.*

Pause.

If you feel ready, try closing your eyes—you can always open them, if you need to.

Notice if your breathing changes when you do this. Try to keep it smooth to calm and center you.

Another option, instead of closing your eyes, is to try looking up at a spot on the ceiling as you balance. Choose which option you would like to try.

(Student name), *can you lead us in 3 breaths please?*

Once students finish 3 breaths:

- ❖ Have them slowly come out of the pose and shake out their legs.
- ❖ Lead them through the pose and options with the left leg lifted.
- ❖ Shake the legs out when finished.
- ❖ Instruct students to have a seat.

Robin (Seated)

For Robin Pose, it helps to scoot up to the edge of your chair and put both feet on the floor.
- *Feel free to start really small and make the movement bigger, as you feel comfortable.*
- *When you breathe in, draw the shoulders back.*
- *When you breathe out, bring the shoulders forward and the chin down.*

Guide students while they try a few rounds.

If you want to make it bigger:
- *When you breathe in take the shoulders back and arch the upper back.*
- *When you breathe out round the back, pulling the belly in and letting the head drop forward.*
- *Try a few more rounds, noticing what this movement feels like in your back and shoulders.*

Allow students to do a few more rounds with their breath. Then instruct them to return to normal breathing and to sit comfortably with a straight spine. Proceed to the Mindful Breathing section.

MINDFUL BREATHING (3 MINUTES)

Sit comfortably with your back straight. You can close your eyes at any time, or just look down at your desk to help you focus inward.

I'm going to share with you a trick that helps me to keep my mind focused on my breath, so I don't get carried away by my thoughts. If you get carried away by your thoughts, you can't actually see what they are because you're lost in them. But if you stay focused on your breath, you can notice your thoughts as they come and go. You can use the movement of your hands to keep you focused on your breath.

- *Take a look at your hands.*
- *When you breathe in, touch your index finger to your thumb.*
- *When you breathe out, touch your middle finger to your thumb.*
- *When you breathe in, touch your ring finger to your thumb.*
- *When you breathe out, touch your pinky finger to your thumb.*
- *Keep doing this as you breathe, one finger per breath.*
- *You can close your eyes as you do this or look at your hands.*

We're going to practice this for 1 minute. If you notice you get caught up following one thought to the next to the next, and you lose track of your fingers, just start again on an inhale.

Allow students to practice for 1 minute, giving verbal cues to help them stay focused.

Now, if you'd like, you can relax your hands. We'll take 3 deep breaths together.
- *If you noticed any negative thoughts in your head, you can imagine breathing them out on the exhale.*
- *Deep breath in, and then breathe negative thoughts out.*
- *Do this 2 more times.*
- *Deep breath in, breathe out and let it all go.*
- *In, out.*

WRAP-UP

GUIDED MEDITATION AND CLOSING BELL (1 MINUTE)

We're going to end class by sitting silently for 1 minute, just noticing your breathing and how your body feels.

Feel free to close your eyes or look down to help you concentrate only on yourself.

If you like, you can even put your head down and rest it on your arms.

Pause.

> *Notice your feet resting on the floor, your legs relaxed on the seat.*
>
> *Notice where your arms and hands are. Maybe you can allow your arms and shoulders to relax a bit more.*
>
> *Notice how you're breathing.*
>
> *You might even allow the muscles of your face to relax as you breathe.*

Long pause, allow students to sit silently for remainder of the minute.

> *I will now ring the bell one last time. Listen to the bell and when you can't hear it anymore, please look up at me.*

Ring bell and allow it to vibrate to completion.

CONNECTION QUESTIONS (3 MINUTES)

What did you notice today about the quality of the different thoughts that came up for you?

Were they positive or negative? Were they about yourself, someone else, or a situation?

Where they reassuring, or did they contribute to you feeling stressed, anxious, or mad?

Is there anything we learned in class today that you can use to help yourself notice your thought patterns?

Ask students if they have any questions about what we did today or about TLS or mindfulness in general, and thank them for their participation.

LESSON 2.10: FOCUSING INWARD VS. FOCUSING OUTWARD

In this lesson, students will be introduced to Warrior III. Physically, this pose:

❖ Strengthens the muscles in the legs, abdomen, and back
❖ Stretches the hamstrings
❖ Improves balance and concentration

Lesson objectives are (a) students will be able to distinguish between focusing their attention outward and focusing their attention inward, and understand why it is important to be able to focus inward, and (b) students will practice focusing their attention inward.

STUDENT OVERVIEW

REVIEW EXPECTATIONS (2 MINUTES)

Review the expectations for TLS sessions, including:

❖ Students clear desks of all distractions including books, papers, food, cell phones, and music.
❖ One-mic rule: one person talks at a time. If students have questions, they can raise a hand or ask at the end of class. Assure students that there will be a few minutes dedicated to questions at the end of each session.
❖ Students focus on their own body and breath. That means not making comments about self or others, not touching others, and not distracting others from their experience.
❖ Students try their best to participate at all times. (However, participation may look different for each student. For some students, it may mean doing only the breathing for as long as they need, until they choose to engage with the movement. Allow students to come to the practice at their own pace, as long as they are not being distracting or disrespectful toward others. Engaging with one's body and mind through TLS is always a choice, and every day is a different experience.)

ACTIVATE BACKGROUND KNOWLEDGE (3 MINUTES)

In response to the class environment each day, you may wish to provide this information to students when you feel it would be best received—that may be at the beginning of class, woven into the mindful movement, or before the silent sitting.

> *You always have the ability to focus outward or focus inward. Focusing outward means paying attention to what's happening around you. Focusing inward means paying attention to what's happening inside you: your breath, your feelings, and your thoughts. Most people are good at focusing their attention outward—on their friends, on their phone, or on what people around them are doing. Focusing outward can keep us safe and help us read social cues.*

> *But it is equally important to be able to focus inward. If you don't, you might not notice your thoughts or feelings until they get really strong and start to affect your behavior.*

You may give the following examples:
- ❖ Noticing you are angry, and stepping away from the situation before you do something you regret;
- ❖ Noticing you are tired and irritated, and taking a nap before you say something mean to someone you care about.

> *Another reason to practice focusing inward is that we tend to hold onto negative comments from others much more strongly than positive ones. If we're not careful, negative comments can affect us for weeks, months, even years! In TLS we practice letting let them go and refocusing inward, where we can notice all the positive that is inside of us.*

Activation Question 2.10

Do you think you spend more time focused outward on what's going on around you, or focused inward on yourself?

Give students a chance to reflect, and choose a few students to share their responses with the class.

TLS helps us practice bringing our attention from outward to inward. As we practice today, if you notice yourself thinking about what others are doing or might be thinking, try to refocus your attention on what you feel and how you are breathing.

ACTION, BREATHING, CENTERING

OPENING BELL AND FOCUSED BREATHING (2 MINUTES)

We will start our time together today by trying to focus our attention on a sound. I would like to ask you all to listen to the sound of the bell I am going to ring.

Try to keep your attention on the sound of the bell for as long as you can, and when you can't hear it anymore, please raise your hand.

Ring bell or singing bowl.

- ❖ Allow to vibrate to completion and until all students have raised their hands.
- ❖ Then ask students to do the same thing, this time closing their eyes or looking down at their desks to focus just on their hearing, and ring the bell again.
- ❖ Wait until all students have raised their hands.

  That was very good. Now I'll lead you in a breathing exercise:
  - *You can keep your eyes closed, or just look down.*
  - *Let all the air out of your lungs.*
  - *Now breathe in, breathe out.*

Lead class in simple breathing, encouraging them to breathe deeply and smoothly.

Continue for 3–4 rounds.

Then tell students that you are going to do the bell exercise one more time. Ring the bell again, and students raise their hands when they can no longer hear it.

MINDFUL MOVEMENT AND POSE OF THE DAY (6 MINUTES)

For the Mindful Movement today, we will be folding forward. It is best that students don't stand behind each other. You may wish to position students in a circle around the room before beginning this section.

Mountain

Let's all stand up in Mountain Pose.

If needed, review the elements of Mountain Pose:
- ❖ Feet parallel and hip-width distance apart
- ❖ Shoulders relaxed
- ❖ Standing tall

Press your hands together at your chest, and either close your eyes or look down at the place where your hands meet. Can someone lead us in 3 breaths, saying, "breathe in, breathe out"?

Choose a student to lead the breaths, making sure the student leads them slowly to allow for deep breathing.

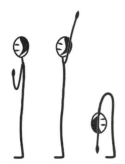

Half Sun Salutation

Let's prepare for some Half Sun Salutations.
- *On your next inhale, raise your arms high, reaching toward the ceiling.*
- *If it feels okay, reach your arms back slightly for a mini-backbend in your upper back and shoulders.*
- *On the exhale, fold forward. You can fold forward a lot, feeling a*

stretch in the back of the legs. Or if you feel more comfortable, you can just fold forward a little, letting your arms and neck relax and your upper back round.

- *Take a breath here and notice where you feel a stretch.*

Pause.

Notice if you're focused on others or on yourself. If you feel comfortable with it, try to focus on the sensations in the back of your legs, back and neck.

When you inhale, if it feels okay, place your hands on the front of your legs and flatten out your back like a table top.

- *Feel the muscles on your back get firmer here.*
- *On your next exhale, relax your back and fold forward again.*
- *Inhale, come back to standing, reaching the arms straight up.*
- *Exhale, hands to the front of the chest, Mountain Pose.*

Good, that was 1 round.

We are going to repeat that series 3 times, but with only 1 breath per movement. Try to focus on connecting your breath with your movement. Ready?

- *On your next inhale, raise your arms high and maybe a little back.*
- *Exhale, fold forward.*
- *Inhale, flat back.*
- *Exhale, fold forward.*
- *Inhale, reach your arms straight up.*
- *Exhale, hands to chest.*

Repeat 2 more times, having a student lead the breath. When you finish, instruct students to stay in Mountain Pose and focus inward, noticing how they are breathing, if their heart is beating faster, or any other sensations in their body. Have one student lead everyone in 3 breaths in Mountain Pose.

Lunge

Let's come into Lunge Pose.

Remember, Lunge is like Forward Warrior, but with the back heel lifted up toward the ceiling.
- *Start by bringing the left leg back.*
- *Place your legs far apart for more of a stretch. You can move them closer together if you feel like that's too much.*
- *In Lunge, the front leg is bent with the knee right above the ankle, not in front of it. If the knee goes farther forward than the ankle, make your stance wider.*
- *If it feels comfortable, straighten you back leg.*

Breathe in, and either raise your arms up toward your ears or press your hands together at your chest. Feel the center of your chest lift up when you breathe in, and draw your belly gently in when you breathe out. Can someone lead us in 2 breaths?

Warrior III—Pose of the Day

Now we'll lift into Bird Pose, and from there we'll go into the main pose of the day, Warrior III.
- *When you're ready, extend your arms out to the sides.*
- *Lean forward and lift your left leg off the floor.*
- *Pull in your belly gently, and reach your left heel back.*
- *If you lose your balance, take a moment to take a deep breath before you try it again.*
- *You might notice that it's hard to balance if your attention is on others—it helps to focus on yourself.*

Pause.

Now either stay here, or if you feel ready, extend the arms straight forward into Warrior III. Wherever you choose to place your arms, try to find your balance.

Can someone lead us in 3 breaths?

Choose a student to lead the breaths. Come out of the pose by lowering the left leg into Lunge, then brining it forward to Mountain Pose.

Warrior III is a balancing pose that strengthens the muscles in your lower body, upper body, and core. In this pose you're reminded of the importance of being able to focus on yourself and not what others are doing, otherwise you might fall!

Let's try it on the other side.

Lead students through Lunge with the right foot back, Bird, and Warrior III. When finished, bring everyone back to Mountain Pose and have one student lead 3 mindful breaths.

Arm Movements

Press your hands together at your chest.
- *When you breathe in, take the hands forward, still pressed together, and then apart and out to the sides.*
- *When you breathe out, bring the hands back together and then in to the chest.*
- *Continue the movement, breathing in for 4 counts and out for 8.*

Lead students by counting a few rounds.

Now as you do it, count silently in your head.
- *In for 4.*

Pause.

- *Out for 8.*

Pause as students continue for a few more rounds.

❖ Once students finish the arm movements, pause in Mountain Pose.
❖ Invite students to notice whether their attention is focused outward or inward. Then instruct students to have a seat. Proceed to the Mindful Breathing section.

MINDFUL BREATHING (3 MINUTES)

Sit comfortably with your back straight. You can close your eyes at any time, or just look down at your desk to help you focus inward. We're going to practice changing our focus from outward to inward.
- *For the next 30 seconds, we will focus on the sounds we hear in our environment.*
- *Notice any sound that you can hear, loud or soft, without judging it as a bad sound or a good sound. Just noticing sounds as they come and go.*
- *See how many different sounds you can notice.*
- *I'll ring the bell to start and end the 30 seconds.*

Ring bell.
Wait for 30 seconds and ring bell again.

Now bring your attention inside. To help you do this, we'll do some focused breathing first. Let your breath get deeper.
- *Focus on your breath as you breathe in.*
- *Notice when you get to the end of the inhale.*
- *Feel your breath as you slowly breathe out.*
- *Notice when you get to the end of the exhale.*
- *Breathing in deeply.*

Pause.

- *Breathing out slowly.*

Pause while students breathe a few more rounds.

For the next 30 seconds, focus only on yourself:
- *On your breathing,*

- *On your heart beating, or*
- *On how your body feels in your seat.*
- *Just focusing inside.*

Ring bell.
Wait for 30 seconds and ring bell again.

Good job everyone.

WRAP-UP

GUIDED MEDITATION AND CLOSING BELL (1 MINUTE)

We're going to end class by sitting silently for 1 minute.
- *Feel free to close your eyes or look down.*
- *Try to sit up straight, but be relaxed and comfortable.*

During this minute, you can choose to focus on the sounds you hear, your breathing, or relaxing your body.

Long pause, allow students to sit silently for remainder of the minute.

I will now ring the bell one last time. Listen to the bell and when you can't hear it anymore, please look up at me.

Ring bell and allow it to vibrate to completion.

CONNECTION QUESTIONS (3 MINUTES)

How are you all feeling?

Was it easier for you to focus on sounds, or on yourself?

Why do you think it's important to be able to choose when you focus outward and inward?

Ask students if they have any questions about what we did today or about TLS or mindfulness in general, and thank them for their participation.

LESSON 2.11: CHOOSING WHERE TO FOCUS YOUR MIND

In this lesson, students will be introduced to Eagle Pose. Physically, this pose:

- ❖ Promotes circulation of the blood in the hips
- ❖ Relieves stiffness in the shoulders and sacroiliac region
- ❖ Strengthens the legs
- ❖ Improves balance and concentration

Lesson objectives are (a) students will build awareness that they have a choice as to where to focus their attention, and (b) students will practice focusing their attention on different aspects of their experience.

STUDENT OVERVIEW

REVIEW EXPECTATIONS (2 MINUTES)

Review the expectations for TLS sessions, including:

- ❖ Students clear desks of all distractions including books, papers, food, cell phones, and music.
- ❖ One-mic rule: one person talks at a time. If students have questions, they can raise a hand or ask at the end of class. Assure students that there will be a few minutes dedicated to questions at the end of each session.
- ❖ Students focus on their own body and breath. That means not making comments about self or others, not touching others, and not distracting others from their experience.
- ❖ Students try their best to participate at all times. (However, participation may look different for each student. For some students, it may mean doing only the breathing for as long as they need, until they choose to engage with the movement. Allow students to come to the practice at their own pace, as long as they are not being distracting or disrespectful toward others. Engaging with one's body and mind through TLS is always a choice, and every day is a different experience.)

ACTIVATE BACKGROUND KNOWLEDGE (3 MINUTES)

In response to the class environment each day, you may wish to provide this information to students when you feel it would be best received—that may be at the beginning of class, woven into the mindful movement, or before the silent sitting.

You might have noticed by now that you have a choice as to where to focus your attention. It's helpful to think of your attention or awareness as a spotlight, like they use on stage. If you shine it on what you feel in your body, or on your breath, you will focus inward. If you shine the light of your attention on what people are doing or saying around you, you will focus outward. You can choose to focus your attention on people that make you feel irritated or unsure of yourself. Or you can choose to focus your attention on people that make you feel good. Maybe that person is yourself.

Activation Question 2.11

Do you think that when people focus their attention on what other people think it changes their behavior? Can you give an example?

Give students a chance to reflect, and choose a few students to share their responses with the class.

Today as we practice, you'll have the opportunity to focus on various aspects of your experience. If you find yourself focused on other people, shine your attention on your breath or your body sensations, and see if it helps you focus on yourself.

ACTION, BREATHING, CENTERING

OPENING BELL AND FOCUSED BREATHING (2 MINUTES)

We will start our time together today by trying to focus our attention on a sound. I would like to ask you all to listen to the sound of the bell I am going to ring.

Try to keep your attention on the sound of the bell for as long as you can, and when you can't hear it anymore, please raise your hand.

Ring bell or singing bowl.

- ❖ Allow to vibrate to completion and until all students have raised their hands.
- ❖ Then ask students to do the same thing, this time closing their eyes or looking down at their desks to focus just on their hearing, and ring the bell again.
- ❖ Wait until all students have raised their hands.

That was very good. Now I'll lead you in a breathing exercise:
- *You can keep your eyes closed, or just look down.*
- *Let all the air out of your lungs.*
- *Now breathe in, breathe out.*

Lead class in simple breathing, encouraging them to breathe deeply and smoothly.

Continue for 3–4 rounds.

Then tell students that you are going to do the bell exercise one more time.

Ring the bell again, and students raise their hands when they can no longer hear it.

MINDFUL MOVEMENT AND POSE OF THE DAY (6 MINUTES)

Mountain

Let's all stand up in Mountain Pose.

Press your hands together at your chest, and either close your eyes or look down at the place where your hands meet. As you breathe in, lift the top of your head up toward the ceiling. As you breathe out, let your shoulders and arms relax. Breathe in and stand tall, reaching your head toward the ceiling. Breathe out and feel your feet on the floor, wiggling your toes if that helps you feel them. Take 1 more deep breath: standing tall, feeling your feet on the floor, and shoulders relaxed.

Pause to allow students to breathe and focus.

Wide-Legged Crescent

If it feels comfortable, bring your feet wider apart.
- *When you breathe in, lift both arms high above your head.*
- *When you breathe out, take your right hand down to your right thigh and reach your left arm over your head. Do you feel a stretch in your left side? If having the arms up doesn't work for you, you can also do the pose with your hands on your hips.*
- *Keep leaning to the right, but see if you can put equal weight into both feet on the floor.*
- *When you breathe in, come back to standing straight up, maybe reaching your arms high.*
- *When you breathe out, lean to the other side.*
- *Continue to move with your breath, concentrating on the sensations your feel in your body as you move. Maybe you feel a stretching sensation in your ribs, or in your hips, or somewhere else.*

Can someone lead us by saying, "Breathe in, breathe out," nice and slow?

Repeat movement 3 times on each side, breathing in to stand up straight, and breathing out to lean. When finished, lower arms to sides.

Arched Warrior

Bring your feet back in close together to Mountain Pose.

We're going to do Arched Warrior.
- *We'll start in Forward Warrior with the left leg back. You can reach the arms up to the ceiling or place your hands together at your chest.*

- *Take a few breaths, and face your hips and chest toward the front as much as feels comfortable.*
- *Notice if you can straighten your back leg a little bit more, or bend your front leg a little more.*
- *Keep your breath flowing.*
- *If you feel an arch in your lower back, try to straighten it out by drawing the belly in and up, and dropping your tailbone downward.*

Pause.

Now if it feels okay, as you breathe in, straighten the front leg and reach up.

As you breathe out, bend the front leg and bring the hands together at the chest.

Let's do this 2 more times.
Choose a student to lead the breathing for 2 more rounds.

Great. The next time you breathe in, keep your front leg bent. Either keep your hands pressed together at your chest, or reach the arms high.

From here, lift the center of the chest and take your shoulders back.
Keep your breath flowing as you do this.
- *If you feel pain or your breath stops, back off a bit or take a rest.*
- *1 more breath. Good!*
- *Next time you breathe in, lift up and forward to come back to regular Forward Warrior.*
- *Exhale.*
- *Bring the left foot forward to Mountain Pose. Let's take 3 breaths here with the hands at the chest. Look down at your hands or close your eyes to help you focus inward.*
- *Notice if you can feel your heart beating. How are you breathing?*

Pause to let students observe for a few breaths. Then repeat the Front Warrior/
Arched Warrior sequence with the right leg back. End in Mountain Pose again
with 3 focused breaths.

Chair

Now we're going to do Chair Pose, and we'll only do it one time, so give it your best shot.

Start by placing the feet together. You have a choice here: Either, (1) reach your arms straight over your head, or (2) place your hands together at your chest.
- *Breathe in lifting up your chest, breathe out bending your legs, as if you were sitting down on a chair behind you.*
- *See if you can bend a little deeper.*
- *Notice if this gets difficult and your mind wanders, or if you come out of the pose as a reaction to how difficult it is.*
- *You might choose to focus on the feelings in your legs or arms, or maybe on the pressure of your feet against the floor, or your breathing.*
- *Let's try to hold it for 3 more breaths—you can do it!*

Choose a student to say the breaths.

> Breathe in to straighten your legs. Breathe out, and let your arms relax. Very good.

Eagle—Pose of the Day

The main pose of the day is Eagle. Eagle stretches your shoulders and hips as you balance. You can choose whether to focus on your upper body, your lower body, or your balance, or you can try to be aware of all three at once!

The arms go like this:
- *Extend your arms straight forward.*
- *Cross the right arm on top of the left.*
- *If you can cross the arms above the elbows, keep twisting the arms around each other until you can press the palms of the hands together.*
- *If that doesn't work for you, you can get the same stretch by giving yourself a tight hug.*
- *Breathe in and stand up straight.*
- *Breathe out and bring your shoulders down away from your ears.*

Notice if you feel more of a stretch in your shoulder blades by lowering your shoulders.

Now if it feels okay, bend your legs like in Chair Pose. Cross your left leg on top of your right and balance on your bent right leg.

If you prefer to focus just on the arms, stay in Chair Pose with both feet on the floor, or stand with your legs straight as you do the arms. If you are in the balance, notice what you feel in your legs. Steady your balance by steadying your breath.

Have a student lead the class in 3 breaths.

To come out of the pose, untwist everything and straighten your legs. Take a couple of Trunk Twists to release tension.

Twist the upper body from side to side for a few breaths.

Then do Eagle Pose on the opposite side: Left arm on top of right, right leg on top of left.

Do some Trunk Twists again when you are done with the second side.

End in Mountain Pose for 3 breaths.

Instruct students to take a seat. Proceed to the Mindful Breathing section.

MINDFUL BREATHING (3 MINUTES)

Find a way to sit comfortably with your back straight.
- *You can close your eyes at any time, or just look down at your desk to help you focus inward.*
- *If it feels comfortable, bring your left hand to your belly and right hand to the left side of your chest.*
- *With your right hand, notice if your chest moves as you breathe.*
- *With your left hand, notice if your belly moves as you breathe.*

Pause for 3–4 breaths.

Now, with your hand to your heart see of you can find the beating of your own heart.

It is normal to have a hard time doing this, but for the next 30 seconds, see if you can make the beating of your heart the loudest thing in your awareness.

Remain quiet for 30 seconds and allow students time to focus.

Is anyone having a hard time feeling your heart beat? If so, why do you think that is?

Allow students to respond.

We can agree that all of our hearts are beating, but maybe it is that we are having trouble focusing our minds. We spend so much time focused outside of our bodies that it takes awhile to develop the skill to be able to focus inside.

Using things like our heartbeat and breath can help to teach us how to focus on ourselves. It is important to remember that we have a choice of what we pay attention to from moment to moment. If something is bothering you, it might seem like you don't have a choice because your mind keeps focusing on that one thing. But remember that you still do have the power to choose where you focus—even if you have to keep refocusing over and over, you are practicing and getting better at managing your attention.

Let's try one more time practicing choosing to focus on the beating of our hearts, letting all the other noises and thoughts in our heads fade into the background. Continue to breathe as you notice your heartbeat. If your breathing makes it harder to feel your heart beating in your chest, feel free to tune into the feeling of your heart beating elsewhere in your body, like below your jawbone or in your wrist.

Allow students 30 seconds to focus.

WRAP-UP

GUIDED MEDITATION AND CLOSING BELL (1 MINUTE)

We're going to end class by sitting silently for 1 minute, just noticing your breathing and how your body feels.

Feel free to close your eyes or look down to help you concentrate only on yourself.

If you like, you can even put your head down and rest it on your arms.

Pause.

Notice your feet resting on the floor, your legs relaxed on the seat.

Notice where your arms and hands are. Maybe you can allow your arms and shoulders to relax a bit more.

Notice how you're breathing.

You might even allow the muscles of your face to relax as you breathe.

Long pause, allow students to sit silently for remainder of the minute.

I will now ring the bell one last time. Listen to the bell and when you can't hear it anymore, please look up at me.

Ring bell and allow it to vibrate to completion.

CONNECTION QUESTIONS (3 MINUTES)

How is everyone feeling?

Can you think of a situation where it would be helpful to be able to focus on one thing and tune others out? When might you do this?

Ask students if they have any questions about what we did today or about TLS or mindfulness in general, and thank them for their participation.

LESSON 2.12: REVIEW AND RETEACHING

The purpose of this lesson is to review and reteach any essential skills before moving on to Unit 3. Although this lesson is optional, we encourage instructors to review their fidelity checklists and instructor notes, and formulate a lesson plan based on what they think students would benefit from most. If content was covered equally well, instructors may want to attempt to reteach lessons during which students did not appear well engaged and attempt new strategies to motivate and engage students. Or instructors may choose to review a lesson during which a high percentage of students were absent. After reviewing your notes, make a plan for what you intend to reteach and why.

UNIT 2 REVIEW FORM

UNIT 2. Lesson	% Implementation	% Students absent	Overall engagement
2.1: Understanding Self-Awareness			
2.2: Building Body Awareness			
2.3: Being Aware of Your Body as You Move			
2.4: Building Awareness of the Breath			
2.5: The Connection between Breath and Emotion			
2.6: Building Awareness of Your Intentions			
2.7: Building Awareness of Thought Patterns			
2.8: Thoughts and Feelings Always Change			
2.9: Watching Your Thoughts			
2.10: Focusing Inward vs. Focusing Outward			
2.11: Choosing Where to Focus Your Mind			

_____ I choose to reteach lesson(s) because _____.

_____ All students have mastered skills. No reteaching is necessary.

UNIT 3

Emotion Regulation

Emotion regulation is the ability to experience emotions as they come up without allowing them to negatively alter your behavior or health. Closely related to self-control or self-regulation, it allows you to choose your actions rather than follow impulses. Studies have shown that greater self-control correlates with higher grade point average, better adjustment (fewer reports of psychopathology, higher self-esteem), less binge eating and alcohol abuse, better relationships and interpersonal skills, and more optimal emotional responses. Low self-control is a significant risk factor for a broad range of personal and interpersonal problems. In this unit, we learn tools for emotion regulation and how to apply them in our lives.

One tool that TLS gives us for self-regulation is the idea of centering yourself before you act. Centering yourself means pausing to notice what's happening right now. By centering yourself, you can notice the urges and motivations pushing you to act, and choose whether to follow them or not. If you notice that you are really stressed or angry, you can choose to calm yourself before making a decision, knowing that your brain works better when you are calm and steady.

Mahatma Gandhi once said: "Your thoughts become your words, your words become your actions, your actions become your behavior." What scientists have found out is that your behavior, in turn, can change your brain. By practicing centering yourself in TLS, you can become better at doing it in your everyday life. If you keep practicing, self-regulation skills can become part of your normal behavior, helping you to become more in control of your actions and be more successful at whatever you set out to do.

Objectives

❖ Define emotion regulation and how it relates to self-awareness and stress management

❖ Understand the connection between thoughts, words, actions, and behavior

❖ Understand how practicing a behavior can change the brain

❖ Learn to pause before choosing to act

❖ Increase and strengthen emotion regulation, healthy adaptive coping strategies, and balance

❖ Learn what it means to center yourself and why it is important

LESSON 3.1: YOUR ENVIRONMENT AFFECTS YOUR THOUGHTS AND FEELINGS

In this lesson, students will be introduced to the Triangle Pose. Physically, this pose:

❖ Strengthens the legs and ankles
❖ Relieves stiffness in the legs and back
❖ Increases mental focus and clarity

Lesson objectives are (a) students will recognize how what happens to them and around them affects their thoughts and emotions, and (b) students will practice noticing their thoughts and feelings.

STUDENT OVERVIEW

REVIEW EXPECTATIONS (2 MINUTES)

Review the expectations for TLS sessions, including:

❖ Students clear desks of all distractions including books, papers, food, cell phones, and music.
❖ One-mic rule: one person talks at a time. If students have questions, they can raise a hand or ask at the end of class. Assure students that there will be a few minutes dedicated to questions at the end of each session.
❖ Students focus on their own body and breath. That means not making comments about self or others, not touching others, and not distracting others from their experience.
❖ Students try their best to participate at all times. (However, participation may look different for each student. For some students, it may mean doing only the breathing for as long as they need, until they choose to engage with the movement. Allow students to come to the practice at their own pace, as long as they are not being distracting or disrespectful

toward others. Engaging with one's body and mind through TLS is always a choice, and every day is a different experience.)

ACTIVATE BACKGROUND KNOWLEDGE (3 MINUTES)

In response to the class environment each day, you may wish to provide this information to students when you feel it would be best received—that may be at the beginning of class, woven into the mindful movement, or before the silent sitting.

Activation Question 3.1

Do you think your environment affects your thoughts and feelings? If so, how?

Give students a chance to reflect, and choose a few students to share their responses with the class.

Our thoughts and feelings are affected by the people around us. Human beings are social animals—we need other people to survive, and we respond to their emotions. You could be in a good mood, but then your parent says something that makes you angry. You could be having a horrible day, but then the person you like texts you and you start smiling.

Since the world around us is constantly changing, so are our thoughts and feelings. The good news is that you are not your thoughts, and you are not your feelings. All thoughts and feelings will change eventually. Just by noticing that, you can take away some of the power they have over you.

During class today, notice how your thoughts and feelings come and go in response to what's happening around you.

ACTION, BREATHING, CENTERING

OPENING BELL AND FOCUSED BREATHING (2 MINUTES)

We will start our time together today by trying to focus our attention on a sound. I would like to ask you all to listen to the sound of the bell I am going to ring.

Try to keep your attention on the sound of the bell for as long as you can, and when you can't hear it anymore, please raise your hand.

Ring bell or singing bowl.

❖ Allow to vibrate to completion and until all students have raised their hands.

❖ Then ask students to do the same thing, this time closing their eyes or looking down at their desks to focus just on their hearing, and ring the bell again.

❖ Wait until all students have raised their hands.

That was very good. Now I'll lead you in a breathing exercise:
- *You can keep your eyes closed, or just look down.*
- *Let all the air out of your lungs.*
- *Now breathe in, breathe out.*

Lead class in simple breathing, encouraging them to breathe deeply and smoothly.

Continue for 3–4 rounds.

Then tell students that you are going to do the bell exercise one more time.

Ring the bell again, and students raise their hands when they can no longer hear it.

MINDFUL MOVEMENT AND POSE OF THE DAY (6 MINUTES)

Mountain

Let's all stand up in Mountain Pose.

If needed, review the elements of Mountain Pose:

❖ Feet parallel and hip-width distance apart
❖ Shoulders relaxed
❖ Standing tall

If you'd like, press your hands together at your chest, and either close your eyes or look down at the place where your hands meet. Can someone lead us in 3 breaths, saying, "breathe in, breathe out"?

Choose a student to lead the breaths, making sure the student leads them slowly to allow for deep breathing.

Shoulder Isolations

Let your arms rest at your sides. Let's start making circles with the right shoulder.
  • *The circles can be as big or small as you'd like.*
  • *Try not to move anything else but your right shoulder.*

Pause while students do 4–5 circles.

Now try it with your left shoulder.

Pause for the same amount of time.

You can let both shoulders relax. Now we'll combine the two:
  • *One circle with right*
  • *One with left*
  • *One with both*
  • *Right, left, both*

Repeat 4–5 times, going faster if you want, or switching the order to left to right. Then invite students to shake out their arms and let them relax.

Tree

Let's do a balancing pose to help us focus our minds—we'll do Tree. Feel your left foot planted firmly on the floor. When you're ready, bring your right foot to your ankle, or to your calf, or to your thigh, avoiding your knee. Remember, it might help you balance if you focus your eyes on one spot in front of you. Standing up a little straighter can also help you balance. If you'd like, bring your hands to your chest. Take a few breaths here.

Pause.

Feel free to stay in Tree Pose, or if you would like, raise your arms up toward the ceiling. Take a few breaths and see if you can find your balance here. If this is still easy for you, try looking up at the ceiling as you balance. (Student name), can you lead us in 3 breaths?

If students have a hard time balancing, have them take a deep breath and try to clear their minds of other thoughts. If other students in the class are being distracting, have students notice whether being distracted makes it harder to balance.

When you finish taking 3 breaths, shake out your legs and arms and try the pose on the other side. End in Mountain Pose with your hands at your chest and take 3 breaths together.

Side Warrior

Make sure you have space behind you because we're going to take a big step back for Side Warrior. Start in Mountain Pose and take your left leg back. Press your left heel to the floor and face your hips and chest to the left. Notice how it feels to bend your right leg as you keep your left leg straight—you might feel a stretch in your thigh or hip. Make sure your right knee is bent straight forward, not to the side, and it doesn't go further forward than your ankle. If it feels okay to you, raise your arms to shoulder height and look over the fingers of your right hand. Notice the strength in your legs here.

Now as we breathe in, we'll straighten our legs and reach our arms up, palms together. As we breathe out, we'll bend our front leg and bring our arms back out to the sides, palms down. Let's do this 2 more times with the breath.

Good. We'll now stay Side Warrior with the right leg bent. We'll try to stay here for 3 breaths. Focus on your breath and notice whatever you feel in your legs right now. If it feels intense, notice if you need to exit the pose, or if you can use your breath to give you patience. Who can lead us in 3 breaths?

Choose a student to lead the breaths. When they are done, have students come back into Mountain Pose by bringing the left leg forward. Take a few mindful breaths in Mountain before doing the whole Side Warrior sequence with the right leg back. When you finish, come back to Mountain Pose again and have one student lead the class in 3 breaths.

Triangle—Pose of the Day

The pose of the day is Triangle. Triangle stretches and releases stress in the hips and shoulders. The pose also helps build body awareness and focus.

To do Triangle, we'll start in Side Warrior with the left leg back. Your chest and belly are facing the left side, and your right foot is facing forward. Straighten your front leg. If you feel your legs are too far apart as we do this pose, you can scoot them closer together.

If you'd like, take your hands to your hips. Breathe in and try pressing your right hip back toward the left leg. Notice your left hip rise up higher than your right hip. When you're ready, reach your arms out to the sides. Breathe in and lean over the right leg, reaching forward with the right hand. Breathe out, lowering your right hand to your right leg. If it feels okay, try lifting your left arm to the sky, with your palm facing the same way as your chest.

In this shape, your two legs and the floor form a Triangle. Notice both of your feet pressing flat on the floor. See if you can make both sides of your waist long—the right as well as the left side. If you want, you can look up at your left hand, but if that feels uncomfortable just let your head hang down. Notice if this pose feels good or uncomfortable to you. Breathe and try to notice where exactly you feel stretching or other sensations.

(Student name), can you lead us in 3 breaths, please?

Good. As you breathe in, lift up to stand up straight. Breathe out, and bring your left leg forward to Mountain Pose. Let's take 3 breaths here. As you breathe, notice your feet in contact with the floor, and any other sensations in your body.

Choose a student to lead 3 breaths. Invite students to notice how their environment might be affecting their experience, whether there is a lot of side talk or students are practicing quietly. Then lead students through Triangle Pose with the right leg back, starting in Side Warrior. Finish in Mountain Pose.

Arm Movements—Reaching Overhead

For our final movement, we'll connect the movement with the breath. Breathe in and lift your arms up toward the ceiling as high as feels comfortable to you. Breathe out and press your palms together, lowering them down to your chest. You can look at your hands as they lower down, or close your eyes. Let's do this 3 more times, moving slowly to be aware of your body as you move.

Lead students in 3 more breaths, or choose a student to lead the breaths. When done, have students notice how they are feeling. You can provide examples of calm, sleepy, focused, agitated, excited, and so on. Invite students to take a seat.

Proceed to the Mindful Breathing section.

MINDFUL BREATHING (3 MINUTES)

Find a way to sit comfortably with your back straight. You can close your eyes at any time, or just look down at your desk to help you focus inward.

It's hard to know how you feel if you don't first pause and take the time to notice. Sometimes we move through our activities and thoughts at such a fast pace that it's hard to recognize our feelings. Let's practice slowing down your breath and your thoughts for a minute so that it's easier to notice how you feel.

We'll take deep inhales for 4 counts and slow exhales for 8 counts. I'll start the first few for you, and then you can do the breathing on your own. Feel free to go slower or faster than my counting if you'd like.

Let all the air out of your lungs.

Pause.

- *Breathe in 1, 2, 3, 4.*
- *Breathe out 1, 2, 3, 4, 5, 6, 7, 8.*

Repeat counting 2 more times.

Now count silently to yourself:
- *Breathing in for 4.*

Pause.

- *Breathing out for 8.*

Pause.

Now I'm going to be quiet and let you practice 3 rounds on your own. See if you can keep your mind on the counting and the feeling of the breath. If your mind wanders to other thoughts, bring it back to focus on your breathing as soon as you realize it.

Pause, allow students to breathe on their own for 3 rounds.

Good! You can go back to breathing normally. Notice how you're feeling now. Did you notice that it helped you to concentrate that the others around you were focused and quiet? (Or, did anyone find yourself distracted by what was going on around you?)

WRAP-UP

GUIDED MEDITATION AND CLOSING BELL (1 MINUTE)

We're going to end class by sitting silently for 1 minute, just noticing your breathing and how your body feels.

Feel free to close your eyes or look down to help you concentrate only on yourself.

If you like, you can even put your head down and rest it on your arms.

Pause.

Notice your feet resting on the floor, your legs relaxed on the seat.

Notice where your arms and hands are. Maybe you can allow your arms and shoulders to relax a bit more.

Notice how you're breathing.

You might even allow the muscles of your face to relax as you breathe.

Long pause, allow students to sit silently for remainder of the minute.

I will now ring the bell one last time. Listen to the bell and when you can't hear it anymore, please look up at me.

Ring bell and allow it to vibrate to completion.

CONNECTION QUESTIONS (3 MINUTES)

How is everyone feeling?

Do you think it is possible to stay calm and focused if you are surrounded by chaos? Why or why not?

Ask students if they have any questions about what we did today or about TLS or mindfulness in general, and thank them for their participation.

LESSON 3.2: YOU CAN MANAGE YOUR THOUGHTS AND FEELINGS

In this lesson, students will be introduced to Half Moon Pose. Physically, this pose:

❖ Strengthens the knees
❖ Tones the nervous system
❖ Improves balance and focus

Lesson objectives are (a) students will learn what self-regulation means and the importance of noticing thoughts and feelings, rather than trying to get rid of them, and (b) students will practice noticing their feelings and shifting their awareness to the body or the breath.

STUDENT OVERVIEW

REVIEW EXPECTATIONS (2 MINUTES)

Review the expectations for TLS sessions, including:

❖ Students clear desks of all distractions including books, papers, food, cell phones, and music.
❖ One-mic rule: one person talks at a time. If students have questions, they can raise a hand or ask at the end of class. Assure students that there will be a few minutes dedicated to questions at the end of each session.
❖ Students focus on their own body and breath. That means not making comments about self or others, not touching others, and not distracting others from their experience.
❖ Students try their best to participate at all times. (However, participation may look different for each student. For some students, it may mean doing only the breathing for as long as they need, until they choose to engage with the movement. Allow students to come to the practice at

their own pace, as long as they are not being distracting or disrespectful toward others. Engaging with one's body and mind through TLS is always a choice, and every day is a different experience.)

ACTIVATE BACKGROUND KNOWLEDGE (3 MINUTES)

In response to the class environment each day, you may wish to provide this information to students when you feel it would be best received—that may be at the beginning of class, woven into the mindful movement, or before the silent sitting.

> *Self-regulation is the ability to manage your thoughts and feelings. It can take a long time to learn how to self-regulate, but once you understand the concept it can be very powerful. Self-regulation does not mean labeling certain thoughts or feelings as "bad," or trying to get rid of certain thoughts and feelings. It's about noticing your thoughts and feelings when they come up. Once you notice them, you can decide how to react to them. You can choose to do something to help yourself feel better, or just notice your emotions and give yourself space to process them. You can decide which thoughts help you, and which ones keep you from being happy and reaching your goals.*

> *Whether your goals are immediate or long-term, your thoughts and feelings will impact the outcome. If you are constantly thinking about what you don't have or can't do, it can make it harder to feel confident. Focusing on what we do have and what we can do right now will create positive feelings and help us to succeed.*

Activation Question 3.2

Have you ever had thoughts or feelings that you tried to get rid of? Did it work?

Give students a chance to reflect, and choose a few students to share their responses with the class.

> *When you try to get rid of a thought or emotion, it usually doesn't work. But if you take time to notice it, it will have less power over you.*
>
> *If you notice you get frustrated, bored, or irritated in class today, first take time to notice how you feel. Then you can choose what to do next: maybe try to shift your focus to something more positive, take deeper breaths, or change the pose you're doing to make it feel better for you. Or maybe just have compassion for yourself and acceptance for your feelings, knowing that they will not last forever. Throughout this unit we will go deeper into these different options for managing thoughts and feelings.*

ACTION, BREATHING, CENTERING

OPENING BELL AND FOCUSED BREATHING (2 MINUTES)

We will start our time together today by trying to focus our attention on a sound. I would like to ask you all to listen to the sound of the bell I am going to ring.

Try to keep your attention on the sound of the bell for as long as you can, and when you can't hear it anymore, please raise your hand.

Ring bell or singing bowl.

❖ Allow to vibrate to completion and until all students have raised their hands.
❖ Then ask students to do the same thing, this time closing their eyes or looking down at their desks to focus just on their hearing, and ring the bell again.
❖ Wait until all students have raised their hands.

That was very good. Now I'll lead you in a breathing exercise:
- *You can keep your eyes closed, or just look down.*
- *Let all the air out of your lungs.*
- *Now breathe in, breathe out.*

Lead class in simple breathing, encouraging them to breathe deeply and smoothly.

Continue for 3–4 rounds.

Then tell students that you are going to do the bell exercise one more time.

Ring the bell again, and students raise their hands when they can no longer hear it.

MINDFUL MOVEMENT AND POSE OF THE DAY (6 MINUTES)

Mountain

Let's all stand up in Mountain Pose.

If needed, review the elements of Mountain Pose:

- ❖ Feet parallel and hip-width distance apart
- ❖ Shoulders relaxed
- ❖ Standing tall

Choose a student to lead the breaths, making sure the student leads them slowly to allow for deep breathing.

Standing Backbend as a Movement

For the next pose, we are going to do a Standing Backbend as a movement. Pay attention to how your back feels and only go as far as feels comfortable, so you don't get hurt.

- *Inhale, reaching up.*
- *Exhale, bringing your hands to your lower back.*

- *Support your lower back as you inhale, opening up your chest as you lean back a bit.*
- *Exhale, returning to standing.*

We will repeat this movement 3 times.

Notice if your breath gets shallow—try to keep breathing deeply.

Ask a student to lead the movement. When done, have students stand in Mountain Pose with hands to chest. Have them take 1–2 deep breaths.

Triangle

To do the pose of the day, we'll start in Triangle Pose:

- *Bring the left leg back directly behind the right leg.*
- *Your chest and belly are facing the left side, and your right foot is facing forward.*
- *Straighten your front leg.*
- *If you'd like, take your hands to your hips.*
- *Breathe in and try pressing your right hip back toward the left leg.*

Notice your left hip rise up higher than your right hip.

When you're ready, reach your arms out to the sides.
- *Breathe in, reaching the right hand forward.*
- *Breathe out, lowering your right hand to your right leg.*
- *If it feels okay, try lifting your left arm to the sky, palm facing the left.*

Notice how your body feels as you reach up with your hand and lengthen your spine. Maybe your shoulders can relax a little bit and come away from your ears. Bring your attention to your breathing as we take 3 deep breaths together. (Student name), *can you lead us in 3 breaths, please?*

Pause to take 3 mindful breaths in Triangle.

Half Moon—Pose of the Day

Good. From here we'll come into the main pose of the day, Half Moon. When you're ready, bend your right leg and look down at a spot on the floor in front of you. Keep breathing! Experiment with lifting your back leg off the floor and finding your balance. You can choose how high to lift your foot—from an inch or two off the floor to the height of the hip. If you feel yourself getting overwhelmed or frustrated or unfocused, try taking some deep breaths to help you refocus.

It's more important to keep breathing than to balance the whole time. If you fall out of balance, take a deep breath, focus your eyes on a spot on the floor, and try again.

Let's try Half Moon for 3 breaths (slowly):

Three. Focusing on breathing deeply.

Two. Noticing any unneeded stress in your shoulders.

One. When you're ready, the next time you breathe in, take your left foot to the floor behind you and stand up. Breathe out and bring your left leg forward to Mountain Pose.

As you breathe in Mountain Pose, feel both feet on the floor. You may have noticed that Half Moon requires you to clear your mind and concentrate. It also gives us a chance to practice using the breath to manage our thoughts and feelings when we need to focus.

Lead students through Triangle Pose and then Half Moon with the right leg back. Remind them to focus on the breath to keep calm.

Finish in Mountain Pose, and take 3 breaths with the hands at the chest.

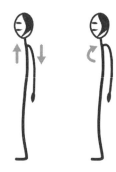

Shoulder Movements

Let's do some movements to release tension in the shoulders.
- *On your next inhale, shrug your shoulders up toward your ears.*
- *On the exhale, let them drop. Let's do that 3 more times.*
- *Imagine bringing tension into that area and letting it go, as your shoulders drop.*

Lead 3 rounds of shoulder shrugs.

For the next movement, we are going to rotate our shoulders in small circles:
- *As you inhale, roll the shoulders up and back.*
- *As you exhale. bring them down and forward.*
- *If you notice yourself getting impatient or bored and wanting to make the movement faster, try deepening your breath and keeping the movement slow, so you can feel each little detail of movement in the shoulders.*
- *You might notice little stretching sensations, or clicking, or warmth building, or something else.*

Repeat 3 times.

Reverse direction and repeat 3 times.

When done, have students take a seat. Proceed to the Mindful Breathing section.

MINDFUL BREATHING (3 MINUTES)

Sometimes it can be hard to manage your thoughts and feelings, especially when they are very strong or persistent. When you get overwhelmed by your thoughts or feelings and would like to calm yourself down, there's a breathing technique that can be really helpful. It's called "Count Down to Calm Down." We'll practice it now.

First, sit in a comfortable position with your back straight. You can close your eyes at any time, or just look down at your desk to help you focus inward.

Notice how you're breathing. Feel free to close your eyes if that helps.

- *Notice if you can feel your belly move as you breathe. If not, try to relax the muscles around your belly so that it moves out a little on the inhale and in toward your spine on the exhale. Practice this a few times, with the belly expanding as you breathe in, and contracting as you breathe out.*

Pause.

We're going to do 10 belly breaths just like this, counting down from 10.

Try to concentrate on the movement of your belly as you breathe, and let the rest of your body relax.

Ready?

Breathe in, breathe out: 10. In, out. 9 . . .

Count down slowly to 1, giving students time and encouragement to inhale and exhale slowly with the abdomen for each count. After you finish, instruct students to return to breathing normally.

WRAP-UP

GUIDED MEDITATION AND CLOSING BELL (1 MINUTE)

We're going to end class by sitting silently for 1 minute, just noticing your breathing and how your body feels.

Feel free to close your eyes or look down to help you concentrate only on yourself.

If you like, you can even put your head down and rest it on your arms.

Pause.

Notice your feet resting on the floor, your legs relaxed on the seat.

Notice where your arms and hands are. Maybe you can allow your arms and shoulders to relax a bit more.

Notice how you're breathing.

You might even allow the muscles of your face to relax as you breathe.

If there are any thoughts that keep coming up for you, see if you can just notice they're here, without trying to "figure them out" or get rid of them, and then bring your attention back to your breathing.

Long pause, allow students to sit silently for remainder of the minute.

I will now ring the bell one last time. Listen to the bell and when you can't hear it anymore, please look up at me.

Ring bell and allow it to vibrate to completion.

CONNECTION QUESTIONS (3 MINUTES)

How is everyone feeling? What advice might you give to a friend who is dealing with difficult or unpleasant emotions, like fear, anger, or grief?

Ask students if they have any questions about what we did today or about TLS or mindfulness in general, and thank them for their participation.

LESSON 3.3: CENTERING YOURSELF

In this lesson, students will be introduced to Twisting Flamingo Pose. Physically, this pose:

❖ Firms the leg muscles
❖ Increases flexibility in the spine
❖ Improves balance and focus

Lesson objectives are (a) students will explore what it means to be centered, and (b) students will practice getting twisted up and then finding their center again.

STUDENT OVERVIEW

REVIEW EXPECTATIONS (2 MINUTES)

Review the expectations for TLS sessions, including:

❖ Students clear desks of all distractions including books, papers, food, cell phones, and music.
❖ One-mic rule: one person talks at a time. If students have questions, they can raise a hand or ask at the end of class. Assure students that there will be a few minutes dedicated to questions at the end of each session.
❖ Students focus on their own body and breath. That means not making comments about self or others, not touching others, and not distracting others from their experience.
❖ Students try their best to participate at all times. (However, participation may look different for each student. For some students, it may mean doing only the breathing for as long as they need, until they choose to engage with the movement. Allow students to come to the practice at their own pace, as long as they are not being distracting or disrespectful toward others. Engaging with one's body and mind through TLS is always a choice, and every day is a different experience.)

ACTIVATE BACKGROUND KNOWLEDGE (3 MINUTES)

In response to the class environment each day, you may wish to provide this information to students when you feel it would be best received—that may be at the beginning of class, woven into the mindful movement, or before the silent sitting.

Activation Question 3.3

What does it mean to be "centered"?

Give students a chance to reflect, and choose a few students to share their responses with the class.

When you are centered:
- *Your mind is focused on yourself rather than scattered among all the things going on around you.*
- *You are focused on what's happening right now, rather than on the past or the future.*
- *When you are centered, you feel your feet on the floor. You are able to notice your thoughts and feelings, but you don't feel out of control.*

It's important to know how to center yourself so that you can stay strong, confident, and in control of your actions, and not get pressured into doing things that aren't right for you.

Today we're going to practice getting all twisted up, and then finding our center again.

ACTION, BREATHING, CENTERING

OPENING BELL AND FOCUSED BREATHING (2 MINUTES)

We will start our time together today by trying to focus our attention on a sound. I would like to ask you all to listen to the sound of the bell I am going to ring.

Try to keep your attention on the sound of the bell for as long as you can, and when you can't hear it anymore, please raise your hand.

Ring bell or singing bowl.

❖ Allow to vibrate to completion and until all students have raised their hands.

❖ Then ask students to do the same thing, this time closing their eyes or looking down at their desks to focus just on their hearing, and ring the bell again.

❖ Wait until all students have raised their hands.

That was very good. Now I'll lead you in a breathing exercise:
* *You can keep your eyes closed, or just look down.*
* *Let all the air out of your lungs.*
* *Now breathe in, breathe out.*

Lead class in simple breathing, encouraging them to breathe deeply and smoothly.

Continue for 3–4 rounds.

Then tell students that you are going to do the bell exercise one more time.

Ring the bell again, and students raise their hands when they can no longer hear it.

MINDFUL MOVEMENT AND POSE OF THE DAY (6 MINUTES)

Mountain

Let's all stand up in Mountain Pose. Mountain pose is a great thing to do when you feel yourself swept away by worries, anger, or other emotions and need to center yourself. You can do it anywhere and anytime, and people don't even have to know you are doing TLS.

If needed, review the elements of Mountain Pose:

❖ Feet parallel and hip-width distance apart
❖ Shoulders relaxed
❖ Standing tall

Each time you breathe in, see if you can reach the top of your head toward the ceiling. Each time you breathe out, feel where your feet are touching the floor, wiggling your toes if that helps. Breathing in, allowing your chest to lift; breathing out, letting your arms hang down from your shoulders and feeling your feet on the floor.

Choose a student to lead 3 more breaths, making sure the student leads them slowly to allow for deep breathing.

Arm Movements—Reaching Overhead

Next time you breathe in, reach your arms up as high as feels comfortable.
• *Breathe out, press your palms together, and bring your hands down to your chest.*
• *To help you focus on yourself, you can close your eyes or watch your hands as they come down to your chest.*

Now we'll add the breath, breathing in for 4 counts as we reach up, and breathing out for 8 counts as we bring the hands to the chest.

Lead students by counting a few rounds.

Now as you do it, count silently in your head.
- *In for 4.*

Pause.

- *Out for 8.*

Pause as students continue for a few rounds.

After this round, you can relax your arms at your sides.

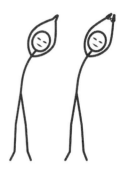

Crescent Moon

Now we'll stretch out the sides and shoulders with Crescent Moon. When you breathe in, try reaching your arms up straight, and if it feels good, clasp your hands together. If reaching up doesn't feel good to you right now, you can place your hands on your hips. Each time you breathe in, see if you can reach your hands up a little higher or stand a little taller. Feel your feet on the floor.

When you breathe out, lean to the right, just enough to feel a stretch somewhere in your left side.
- *Try to keep equal weight in both your feet as you lean.*
- *Continue moving with your breath: breathing in to stand straight, out to bend.*
- *When you come through center, notice yourself standing tall before you move on to the next side. Can someone lead the breath for us?*

Choose a student to lead the breath for 2 more rounds to each side.

The next time you breathe out, release your arms at your sides and shake them out a little.

Thank the student for leading the breath

This time we'll try holding the pose for 3 breaths per side. Notice if your body or mind start to feel stressed out or you get the urge to come out of the pose early. Try to keep breathing smoothly and notice the sensations in your body before you decide to come out of the pose.

Lead students in Crescent Moon to the right and then to the left. For each side, choose a student to lead the class in 3 breaths. After doing both sides, breathe in to stand tall, breathe out to relax and release.

Flamingo

We're going to do Flamingo, moving with the breath.
- *Breathe in and stand tall, reaching the top of your head toward the ceiling.*
- *When you exhale, bend your right leg and grab your shin or thigh with your hands. If you'd like, raise your knee up toward your chest.*
- *Inhale, place both feet firmly on the floor and stand tall.*
- *Exhale, and raise the left leg in the same way.*
- *Inhale, place your left foot down, and feel both feet on the floor.*
- *Try to make your breath and your movements smooth.*
- *Each time you inhale, feel yourself centered with both feet on the floor before moving on.*

Choose a student to lead the breath and repeat 2 more times on each side.

To help with balance, look at a spot that's not moving, like a spot on the floor or the wall in front of you. It can also help to draw the belly in toward the spine as you breathe out to balance.

End in Mountain Pose and take 3 breaths with the palms pressed together at the chest.

Twisting Flamingo—Main Pose of the Day

We're going to do the pose of the day, Twisting Flamingo. Twisting Flamingo is a balancing pose that helps us to clear and focus the mind. It also helps us learn to center ourselves—even in the midst of stressful situations.

It's important to center yourself before trying Twisting Flamingo. Take a breath or 2 in Mountain Pose, feeling your feet evenly on the floor and your arms relaxed at your sides. Breathe in. When you breathe out, lift your right leg up to Flamingo.

Pause here.

- *Take your right knee into your left hand.*
- *If your body feels wobbly, take a few breaths to center yourself before you move on.*
- *If you feel ready, twist your chest to face the right side of the room, keeping your right knee pointed forward.*
- *Reach your right arm back toward the wall behind you.*
- *Pause. Breathe.*
- *Notice if you could stand up straighter. Stay here for a few breaths, or if you want an extra challenge, begin to turn your head until you're looking behind you at your right thumb.*

(Student name), *could you lead us in 3 breaths please?*

After students finish 3 breaths in the pose, instruct them to slowly and carefully face forward on the next inhale, and exhale to put the right foot on the floor. Take a few centering breaths in Mountain Pose before doing Twisting Flamingo on the left side.

When finished, shake out the arms and legs and take 3 mindful breaths in Mountain Pose.

Seated Twist

Let's all take a seat. Sit facing the front, and place your feet on the floor.

Pause.

The last pose we'll do today is a Seated Twist.
- *As you breathe in, see if you can sit up a little straighter.*
- *As you breathe out, turn to face the right.*
- *You can take your right hand to the back of your seat and your left hand to your right thigh to help you twist, if you'd like.*
- *When you breathe in, face front again and feel your legs resting on your seat, hands resting on your legs.*
- *As you breathe out, twist to the left.*
- *Each time you breathe in, face the front and feel yourself centered and sturdy in your seat.*
- *Then twist again with an exhale.*
- *Keep going with your own breath.*

Allow students to continue for about 3 more rounds on their own.

You may wish to have a student say "breathe in, breathe out," as they twist.

After students return to face forward, have them take a deep breath and notice any sensations they feel in their bodies after twisting.

Proceed to the Mindful Breathing section.

MINDFUL BREATHING (3 MINUTES)

Today we'll practice a breathing technique that helps you to center yourself. Allow your arms and legs to relax as much as feels comfortable. You can close your eyes as we do this or just look down at your desk.

Notice your breath as it comes in and goes out.

Pause.

Experiment with breathing in a little bit more deeply each time, and breathing out a little bit longer each time.

Pause.

Now when you're ready, breathe in deep, and notice the moment when the inhale turns into an exhale.

Pause.

Breathe out, and notice the moment when the exhale becomes an inhale.

Pause.

Breathing in, noticing the very top of the inhale.

Pause.

Breathing out, noticing the very bottom of the exhale.

Pause.

Continue to breathe, noticing the end point of each breath and when the new breath starts. If it feels comfortable to you, you can experiment pausing for a second before starting each new inhale or exhale. If it's helpful for you, connect your breath to a movement: perhaps opening your hands as you breathe in and closing them into fists as you breathe out.

We will practice this for 1 minute. I will ring the bell to start and stop. If you get stuck in a thought, try to bring your focus back to your breath as soon as you notice it, noticing whether you are on an inhale or an exhale. You can start now.

Ring the bell. Allow students to breathe silently for 1 minute, providing verbal cues to help them remain present as needed. Then ring the bell to signify the end of the minute.

WRAP-UP

SILENT SITTING AND CLOSING BELL (1 MINUTE)

We're going to end class by sitting silently for 1 minute, just noticing your breathing and how your body feels.

Feel free to close your eyes or look down to help you concentrate only on yourself.

If you like, you can even put your head down and rest it on your arms.

Pause.

Notice your feet resting on the floor, your legs relaxed on the seat.

Notice where your arms and hands are. Maybe you can allow your arms and shoulders to relax a bit more.

Notice how you're breathing.

You might even allow the muscles of your face to relax as you breathe.

Long pause, allow students to sit silently for remainder of the minute.

I will now ring the bell one last time. Listen to the bell and when you can't hear it anymore, please look up at me.

Ring bell and allow it to vibrate to completion.

CONNECTION QUESTIONS (3 MINUTES)

How is everyone feeling?

How can you use the idea of being "centered" in your daily life?

Ask students if they have any questions about what we did today or about TLS or mindfulness in general, and thank them for their participation.

LESSON 3.4: YOUR THOUGHTS AND FEELINGS AFFECT YOUR ACTIONS

In this lesson, students will be introduced to Tip Toe Pose. Physically, this pose:

❖ Strengthens the calves
❖ Builds core strength
❖ Improves balance and focus

Lesson objectives are (a) students will reflect on how their thoughts and feelings affect their actions, and (b) students will practice using the breath and body sensations to help them clear their mind and find balance, and will notice when their own thoughts and feelings affect their ability to balance.

STUDENT OVERVIEW

REVIEW EXPECTATIONS (2 MINUTES)

Review the expectations for TLS sessions, including:

❖ Students clear desks of all distractions including books, papers, food, cell phones, and music.
❖ One-mic rule: one person talks at a time. If students have questions, they can raise a hand or ask at the end of class. Assure students that there will be a few minutes dedicated to questions at the end of each session.
❖ Students focus on their own body and breath. That means not making comments about self or others, not touching others, and not distracting others from their experience.
❖ Students try their best to participate at all times. (However, participation may look different for each student. For some students, it may mean doing only the breathing for as long as they need, until they choose to engage with the movement. Allow students to come to the practice at their own pace, as long as they are not being distracting or disrespectful

toward others. Engaging with one's body and mind through TLS is always a choice, and every day is a different experience.)

ACTIVATE BACKGROUND KNOWLEDGE (3 MINUTES)

In response to the class environment each day, you may wish to provide this information to students when you feel it would be best received—that may be at the beginning of class, woven into the mindful movement, or before the silent sitting.

Even when you don't realize it, your thoughts and feelings affect what you do. When you're stressed out, upset, or having negative thoughts about yourself or others, you often have a hard time concentrating and motivating yourself to do things. It can even cause you to say or do things you don't mean. This can add to your stress and make you feel even worse—like a vicious cycle. On the other hand, when you feel good and think positively, it can affect your words and actions in a positive way.

Activation Question 3.4

Can you think of an example of when your thoughts or feelings affect how you act?

Give students a chance to reflect, and choose a few students to share their responses with the class.

In TLS, we learn ways to manage our thoughts and feelings so that we can still make good decisions, reach our goals, and feel good about ourselves despite life's ups and downs. Today let's focus on noticing how our thoughts and feelings affect our ability to move and balance.

ACTION, BREATHING, CENTERING

OPENING BELL AND FOCUSED BREATHING (2 MINUTES)

We will start our time together today by trying to focus our attention on a sound. I would like to ask you all to listen to the sound of the bell I am going to ring.

Try to keep your attention on the sound of the bell for as long as you can, and when you can't hear it anymore, please raise your hand.

Ring bell or singing bowl.

❖ Allow to vibrate to completion and until all students have raised their hands.

❖ Then ask students to do the same thing, this time closing their eyes or looking down at their desks to focus just on their hearing, and ring the bell again.

❖ Wait until all students have raised their hands.

That was very good. Now I'll lead you in a breathing exercise:
- *You can keep your eyes closed, or just look down.*
- *Let all the air out of your lungs.*
- *Now breathe in, breathe out.*

Lead class in simple breathing, encouraging them to breathe deeply and smoothly.

Continue for 3–4 rounds.

Then tell students that you are going to do the bell exercise one more time.

Ring the bell again, and students raise their hands when they can no longer hear it.

MINDFUL MOVEMENT AND POSE OF THE DAY (6 MINUTES)

Mountain

Let's all stand up in Mountain Pose. Stand up tall, lifting the very top of your head up toward the ceiling.

If needed, review the elements of Mountain Pose:

❖ Feet parallel and hip-width distance apart
❖ Shoulders relaxed
❖ Standing tall

If you'd like, press your hands together at your chest, and either close your eyes or look down at the place where your hands meet.

Notice how you feel, and any thoughts that are really loud in your mind right now.

Can someone lead us in 3 breaths, saying, "breathe in, breathe out"?

Choose a student to lead the breaths, making sure the student leads them slowly to allow for deep breathing.

Wrist-Cross Crescent

Cross your right wrist over your left in front of you. Feel the backs of your hands pressing together. If it feels alright, lift your arms above your head. Breathe in, lift your arms a little higher. Breathe out, lean to the left. Breathe in, lift your arms up straight again. Breathe out, lean to the left again. Notice if you get a stretch somewhere in your right side. Breathe in, come up straight. One more time!

Breathe out lean, breathe in come up. Now bring your arms forward and cross them more, more, more, until your arms are crossed above the elbows. Give yourself a big hug, grabbing onto your shoulder blades with your hands. Take a big breath in, allowing your ribs to expand as you breathe. Breathe out, and see if you can keep your grip on your shoulder blades as you lower your shoulders down away from your ears. Take 1 more breath here, perhaps feeling a stretch in the upper back or shoulders. Good! Shake out your arms. Let's do the other side.

Lead class in the same movements on the other side: left wrist crosses over right, lean to the right, then cross more until you are giving yourself a hug. Once you are done, have students shake out their arms.

Standing Backbend

When you're ready, place your hands together at your chest. As you breathe in, feel your upper chest rise up toward your thumbs.

As you breathe out, pull your belly in a little and bring your shoulders back. This is a small movement that has a big impact, so pay attention to how you feel and don't go too far. Keep breathing as you try to lift your upper chest toward your hands. Now either keep your hands at your chest, or if you'd like, raise your arms high above your head and slightly back.

Notice where your mind is at. Try to focus on how your back feels and only do what feels good for you.

See if you can hold this pose for 3 deep breaths.

If you feel any crunching in your lower back, come out of the bend a little and pull the belly in, so that you feel the arch more in your upper back.
- *2 more breaths.*
- *Last one.*
- *Breathe in and lift yourself out of the backbend, standing tall.*

Breathe out, hands to the chest. Is your heart beating any faster? How are you breathing?

Take 3 mindful breaths in Mountain Pose.

Lunge

Let's come into Lunge Pose. Remember, Lunge is like Forward Warrior, but with the back heel lifted up toward the ceiling. Start by bringing the left leg back. Step really far back for more of a stretch, or not as far is you want less of a stretch. In Lunge, the front leg is bent with the knee right above the ankle, not in front of it. If the knee goes farther forward than the ankle, make your stance wider. Notice if you can straighten you back leg a little more.

Breathe in, and either raise your arms up toward your ears or press your hands together at your chest, lifting the center of your chest as you breathe. Can someone lead us in 2 breaths?

After the breaths, return to Mountain Pose.

You might have noticed that Lunge is also a balancing pose. What might affect your ability to balance?

Possible answers: where you are looking, whether you are breathing, where your mind is focused.

If you are thinking of other things rather than focused on what's happening right now, that might make it harder to balance. As we do the other side, notice if it is easier to balance if you can just focus on your breathing and your body.

Repeat the pose on the other side, and then return to Mountain Pose.

Tip Toe—Pose of the Day

The pose of the day is Tip Toe Pose. Tip Toe strengthens the muscles in the legs. It also makes us more aware of the thoughts and feelings that we are having, as they affect our ability to balance. To practice Tip Toe, we'll start in Mountain Pose. On an inhale, if you'd like, lift your arms up above your head. As another option, you might choose to reach your arms out to the sides. You can also put a hand on a desk during this pose if you feel you need more support.

Lift your heels off the floor so that you are just balancing on the balls of your feet. Keep the breath moving. If you have to come out of the pose, experiment with taking a breath to clear your mind and then trying the pose again.

Notice if your mind is clear and focused on what your body is doing. Or if you are having a hard time balancing, notice what emotions or thoughts might be getting in the way. Let's try holding Tip Toe for 3 more breaths. (Student name,) can you lead us in 3 breaths?

Pause for 3 breaths.

Good! Go ahead and lower the heels. If you'd like, shake out your legs and arms. Rest your arms at your sides, and take a few breaths, feeling your feet where they have contact with the floor.

Trunk Twists

For our last movement, bring your feet a little farther apart. Let your arms swing or bend them at chest height as you twist from side to side.

Feel the air brush past your hands.

Pause.

Lift the opposite heel as you twist to the side to protect your knees. If you'd like, use your breath to twist more, breathing out each time you turn to the side.

Demonstrate twisting and breathing out in short, audible spurts each time you twist to the side.

Now let your twists get smaller and smaller until you are still. Come back to Mountain Pose with your palms together at your chest and take a few breaths, noticing how your body feels and any thoughts that are coming up for you.

Have another student lead 3 breaths.

Instruct students to take a seat. Proceed to the Mindful Breathing section.

MINDFUL BREATHING (3 MINUTES)

Find a way to sit comfortably with your back straight. You can close your eyes at any time, or just look down at your desk to help you focus inward. Notice your breath as it comes in and goes out.

Pause.

We'll practice the relaxation breath, breathing in to a count of 4 and out to a count of 8. Breathing like that for a while helps us to slow down our thoughts, so that we can be more aware of them. Feel free to go with your own counting if I go too fast or too slow.

Let all the air out of your lungs.

Pause.

- *Breathe in 1, 2, 3, 4.*
- *Breathe out 1, 2, 3, 4, 5, 6, 7, 8.*
- *Breathe in 1, 2, 3, 4.*
- *Breathe out 1, 2, 3, 4, 5, 6, 7, 8.*

Now count silently to yourself, breathing in for 4.

Pause.

And out for 8.

Pause.

In deeply, and out slowly.

Pause to allow students to practice 3 more rounds on their own.

Now you can continue with the 4:8 breathing, or just breathe normally. We will do 1 minute of meditation.

As you pay attention to your breath coming in and out, notice if any thoughts come up. Notice what the thoughts are, but try not to follow any one thought. Instead keep your attention on your breath, and try to watch your thoughts come and go. If you find it helpful, move your hands with your breath to help you stay focused on the present: opening your hands as you breathe in and closing them into fists as you breathe out. Start now.

Pause, allow students to breathe for a minute, providing verbal reminders to help them focus.

Good job! Was it hard or easy for you to watch your thoughts without getting carried away by them?

WRAP-UP

GUIDED MEDITATION AND CLOSING BELL (1 MINUTE)

We're going to end class by sitting silently for 1 minute, just noticing your breathing and how your body feels.

Feel free to close your eyes or look down to help you concentrate only on yourself.

If you like, you can even put your head down and rest it on your arms.

Pause.

Notice your feet resting on the floor, your legs relaxed on the seat.

Notice where your arms and hands are. Maybe you can allow your arms and shoulders to relax a bit more.

Notice how you're breathing.

You might even allow the muscles of your face to relax as you breathe.

Long pause, allow students to sit silently for remainder of the minute.

I will now ring the bell one last time. Listen to the bell and when you can't hear it anymore, please look up at me.

Ring bell and allow it to vibrate to completion.

CONNECTION QUESTIONS (3 MINUTES)

How is everyone feeling?

Speaking of how our thoughts affect our actions, have you ever done or said something because of an assumption that you had, and later realized that your assumption was incorrect? What can we do to avoid making mistakes because of assumptions?

Ask students if they have any questions about what we did today or about TLS or mindfulness in general, and thank them for their participation.

LESSON 3.5: ACTING VS. REACTING

In this lesson, students will be introduced to Baby Dancer Pose. Physically, this pose:

* Stretches the quadriceps
* Improves balance and focus

Lesson objectives are (a) students will learn the importance of pausing before they act rather than reacting to impulses, and (b) students will practice pausing and centering themselves before moving.

STUDENT OVERVIEW

REVIEW EXPECTATIONS (2 MINUTES)

Review the expectations for TLS sessions, including:

* Students clear desks of all distractions including books, papers, food, cell phones, and music.
* One-mic rule: one person talks at a time. If students have questions, they can raise a hand or ask at the end of class. Assure students that there will be a few minutes dedicated to questions at the end of each session.
* Students focus on their own body and breath. That means not making comments about self or others, not touching others, and not distracting others from their experience.
* Students try their best to participate at all times. (However, participation may look different for each student. For some students, it may mean doing only the breathing for as long as they need, until they choose to engage with the movement. Allow students to come to the practice at their own pace, as long as they are not being distracting or disrespectful toward others. Engaging with one's body and mind through TLS is always a choice, and every day is a different experience.)

ACTIVATE BACKGROUND KNOWLEDGE (3 MINUTES)

In response to the class environment each day, you may wish to provide this information to students when you feel it would be best received—that may be at the beginning of class, woven into the mindful movement, or before the silent sitting.

Have you ever heard the expression, "slow is fast?" Slowing down and pausing before you act allows you to be in control of your actions, and it can help you to avoid saying or doing things that you later regret. Learning how to pause and center yourself before you act can help improve your interactions with friends and family as well. In situations when you feel strong emotions, it's often harder to pause before you act. But those are the times when it is most important, because when your brain is overwhelmed by strong emotions you are more likely to make decisions that you regret.

Activation Question 3.5

Has there ever been a time when you did not pause before you acted, and you ended up regretting what you said or did?

Give students a chance to reflect, and choose a few students to share their responses with the class.

During TLS we practice pausing and centering ourselves before we move. When we practice this skill in TLS, we become better at it in real life, so we can make more conscious choices rather than reacting to impulses.

Give students a chance to reflect, and choose a few students to share their responses with the class.

ACTION, BREATHING, CENTERING

OPENING BELL AND FOCUSED BREATHING (2 MINUTES)

We will start our time together today by trying to focus our attention on a sound. I would like to ask you all to listen to the sound of the bell I am going to ring.

Try to keep your attention on the sound of the bell for as long as you can, and when you can't hear it anymore, please raise your hand.

Ring bell or singing bowl.

❖ Allow to vibrate to completion and until all students have raised their hands.

❖ Then ask students to do the same thing, this time closing their eyes or looking down at their desks to focus just on their hearing, and ring the bell again.

❖ Wait until all students have raised their hands.

That was very good. Now I'll lead you in a breathing exercise:
- *You can keep your eyes closed, or just look down.*
- *Let all the air out of your lungs.*
- *Now breathe in, breathe out.*

Lead class in simple breathing, encouraging them to breathe deeply and smoothly.

Continue for 3–4 rounds.

Then tell students that you are going to do the bell exercise one more time.

Ring the bell again, and students raise their hands when they can no longer hear it.

MINDFUL MOVEMENT AND POSE OF THE DAY (6 MINUTES)

Mountain

Let's all stand up in Mountain Pose.

Pause as students stand.

Press your hands together at your chest, and either close your eyes or look down at the place where your hands meet. As you breathe in, lift the top of your head up toward the ceiling. As you breathe out, let your shoulders and arms relax. Breathe in and stand tall, reaching your head toward the ceiling. Breathe out and feel your feet on the floor, wiggling your toes if that helps you feel them. Take 1 more deep breath: standing tall, feeling your feet on the floor and shoulders relaxed.

Pause to allow students to breathe and focus.

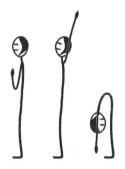

Half Sun Salutation

Let's practice some Half Sun Salutations. We'll start in Mountain Pose with the hands together at the chest.

- *On your next inhale, raise your arms high, reaching toward the ceiling. If it feels okay, you can reach your arms back a little. Notice any sensations in your upper back and shoulders as you reach back.*
- *On the exhale, fold forward. You can fold forward a lot, feeling a stretch in the back of the legs. Or, if it feels more comfortable, you can just fold forward a little, letting your arms and neck relax and your upper back round. Take a breath here and notice where you feel a stretch. Find the spot where you feel a stretch but it's not too much for you.*

Pause.

- *When you inhale, if it feels okay, flatten out your back like a table top. You can rest your hands on the fronts of your legs.*
- *When you exhale, relax and fold forward again.*
- *Inhale, come back to standing, reaching the arms straight up.*
- *Exhale, hands to the front of the chest in Mountain Pose.*

We are going to repeat that series 3 times, but with only 1 breath per movement. Try to keep your movement connected to your breath, and feel free to pause for a rest if you need to. Ready?
- *On your next inhale raise your arms high and maybe a little back.*
- *Exhale, fold forward.*
- *Inhale, flat back.*
- *Exhale, fold forward.*
- *Inhale, reach your arms straight up.*
- *Exhale, hands to chest.*

Repeat 2 more times. Have a student lead the breath and movement if you'd like. When you finish, instruct students to stay in Mountain Pose and notice how they are breathing; notice if their heart is beating faster; notice how their body feels. Have one student lead everyone in 3 breaths in Mountain Pose.

Baby Dancer—Pose of the Day

The pose of the day is Baby Dancer. Baby Dancer stretches out the quadriceps, which are located in the front of the thigh. It is also a balancing pose, which helps us to focus and calm the mind. If you practice keeping your breath flowing while trying to balance, you get better at making slow, smooth adjustments so you can balance better, rather than big reactions that could make you fall.

To do Baby Dancer, we start in Mountain Pose. Notice your feet flat on the floor. Then start to move the weight into your right foot, lifting the left foot lightly off the floor.

Keeping your knees close together, experiment with lifting and lowering your left lower leg behind you. Do you notice the muscles in the back of your thigh working to lift the leg? Now, one option here is to reach back and grab onto your left ankle with your left hand. Another option is to grab onto your pant leg or simply lift the left foot up off the floor without using your hand.

Point your knee down toward the floor and feel yourself stand up tall, reaching up through the top of your head. Notice if it helps you balance if you engage your core muscles, drawing your abs slightly inward. If you'd like, raise your right arm up toward the ceiling. Keep the breath flowing and try to make slow adjustments to keep your balance, rather than quick movements.

(Student name), *would you lead us in 3 breaths?*

Once students finish 3 breaths, lead them in slowly transitioning to the other side. Once both sides have been done, invite students to take 3 breaths in Mountain Pose.

Side Warrior

Let's practice Side Warrior. If you feel the urge to come out of the pose, you might experiment with taking a deep breath and noticing what it is that you feel in your body. Then decide if you want to stay in the pose or get out. Practicing Side Warrior in this way can help you get better at acting rather than reacting.

Start in Mountain Pose and take your left leg back far behind you. Press your left heel to the floor and face your hips and chest to the left.
* *As you bend your right leg, try to keep your knee right above your ankle. Keeping your knee over the ankle or slightly behind it will help protect your knee from injury in this pose.*
* *If it feels okay, raise your arms to shoulder height.*
* *Now as you breathe in, straighten your legs.*
* *As you breathe out, bend your front leg again.*

- *Did you notice the muscles on the top of your right leg start to work harder as you bent the leg? Try it again, straightening the right leg and bending it.*
- *If you'd like, you can even feel the right quadriceps with your hand as they engage.*
- *Try it a few more times if you'd like. Try to keep the breath flowing as you bend and straighten.*

This time, we'll stay in Side Warrior with the right leg bent.
- *You might notice the top of your thigh getting tired here.*
- *If you notice the urge to come out of the pose, see if you can take another breath first and investigate.*
- *If you feel it's best for you to come out of the pose, come out and rest. If you feel like you can stay for another breath, give that a try. You are in control.*

Let's try to stay here for 3 breaths. Who can lead us in 3 breaths?

Choose a student to lead the breaths.

- ❖ When they are done, have students come back into Mountain Pose by bringing the left leg forward.
- ❖ Take a few mindful breaths in Mountain before doing the whole Side Warrior sequence with the right leg back.
- ❖ Allow for the same amount of time in Side Warrior on the second side as on the first.
- ❖ When you finish, come back to Mountain Pose.
  Have students take a seat. Proceed to the Mindful Breathing section.

MINDFUL BREATHING (3 MINUTES)

Today we'll practice a breathing technique that can be helpful for centering yourself. Allow your arms and legs to relax, making yourself comfortable. If you want, you can close your eyes, or just look down at your desk to help you focus on yourself. Notice your breath as it comes in and goes out.

Pause.

Experiment with breathing in a little bit more deeply each time, and breathing out a little bit longer each time.

Pause.

Now when you're ready, breathe in deep, and notice the moment when the inhale turns into an exhale.

Pause.

Breathe out, and notice the moment when the exhale becomes an inhale.

Pause.

Breathing in, noticing the very top of the inhale.

Pause.

Breathing out, noticing the very bottom of the exhale.

Pause.

Continue to breathe, noticing the end point of each breath and when the new breath starts. If it feels comfortable to you, you can experiment with pausing for a second before starting each new inhale or exhale. If it's helpful, you can connect your breath to a movement, perhaps opening your hands on each in breath and closing them into fists on each out breath.

We will practice this for 1 minute. I will ring the bell to start and stop. If you get stuck in a thought, try to bring your focus back to your breath as soon as you notice it, noticing whether you are on an inhale or an exhale. You can start now.

Ring the bell. Allow students to breathe silently for 1 minute providing concrete cues to help students focus on the present. Then ring the bell to signify the end of the minute.

WRAP-UP

GUIDED MEDITATION AND CLOSING BELL (1 MINUTE)

We're going to end class by sitting silently for 1 minute, just noticing your breathing and how your body feels.

Feel free to close your eyes or look down to help you concentrate only on yourself.

If you like, you can even put your head down and rest it on your arms.

Pause.

Notice your feet resting on the floor, your legs relaxed on the seat.

Notice where your arms and hands are. Maybe you can allow your arms and shoulders to relax a bit more.

Notice how you're breathing.

You might even allow the muscles of your face to relax as you breathe.

Long pause, allow students to sit silently for remainder of the minute.

I will now ring the bell one last time. Listen to the bell and when you can't hear it anymore, please look up at me.

Ring bell and allow it to vibrate to completion.

CONNECTION QUESTIONS (3 MINUTES)

How is everyone feeling?

Do you believe that practicing TLS can help you to learn to "pause before you act"? Why or why not?

Ask students if they have any questions about what we did today or about TLS or mindfulness in general, and thank them for their participation.

LESSON 3.6: YOUR ACTIONS AFFECT YOUR BRAIN

In this lesson, students will be introduced to Rag Doll Pose. Physically, this pose:

- ❖ Releases tension in the lower back, shoulders, and neck
- ❖ Stretches the hamstrings
- ❖ Calms the nervous system

Lesson objectives are (a) students will learn that the brain has the ability to change and that any positive or negative actions, practiced enough, will become habits, and (b) students will practice centering themselves when they become distracted or unfocused.

STUDENT OVERVIEW

REVIEW EXPECTATIONS (2 MINUTES)

Review the expectations for TLS sessions, including:

- ❖ Students clear desks of all distractions including books, papers, food, cell phones, and music.
- ❖ One-mic rule: one person talks at a time. If students have questions, they can raise a hand or ask at the end of class. Assure students that there will be a few minutes dedicated to questions at the end of each session.
- ❖ Students focus on their own body and breath. That means not making comments about self or others, not touching others, and not distracting others from their experience.
- ❖ Students try their best to participate at all times. (However, participation may look different for each student. For some students, it may mean doing only the breathing for as long as they need, until they choose to engage with the movement. Allow students to come to the practice at their own pace, as long as they are not being distracting or disrespectful

toward others. Engaging with one's body and mind through TLS is always a choice, and every day is a different experience.)

ACTIVATE BACKGROUND KNOWLEDGE (3 MINUTES)

In response to the class environment each day, you may wish to provide this information to students when you feel it would be best received—that may be at the beginning of class, woven into the mindful movement, or before the silent sitting.

The brain has the ability to change throughout your life. If you practice doing something like dancing, playing a sport, or speaking a language, it will become easier for you the more you practice. If you practice centering yourself regularly, you will soon be able to center yourself more easily in real-life situations. This will help you feel more in control of your reactions to situations. On the other hand, you can "practice" negative behaviors, and your brain will learn to do those more often. For example, some people deal with difficult emotions by using drugs, getting in fights or going shopping, and this can become a habit. All the actions you take repeatedly can change your brain over time to form behaviors and habits.

Activation Question 3.6

Have you ever practiced something regularly and as a result gotten better at it? What was it?

Give students a chance to reflect, and choose a few students to share their responses with the class. If students can't think of something, you can give examples of learning to walk, ride a bike, read, and so on, to show that everyone is capable of learning.

Each time your mind wanders, see it as an opportunity for you to practice refocusing your attention on your body and your breath. The more you practice, the better you'll get at it!

ACTION, BREATHING, CENTERING

OPENING BELL AND FOCUSED BREATHING (2 MINUTES)

We will start our time together today by trying to focus our attention on a sound. I would like to ask you all to listen to the sound of the bell I am going to ring.

Try to keep your attention on the sound of the bell for as long as you can, and when you can't hear it anymore, please raise your hand.

Ring bell or singing bowl.

❖ Allow to vibrate to completion and until all students have raised their hands.
❖ Then ask students to do the same thing, this time closing their eyes or looking down at their desks to focus just on their hearing, and ring the bell again.
❖ Wait until all students have raised their hands.

That was very good. Now I'll lead you in a breathing exercise:
• *You can keep your eyes closed, or just look down.*
• *Let all the air out of your lungs.*
• *Now breathe in, breathe out.*

Lead class in simple breathing, encouraging them to breathe deeply and smoothly.

Continue for 3–4 rounds.

Then tell students that you are going to do the bell exercise one more time.

Ring the bell again, and students raise their hands when they can no longer hear it.

MINDFUL MOVEMENT AND POSE OF THE DAY (6 MINUTES)

For the Mindful Movement today, which includes forward folding poses, it's important to position students so that they aren't standing behind each other. You may wish to orient the class in a circle around the room before beginning the Mindful Movement section.

Mountain

Let's all stand up in Mountain Pose. Stand up tall, lifting the very top of your head up toward the ceiling.

If needed, review the elements of Mountain Pose:

❖ Feet parallel and hip-width distance apart
❖ Shoulders relaxed
❖ Standing tall

If you'd like press your hands together at your chest, and either close your eyes, or look down at the place where your hands meet. Can someone lead us in 3 breaths, saying, "breathe in, breathe out"?

Choose a student to lead the breaths, making sure the student leads them slowly to allow for deep breathing.

Shoulder Movements

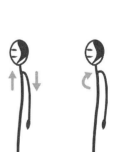

We are going to do some movements to release tension in the shoulders. Let your arms relax to your sides. On your next inhale, we'll shrug our shoulders up toward our ears, and on the exhale, we'll let them drop.

Let's do that 3 more times. Feel yourself bringing tension into that area and letting it go as your shoulders drop.

Pause.

For the next movement, we are going to rotate our shoulders in small circles.

You might experiment with matching your breath to the movement:
- *As you inhale rolling the shoulders up and back, and*
- *As you exhale bringing them down and forward.*

See if you can slow down the movement enough to allow yourself to take full, complete breaths.

Repeat 3 times.
Reverse direction and repeat 3 times.

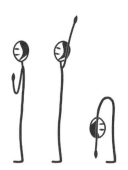

Rag Doll—Pose of the Day

Shake out your arms. Another good pose for releasing stress is the pose of the day, Rag Doll Pose. Rag Doll is a forward-folding pose that stretches the back and the backs of the legs. Doing forward-folds like Rag Doll can help to calm the nerves and refocus the mind.

Start in Mountain Pose. Breathe in, raising your arms up toward the ceiling. Breathe out, folding forward at the hips. If you'd like, fold forward all the way until you feel a stretch in the back of your legs or your back. Or another option is to just fold forward a little, letting your neck and shoulders round forward and release.

The important thing is to breathe and relax the neck. If you're looking around in this position, you will have tension in your neck. Notice how your neck feels if you let your head hang and look at your own legs or torso. If you still feel tension in your neck, you might gently sway your head back and forth to help it release. Hold here and breathe. (Student name), can you lead us in 3 breaths?

Encourage students to relax the neck, arms, and shoulders as they breathe.

On the next inhale, slowly come back to standing and reach your arms up. Exhale and place your hands together at your chest. Notice your breath coming in and out. Pause.

Who felt a stretch in the back of the thighs?

Who felt a stretch in their back? Behind the knees? Somewhere else?

Warrior III

Next we'll do Warrior III.

From Mountain Pose, breathe in and reach the arms up. When you're ready, on an exhale, hinge forward with the upper body and lift your right leg up behind you. Reach your right heel toward the wall behind you, and reach your arms forward. You can draw your belly in gently to give you more stability.

Students can lift the back leg high or keep it close to the floor, according to their comfort level in Warrior III.

If you lose your balance, practice centering yourself with your breathing and try it again. This is good practice for real-life situations when you feel knocked off balance!

Can someone lead us in 3 breaths?

Choose a student to lead the breaths.

Come back to Mountain Pose and repeat the pose with the left leg lifted. When finished, bring everyone back to Mountain Pose and have one student lead 3 mindful breaths.

Chair

For the last pose today, we'll practice using the breath to calm our-selves during stressful situations. Give it your best shot, knowing that you're training your brain so that you can be more self-aware and less reactive.

We're going to come into Chair Pose. If it feels okay, bring your feet together so they're touching.
- *Breathe in, reach the arms high.*
- *Breathe out and bend the legs like you're sitting in a chair.*
- *You might notice the muscles in the front of your thighs working here, as you bend.*

If you notice tension in your shoulders, see if you can let them relax a little as you hold up your arms. Maybe sink down a little more, and notice the strength in your legs. Keep breathing! Now when you're ready, bring your hands together at your chest. Breathe in and reach your arms up but keep the legs bent. Breathe out, and bring your hands down to your chest. We'll practice doing this while counting for 3 breaths. Feel free to go with your own rhythm, if mine doesn't work for you.
- *Breathe in 1, 2, 3, 4.*

Demonstrate reaching the arms up.

- *Breathe out 1, 2, 3, 4, 5, 6, 7, 8.*

Demonstrate bringing the hands to the chest.

- *Try the movement 2 more times, counting to yourself: In for 4. Out for 8.*
- *Experiment with relaxing your face and shoulders, even if your legs are getting tired!*

When students finish the last round, have them straighten their legs and relax. Take 3 breaths in Mountain Pose. Have students take a seat.

Proceed to the Mindful Breathing section.

MINDFUL BREATHING (3 MINUTES)

Sit comfortably with your back straight. You can close your eyes at any time, or just look down at your desk to help you focus inward. We're going to practice breathing while touching different fingers together to help us stay centered and focused. While we do the breathing, if you notice any thoughts come up, rather than reacting to those thoughts or following them, practice keeping your focus on your fingers touching together and your breathing, letting the thoughts come and go. In this way you can practice noticing your thoughts, rather than being swept away by them or reacting to them.

Take a look at your hands.
- *When you breathe in, touch your index finger to your thumb.*
- *When you breathe out, touch your middle finger to your thumb.*
- *When you breathe in, touch your ring finger to your thumb.*
- *When you breathe out, touch your pinky finger to your thumb.*
- *Keep doing this as you breathe, one finger per breath. You can close your eyes as you do this, or look down at your desk.*

We're going to practice this for 1 minute. As soon as you notice you got stuck in a thought, start over again with the breath and fingers. If you feel distracted or aggitated, take a deep breath and notice your feet in contact with the floor and your weight in your seat.

Allow students to practice for 1 minute, providing verbal cues to help them stay focused.

Now you can relax your hands.

If you noticed any negative thoughts in your head, or thoughts you don't need, you can imagine breathing them out on the exhale. Deep breath in, and then breathing negative thoughts out. Let's do this 2 more times.

- *Deep breath in, negative thoughts out.*
- *Breathe in, let it out.*

Good, go back to breathing normally if you'd like.

WRAP-UP

GUIDED MEDITATION AND CLOSING BELL (1 MINUTE)

We're going to end class by sitting silently for 1 minute, just noticing your breathing and how your body feels.

Feel free to close your eyes or look down to help you concentrate only on yourself.

If you like, you can even put your head down and rest it on your arms.

Pause.

Notice your feet resting on the floor, your legs relaxed on the seat.

Notice where your arms and hands are. Maybe you can allow your arms and shoulders to relax a bit more.

Notice how you're breathing.

You might even allow the muscles of your face to relax as you breathe.

Long pause, allow students to sit silently for remainder of the minute.

I will now ring the bell one last time. Listen to the bell and when you can't hear it anymore, please look up at me.

Ring bell and allow it to vibrate to completion.

CONNECTION QUESTIONS (3 MINUTES)

How is everyone feeling?

Have you noticed that you've gotten better at anything we have practiced in TLS? What is it?

Ask students if they have any questions about what we did today or about TLS or mindfulness in general, and thank them for their participation.

LESSON 3.7: USING TOOLS TO CALM DOWN

In this lesson, students will be introduced to Rag Doll Roll-Up Pose. Physically, this pose:

❖ Releases tension in the lower back, shoulders, and neck
❖ Stretches the hamstrings
❖ Calms the nervous system

Lesson objectives are (a) students will learn the importance of being able to calm oneself down, and the different aspects of one's life that that skill can affect, and (b) students will practice using tools to help calm themselves down.

STUDENT OVERVIEW

REVIEW EXPECTATIONS (2 MINUTES)

Review the expectations for TLS sessions, including:

❖ Students clear desks of all distractions including books, papers, food, cell phones, and music.
❖ One-mic rule: one person talks at a time. If students have questions, they can raise a hand or ask at the end of class. Assure students that there will be a few minutes dedicated to questions at the end of each session.
❖ Students focus on their own body and breath. That means not making comments about self or others, not touching others, and not distracting others from their experience.
❖ Students try their best to participate at all times. (However, participation may look different for each student. For some students, it may mean doing only the breathing for as long as they need, until they choose to engage with the movement. Allow students to come to the practice at their own pace, as long as they are not being distracting or disrespectful

toward others. Engaging with one's body and mind through TLS is always a choice, and every day is a different experience.)

ACTIVATE BACKGROUND KNOWLEDGE (3 MINUTES)

In response to the class environment each day, you may wish to provide this information to students when you feel it would be best received — that may be at the beginning of class, woven into the mindful movement, or before the silent sitting.

Being able to calm down when you are upset, angry, or overwhelmed is a very valuable skill. Calming yourself down does not mean being passive—it means being able to take the best and smartest action for yourself and others. If you are able to recognize when you need to calm down and use tools to calm yourself when you need it, it will impact every aspect of your life positively. For example, you could use these tools to do better on tests, fall asleep faster, and avoid getting into fights! The younger you are when you start to learn how to calm yourself down, the better. Learning and using tools to calm yourself down will be a lifelong skill.

Activation Question 3.7

What do you do to help yourself calm down?

Give students a chance to reflect, and choose a few students to share their responses with the class.

In this lesson, we will identify and practice different techniques that you can use as tools to calm down.

ACTION, BREATHING, CENTERING

OPENING BELL AND FOCUSED BREATHING (2 MINUTES)

We will start our time together today by trying to focus our attention on a sound. I would like to ask you all to listen to the sound of the bell I am going to ring.

Try to keep your attention on the sound of the bell for as long as you can, and when you can't hear it anymore, please raise your hand.

Ring bell or singing bowl.

❖ Allow to vibrate to completion and until all students have raised their hands.

❖ Then ask students to do the same thing, this time closing their eyes or looking down at their desks to focus just on their hearing, and ring the bell again.

❖ Wait until all students have raised their hands.

That was very good. Now I'll lead you in a breathing exercise:
- *You can keep your eyes closed, or just look down.*
- *Let all the air out of your lungs.*
- *Now breathe in, breathe out.*

Lead class in simple breathing, encouraging them to breathe deeply and smoothly.

Continue for 3–4 rounds.

Then tell students that you are going to do the bell exercise one more time.

Ring the bell again, and students raise their hands when they can no longer hear it.

MINDFUL MOVEMENT AND POSE OF THE DAY (6 MINUTES)

Just as in the last lesson, for the Mindful Movement today, it's important that none of the students have their back to someone else. You may wish to position students in a circle around the room before beginning the Mindful Movement section.

Mountain

Let's all stand up in Mountain Pose.

Pause as students stand.

Press your hands together at your chest, and either close your eyes or look down at the place where your hands meet. As you breathe in, lift the top of your head up toward the ceiling. As you breathe out, let your shoulders and arms relax. Breathe in and stand tall, reaching your head toward the ceiling. Breathe out and feel your feet on the floor, wiggling your toes if that helps you feel them. Take 1 more deep breath: standing tall, feeling your feet on the floor and shoulders relaxed.

Pause to allow students to breathe and focus.

Arm Movements

The next time we breathe in, we'll take the hands forward, still pressed together, and then apart and out to the sides. Feel your fingers stretching wide. When we breathe out, we'll bring the hands back together and then in to the chest.

Lead students in a couple of rounds, breathing in to reach the hands forward and out, and breathing out to bring them together and in.

Good. Now if it feels comfortable, add some rhythm to the breath, breathing in for 4 counts as you reach wide and breathing out for 8 counts as you bring the arms in.

Lead students by counting a few rounds.

> *Now as you do it, count silently in your head.*
> • *In for 4.*

Pause.

> • *Out for 8.*

Pause.

> *See if you can do 2 more rounds silently, without losing count.*

Pause as students continue.

> *After this round, you can relax your arms at your sides. Notice if you feel the muscles in your arms and shoulders gently relax as your arms hang down.*

Tree

Sometimes balancing poses can help you calm the mind by focusing it on the body and breath. Let's experiment with Tree Pose.

Start in Mountain Pose. Start to shift your weight into your left foot.
• *Notice your left foot planted firmly on the floor.*
• *Bring your right foot to your ankle, or to your calf, or to your thigh, avoiding your knee.*
• *If it feels okay, point the right knee out to the side.*
• *Bring your hands to your chest.*
• *Keep breathing as you balance.*

If you fall out of the pose, it's no big deal. You can focus your eyes on one spot in front of you and try again. (Student name), can you lead us in 3 breaths?

When you finish 3 breaths, shake out the legs and arms and try the pose on the other side. End in Mountain Pose with the palms at the chest and take 3 breaths together.

Rag Doll Roll-Up—Pose of the Day

The main pose of the day is called Rag Doll Roll-Up. Postures where you fold your body forward, like Rag Doll, can help calm the nervous system and release stress. For the pose of the day, we'll add onto Rag Doll, rounding the back to come out of the pose slowly and mindfully. If you get dizzy, try slowing down your movements even more.

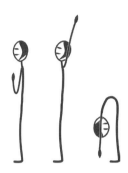

Start in Mountain Pose.
- *When you breathe in, raise your arms up toward the ceiling.*
- *When you breathe out, fold forward at the hips.*
- *Let your arms and head hang down toward the floor.*

You have a choice here:

(1) If you'd like to stretch out the back of your legs or your back, fold forward all the way toward the floor. Keep your legs bent as much as you'd like.

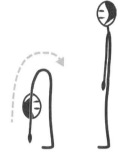

(2) Or if you'd rather focus on the shoulders and upper back, you can just bend forward a little, letting your chin come toward your chest and your arms hang down.

If you notice any tension in your neck, shoulders, back, or thighs, experiment with letting some of it go with each exhale.

(Student name), can you lead us in 3 breaths?

We will now practice rolling up slowly to Mountain Pose. Let your back stay rounded by drawing your abs in, and see how slowly you can roll up to standing. Take your time! Take several breaths to roll up, if you'd like. The last thing to come up will be your head.

Pause.

Once you are back in Mountain Pose, let your shoulders release downward. Notice your arms hanging down below your shoulders.

Notice if you got dizzy, or any other sensations you feel. Maybe you notice your breath coming in and out.

Pause.

Find a comfortable seat.

Robin

For the next movement, you can start really small and make it bigger as you feel comfortable.
- *When you breathe in, draw the shoulders back.*
- *When you breathe out bring the shoulders forward and the chin down.*

Guide students while they try a few rounds.

If you want to make it bigger, when you breathe in take the shoulders back farther and lift the chest; when you breathe out round the back, pulling the belly in and letting the head drop forward. Try a few more rounds, noticing what this movement feels like in your body.

Pause.

After the next round, just sit quietly. Notice if the muscles in the chest and back feel any different from before.

Neck Movements with Scalp Massage

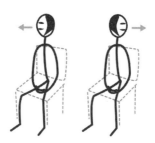

For the last movement today, we'll explore some movements to relax the neck. Start sitting up tall.
- *As you breathe out, look to the right, just turning your head.*
- *You can close your eyes here or look slightly downward.*
- *As you breathe in bring your head back to center, and as you breathe out, look to your left.*
- *Repeat this movement a few more times, noticing if you can feel the muscles in your neck during this movement.*

Pause.

On your next breath in, return your head to center.

Now we'll try another way to move the neck.
- *Tilt your head to the right side, bringing the ear toward the shoulder.*
- *We'll bring the head back to center on the inhale, and tilt it to the left on the exhale.*

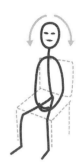

Keep going with your breath.
- *Notice if you feel a stretch in the muscles of the neck or shoulders.*
- *If you'd like, pause with your head tilted.*
- *Place your hand where you feel a stretch and notice if you can feel the spots that are stretching—they might feel like cords. If you'd like, give yourself a gentle massage. Notice how much pressure feels right for you.*

Pause.

You can do this on the other side too.

Pause as students do a self-massage with the head tilted the other way.

When you're ready, bring your head back to center. If you'd like, you can explore massaging your scalp with your fingers.
- *You have muscles in your scalp. See if you can feel them.*
- *Notice how much pressure feels best to you, as you massage the muscles in the scalp.*

Pause, and encourage students to continue to take deep breaths.

Now let the arms relax, and notice any sensations in your neck or head. Notice your feet on the floor. Notice where your hands are resting. Notice your breath flowing.

Proceed to the Mindful Breathing section.

MINDFUL BREATHING (3 MINUTES)

Sometimes it can be hard to calm yourself down, especially when you feel really strong emotions like fear or anger. The "Count Down to Calm Down" breath can be helpful in these situations to take some of the edge off. Let's practice it.

- *Notice how you're breathing.*
- *Feel free to close your eyes if that helps.*
- *Notice if you can feel your belly move as you breathe. If not, you can try relaxing the muscles around your belly so that it moves out a little on the inhale and in toward your spine on the exhale.*
- *Practice this a few times, allowing your abdomen to expand as you breathe in, and bringing it gently in as you breathe out.*

Pause.

We're going to do 10 belly breaths just like this, counting down from 10.

- *Breathe in a way that feels comfortable to you, noticing the movement of your belly as you breathe.*
- *If you need to take a break at any time you can, and join us again as you're ready.*
- *Take a breath in.*
- *Breathe out. 10.*
- *(Slowly) Breathing in, and out. 9 . . .*

Count down slowly to "1," giving students time to inhale and exhale for each count. Give reminders to help students focus on the movement in their body as they breathe. After you finish, invite students to return to normal breathing, and notice how they are feeling.

WRAP-UP

GUIDED MEDITATION AND CLOSING BELL (1 MINUTE)

We're going to end class by sitting silently for 1 minute, just noticing your breathing and how your body feels.

Feel free to close your eyes or look down to help you concentrate only on yourself.

If you like, you can even put your head down and rest it on your arms.

Pause.

Notice your feet resting on the floor, your legs relaxed on the seat.

Notice where your arms and hands are. Maybe you can allow your arms and shoulders to relax a bit more.

Notice how you're breathing.

You might even allow the muscles of your face to relax as you breathe.

Long pause, allow students to sit silently for remainder of the minute.

I will now ring the bell one last time. Listen to the bell and when you can't hear it anymore, please look up at me.

Ring bell and allow it to vibrate to completion.

CONNECTION QUESTIONS (3 MINUTES)

How is everyone feeling? Can you share one pose or breathing technique that we did today that you could use as a tool to calm down?

Ask students if they have any questions about what we did today or about TLS or mindfulness in general, and thank them for their participation.

LESSON 3.8: USING TOOLS TO ENERGIZE

In this lesson, students will be introduced to Arched Lunge Pose. Physically, this pose:

❖ Strengthens and tones the muscles in the legs
❖ Builds flexibility in the hip flexors
❖ Stretches and tones the upper back
❖ Energizes the body

Lesson objectives are (a) students will learn healthy practices that they can use to give themselves more energy when needed, and (b) students will practice using tools to reenergize.

STUDENT OVERVIEW

REVIEW EXPECTATIONS (2 MINUTES)

Review the expectations for TLS sessions, including:

❖ Students clear desks of all distractions including books, papers, food, cell phones, and music.
❖ One-mic rule: one person talks at a time. If students have questions, they can raise a hand or ask at the end of class. Assure students that there will be a few minutes dedicated to questions at the end of each session.
❖ Students focus on their own body and breath. That means not making comments about self or others, not touching others, and not distracting others from their experience.
❖ Students try their best to participate at all times. (However, participation may look different for each student. For some students, it may mean doing only the breathing for as long as they need, until they choose to engage with the movement. Allow students to come to the practice at their own pace, as long as they are not being distracting or disrespectful

toward others. Engaging with one's body and mind through TLS is always a choice, and every day is a different experience.)

ACTIVATE BACKGROUND KNOWLEDGE (3 MINUTES)

In response to the class environment each day, you may wish to provide this information to students when you feel it would be best received—that may be at the beginning of class, woven into the mindful movement, or before the silent sitting.

Practicing dynamic mindfulness can help you to calm down, but did you know that you can also use your breath and movement to help you wake up? Your TLS practice can provide you with some tools for increasing your energy level when you need it.

Activation Question 3.8

What do you do when you want to feel more energetic and awake?

Give students a chance to reflect, and choose a few students to share their responses with the class.

During TLS today, we'll practice some tools for increasing your energy level and mental clarity. We'll also talk about the difference between calming tools and invigorating tools, so you can use them on your own when you need them.

ACTION, BREATHING, CENTERING

OPENING BELL AND FOCUSED BREATHING (2 MINUTES)

We will start our time together today by trying to focus our attention on a sound. I would like to ask you all to listen to the sound of the bell I am going to ring.

Try to keep your attention on the sound of the bell for as long as you can, and when you can't hear it anymore, please raise your hand.

Ring bell or singing bowl.

❖ Allow to vibrate to completion and until all students have raised their hands.

❖ Then ask students to do the same thing, this time closing their eyes or looking down at their desks to focus just on their hearing, and ring the bell again.

❖ Wait until all students have raised their hands.

That was very good. Now I'll lead you in a breathing exercise:
- *You can keep your eyes closed, or just look down.*
- *Let all the air out of your lungs.*
- *Now breathe in, breathe out.*

Lead class in simple breathing, encouraging them to breathe deeply and smoothly.

Continue for 3–4 rounds.

Then tell students that you are going to do the bell exercise one more time.

Ring the bell again, and students raise their hands when they can no longer hear it.

MINDFUL MOVEMENT AND POSE OF THE DAY (6 MINUTES)

Mountain

Let's all stand up in Mountain Pose. Place your feet flat on the floor. Notice if you can feel your feet making contact with the floor. Lift the very top of your head up toward the ceiling. Notice how you're breathing.

If you'd like, press your hands together at your chest, and either close your eyes or look down at the place where your hands meet. Can someone lead us in 3 breaths, saying, "breathe in, breathe out"?

Choose a student to lead the breaths, making sure the student leads them slowly to allow for deep breathing.

Breath of Joy

Next we'll try out a breathing exercise that can help give you energy. We'll take a three-part inhale, raising the arms up.

Demonstrate taking 3 inhales in a row, lifting the arms higher with each inhale until they are overhead.

Then we let the arms drop with one big exhale.

Demonstrate letting your breath out strongly and letting the arms drop.

Let's try it 3 times.

Lead students in 3 "breaths of joy," encouraging them to breathe deeply and stretch their arms.

When finished, have students shake out their arms and hands and notice how they are breathing now – maybe it got faster, deeper, or more spacious.

Standing Backbend as a Movement

We are going to do a standing back bend as a movement. In general, postures where your chest is open and you're bending backward can raise your energy level. This is one example.

- *When you inhale, reach your arms up.*
- *When you exhale, bring your hands to your lower back.*
- *When you inhale, support your lower back, and if it feels comfortable open up your chest and lean back. Only go so far back as is comfortable to you.*

On the exhale, return to standing. Let's repeat this movement 3 times.

Ask a student to lead the movement and breathing.

Trunk Twists

Shake out your arms and bring your feet a little farther apart. Let's do some trunk twists.

If it feels okay to you, let your arms just relax and swing as you twist from side to side as if they were wet noodles. Can you feel the blood rushing to your fingertips as you twist?

Pause.

If there is not much room, give students the alternative to bend the arms at chest height as they twist.

To protect your knees, lift up the opposite heel as you twist to the side. To twist more, breathe out each time you turn to the side.

Pause as students practice for about 30 seconds.

Now let your twists get smaller and smaller until you are still. Come back to Mountain Pose with your palms together at your chest and take a few breaths, noticing how your body feels.

Have another student lead 3 breaths.

Arched Lunge—Pose of the Day

The pose of the day is called Arched Lunge. Arched Lunge stretches and strengthens the legs and hips. It also opens up the chest and shoulders, which can help energize and lift your spirits.

Lets start by coming into Lunge with the left leg back, and right leg forward. For more of a stretch, place your legs farther apart; for less of a stretch, move them closer together. The front leg is bent with the knee right above the ankle. Do you feel your front quad working as you bend?

If the knee goes farther forward than the ankle, it's best to make your stance wider so you don't hurt your knee.

- *When you straighten your back leg, notice if you feel a stretch in the top front of your left thigh. That's called your hip flexor.*

Keep breathing.
- *Let's experiment with the arms a little. Reach your arms high overhead. Notice if you feel your ribs and chest lift as you do that. You might try bending the arms too—notice if that weighs you down or makes them feel heavier. Just notice what you feel, and you can choose whatever one you'd like.*

Can someone lead us in 2 breaths?

Pause here for 2 breaths.

Now as you're ready, either bring your hands behind your head with your elbows out, or bring your hands together at your chest. As you breathe in, lift your chest up and take the shoulders back. Arch as little or as far as you'd like, making sure your back feels okay and you're not crunching the lower back. You can look up at the ceiling if that feels okay on your neck.
- *Keep breathing for 3.*

Pause.

- *Notice the space across the front of your chest: 2.*

Pause.

And 1. . . . Lift up and forward to come out of the arch. And when you're ready, bring your back leg forward to Mountain Pose. Bring your hands to your chest. Can you feel your heart beating? How is your energy level?

(Student name), can you lead us in 3 breaths please? Notice if your heartbeat starts to slow as we breathe.

Lead students through Lunge and Arched Lunge on the other side. Have students hold the pose for the same amount of time on both sides. Then come back to Mountain Pose for 3 breaths.

Tall Tree

The last pose we'll do today is Tall Tree. Plant your left foot firmly on the floor. When you're ready, bring your right foot to your ankle, or to your calf, or to your thigh, avoiding your knee. If it feels okay, point the right knee out to the side. Bring your hands to your chest. Notice your breath.

Pause.

Remember, breathing and focusing your eyes on one spot in front of you can help you balance.

Feel free to stay in Tree Pose, or if you would like, raise your arms up toward the ceiling. Feel your chest lift and expand as you breathe.

Pause.

If this is easy for you, try looking up at the ceiling as you balance.

(Student name), can you lead us in 3 breaths?

If students have a hard time balancing, have them take a deep breath and try to clear their minds of other thoughts. It's also good to remind them that it doesn't matter whether they can balance well today or not. It's more important that they play with trying to do the pose and don't take it too seriously.

When the 3 breaths are finished, shake out the legs and arms and try the pose on the other side. End in Mountain Pose with the palms at the chest and take 3 breaths together.

Proceed to the Mindful Breathing section.

MINDFUL BREATHING (3 MINUTES)

Find a way to sit comfortably. You can close your eyes or just look down to help you focus on yourself. Notice the rhythm of your breathing. Allow each inhale to get a little deeper, and exhale a little longer.

Pause.

- *On your next breath, see if you can notice the very moment when the inhale turns into an exhale. Breathe out, and notice the moment when the exhale turns into an inhale. Pause.*
- *Noticing the top of the inhale, and the bottom of the exhale as you breathe.* Pause.

Now if it feels okay, each time you get to the top of the inhale, pause just a second before you exhale. Then watch the breath come back out. If holding the breath does not feel comfortable, or if you have high blood pressure, don't do the pause. Instead, keep breathing smoothly and noticing the top and the bottom of each breath. So if you're practicing the pause, it looks like this (slowly:)

- *Inhale, pause with the lungs full of air, exhale.*
- *Inhale, pause, exhale.*

Notice how it feels to breathe this way for about 3 more rounds.

Pause for about 3 breaths.

Good. Come back to normal deep breathing. Next we'll experiment with pausing only after the exhale, for just a second. On your next breath, notice the bottom of the exhale. Notice how it feels to be empty and still, and then watch the breath as it comes back in and fills your lungs. Only do the pause if it feels comfortable to you. Exhale, pause with the lungs empty of breath, inhale.

Pause to allow them to take about 3 breaths.

Notice how that one feels. Now you can go back to breathing normally.

Pausing with your lungs full of breath can energize you. Pausing when they are empty of breath can calm you down. If you've been feeling sad or low-energy, try only pausing after each inhale, noticing what it feels like to be full of breath. If you've been feeling anxious, stressed, hyper, or angry, you might try pausing after each exhale, noticing what it feels like to be still and empty of breath. Or you might choose to breathe smoothly without holding if that feels best to you. Choose which option is best for you right now, and try it for about a minute. Feel free to take a break if you feel out of breath. We'll start now.

Pause and let students try the breathing on their own for 30 seconds to a minute.

Good job! Please go back to breathing normally.

WRAP-UP

GUIDED MEDITATION AND CLOSING BELL (1 MINUTE)

We're going to end class by sitting silently for 1 minute, just noticing your breathing and how your body feels.

Feel free to close your eyes or look down to help you concentrate only on yourself.

If you like, you can even put your head down and rest it on your arms.

Pause.

Notice your feet resting on the floor, your legs relaxed on the seat.

Notice where your arms and hands are. Maybe you can allow your arms and shoulders to relax a bit more.

Notice how you're breathing.

You might even allow the muscles of your face to relax as you breathe.

Notice if you feel tired, relaxed, energized, or something else.

Long pause, allow students to sit silently for remainder of the minute.

I will now ring the bell one last time. Listen to the bell and when you can't hear it anymore, please look up at me.

Ring bell and allow it to vibrate to completion.

CONNECTION QUESTIONS (3 MINUTES)

How is everyone feeling?

Who can name one pose or breathing technique that can help you calm down, and one pose or breathing technique that can give you more energy?

❖ Possible answers for calming practice: any movements or poses from lesson 3.7, any poses that bend forward at the waist or neck, abdominal breathing, lengthening the exhale, or pausing after the exhale.

❖ Possible answers for energizing practice: any mindful movements or poses from this lesson, any poses where the chest or arms are lifted or arched backward, thoracic breathing (using the ribs), breath of joy, lengthening the inhale, or pausing after the inhale.

Ask students if they have any questions about what we did today or about TLS or mindfulness in general, and thank them for their participation.

LESSON 3.9: BEING WITH EMOTIONS

In this lesson, students will be introduced to Tip Toe Pose in Chair. Physically, this pose:

❖ Strengthens the quadriceps and calves
❖ Improves balance and focus

Lesson objectives are (a) students will learn strategies for being with and reflecting on emotions, as a foundational practice for emotion regulation, and (b) students will practice noticing their emotions without judgment.

STUDENT OVERVIEW

REVIEW EXPECTATIONS (2 MINUTES)

Review the expectations for TLS sessions, including:

❖ Students clear desks of all distractions including books, papers, food, cell phones, and music.
❖ One-mic rule: one person talks at a time. If students have questions, they can raise a hand or ask at the end of class. Assure students that there will be a few minutes dedicated to questions at the end of each session.
❖ Students focus on their own body and breath. That means not making comments about self or others, not touching others, and not distracting others from their experience.
❖ Students try their best to participate at all times. (However, participation may look different for each student. For some students, it may mean doing only the breathing for as long as they need, until they choose to engage with the movement. Allow students to come to the practice at their own pace, as long as they are not being distracting or disrespectful toward others. Engaging with one's body and mind through TLS is always a choice, and every day is a different experience.)

ACTIVATE BACKGROUND KNOWLEDGE (3 MINUTES)

In response to the class environment each day, you may wish to provide this information to students when you feel it would be best received—that may be at the beginning of class, woven into the mindful movement, or before the silent sitting.

We have been talking a lot about managing our emotions. It's important to point out that managing emotions does not mean changing them or trying not to feel them. We certainly do feel our emotions, but we don't have to be consumed or controlled by them. Sometimes it's good to try to make yourself feel better, and sometimes it is necessary to just be with and observe whatever emotions you are feeling. The practice is how to be with emotions in a skillful way. This includes breathing, relaxing, creating space for your emotions, feeling and reflecting on them, and letting them go when you're ready.

When our emotions are really strong or uncomfortable, it can be hard to just let them be and observe them. But being with strong emotions is an important life skill.

Of course, you have to choose carefully where and with whom you choose to be with strong emotions. You should choose a place where you feel safe and comfortable enough to let yourself feel whatever you are feeling, for as long as you need. For example, you can go to your bedroom, or walk in the woods, or talk with a close friend or mentor.

Activation Question 3.9

Can you think of one situation where it would be useful to observe and be with your emotions, and one situation where it would be best to try to shift your mood?

Give students a chance to reflect, and choose a few students to share their responses with the class.

Today as we practice, try to notice how you are feeling without judging yourself – whatever you are feeling today is just fine.

ACTION, BREATHING, CENTERING

OPENING BELL AND FOCUSED BREATHING (2 MINUTES)

We will start our time together today by trying to focus our attention on a sound. I would like to ask you all to listen to the sound of the bell I am going to ring.

Try to keep your attention on the sound of the bell for as long as you can, and when you can't hear it anymore, please raise your hand.

Ring bell or singing bowl.

❖ Allow to vibrate to completion and until all students have raised their hands.
❖ Then ask students to do the same thing, this time closing their eyes or looking down at their desks to focus just on their hearing, and ring the bell again.
❖ Wait until all students have raised their hands.

> *That was very good. Now I'll lead you in a breathing exercise:*
> • *You can keep your eyes closed, or just look down.*
> • *Let all the air out of your lungs.*
> • *Now breathe in, breathe out.*

Lead class in simple breathing, encouraging them to breathe deeply and smoothly.

Continue for 3–4 rounds.

Then tell students that you are going to do the bell exercise one more time.

Ring the bell again, and students raise their hands when they can no longer hear it.

MINDFUL MOVEMENT AND POSE OF THE DAY (6 MINUTES)

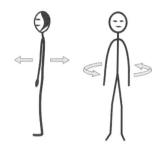

Mountain Variation

Let's all stand up in Mountain Pose. Close your eyes if it feels okay, or just look down.

(1) Experiment with leaning forward slightly and feeling how your weight shifts into your toes. Lean back and feel the weight shift into your heels. Now lean to the right and left, and notice how the weight shifts in the feet.

(2) If you'd like, let your body sway in a slow circle, noticing how the weight shifts in the feet as you do that.

Pause.

Allow your circles to get smaller and smaller, until you settle and find stillness right in the center. That's your center of gravity, where you are strongest. Take a few breaths here, in your center.

Pause.

Feel your feet on the floor and reach the top of your head high. Press your hands together at your chest, with your eyes closed or looking down at the place where your hands meet. Can someone lead us in 3 breaths, saying, "breathe in, breathe out"?

Choose a student to lead the breaths, making sure the student leads them slowly to allow for deep breathing.

Ankle Rolls

Open your eyes and relax your arms at your sides. When you're ready, shift your weight into your left leg until you can lightly lift your right foot off the floor. Take a breath here to center yourself, feeling your left foot firmly planted on the floor. Extending the right leg in front of you, you can start making circles with the foot to warm up the ankle.

They can be small or big circles.

Notice what you feel in there as you make circles—maybe some stretching or clicking or warmth building. Still breathing deeply, see if you can stand a little taller, feeling your left foot on the floor.

If you'd like, switch the direction of your circles.

Pause for students to make 3–4 circles with the foot.

Good. Put the right foot down to find Mountain Pose. Feel both feet on the floor. Then slowly shift your weight to the right foot.

Lead students through Ankle Rolls with their left foot extended. Use cues to remind them to stay centered:

❖ Look at one spot on the floor
❖ Notice your breathing
❖ Press into the floor with the standing foot to stand a little taller

End with 3 breaths in Mountain Pose with palms together at the chest.

Wide-Legged Crescent

If it feels more stable to you, bring your feet wider apart. When you breathe in, take both arms high above your head. When you breathe out, take your right hand down to your right thigh and reach your left arm over your head. Do you feel a stretch in your left side? If having the arms up doesn't work for you, you can also do the pose with your hands on your hips.

Lean to the right, but see if you can put equal weight into both feet on the floor. When you breathe in, come back to standing straight up, maybe reaching your arms high. When you breathe out, lean to the other side.

Continue to move with your breath, concentrating on the sensations your feel in your body as you move. For example, maybe you feel a stretching sensation in your ribs, or in your hips, or somewhere else.

Can some one lead us by saying, "Breathe in, breathe out," nice and slow?

Repeat movement 3 times on each side, breathing in to stand up straight and breathing out to lean. When finished, lower your arms to the sides.

Tip Toe in Chair—Pose of the Day

For the pose of the day, we'll do another variation of Tip Toe. It can be challenging, but do your best to stay aware of your body and your breathing as you try it. If you lose your balance, take a breath or 2 and try it again. Remember, we feel our emotions through sensations in our bodies, so by practicing observing uncomfortable sensations in your body, like your muscles getting tired, you can train yourself to be better at observing uncomfortable emotions without reacting to them. As always, you can come out of the pose if you ever feel it's too much, and try it again as you feel ready.

To start, come into Chair, bending the legs and keeping the feet flat on the floor. If it feels alright, extend your arms in front of you. You always have the option of grabbing onto a desk if you need extra support. Notice your feet flat on the floor. Take a breath.

Pause.

- *When you're ready, lift your heels up, balancing just on the balls of the feet, but keeping your legs bent.*
- *Keep your breath moving.*
- *You might notice the muscles in the front of your thighs working here.*

If you'd like, you can put your hands on your thighs to help you notice the muscles engaging.

Take a moment to move your body up and down by bending your legs more and less, noticing how the thighs feel.

Now we'll experiment with holding still in the pose. Choose where you would like to place your hands—extended in front of you, together at your chest, or lightly touching a desk. Do your best to observe your breath and what you feel in your legs as you attempt the pose.

(Student name), can you lead us in 3 breaths, please?

Pause.

Good effort! To come out, straighten your legs and reach your arms up. Breathe in and stretch. Breathe out, lower your heels to the floor and bring your hands together at your chest.

Can you feel your heart beating?

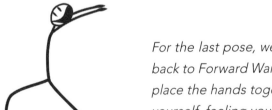

Arched Warrior

For the last pose, we'll come into Arched Warrior. Take the left leg back to Forward Warrior. Either extend the arms up to the ceiling or place the hands together at the chest. Take a few breaths to center yourself, feeling your back leg straight with the heel on the ground and your front leg bent. Keep your breath flowing.

If you feel an arch in your lower back, you can try to straighten it out by bringing the tailbone down and drawing the abdomen slightly in.

Notice how you're breathing.

When you're ready, lift the center of your chest and take your shoulders slightly back. Try to keep your breath smooth as you do this. Feel free to back off a bit or take a rest if you feel any pain or your breath stops.

Keep your breath flowing for 3 counts, feeling your feet flat on the floor to help you feel centered.

3: Being aware of what you feel in your back, and make adjustments if needed.

2: Keep breathing!

And 1.

Come back to regular Forward Warrior. We'll take a breath here, and as we breathe out, we'll bring the left foot forward again to Mountain Pose. Let's take 3 breaths here with the hands at the chest. You can look down at your hands or close your eyes. Notice how your breath feels. Notice if your heart is beating a little faster.

Choose a student to lead 3 breaths. Once they are done, repeat the Forward Warrior/Arched Warrior sequence with the right leg back. Finish in Mountain Pose with 3 mindful breaths.

Invite students to take a seat. Proceed to the Mindful Breathing section.

MINDFUL BREATHING (3 MINUTES)

Sometimes we know we are dealing with difficult emotions, but it's hard to tell what they are or where they're coming from. Focusing on the sensations in your body can help you become more aware of your emotions.

Take a moment to sit comfortably with your back straight. Either close your eyes or look slightly down to help you focus on yourself. Bring your attention to your breathing. Without changing the way you breathe, just notice how you're breathing right now. Notice if you're breathing through your nose or through your mouth.

Pause.

Notice if your breath is deep or shallow, long or short.

Pause.

As you breathe, notice what parts of your body are being moved by your breath.

Pause.

Can you notice your chest move as you breathe?

Pause.

What about your ribs? Feel free to place your hands on your ribs to see if you can feel them moving.

Pause.

Maybe you can even feel your back move, as your ribs go all the way around to the back of your body.

Pause for longer as students focus on the movements.

Can you feel your breath move your belly?

Pause.

If you'd like, bring one hand to your belly, or just try to focus on it moving from the inside. If you breathe deeply, you might notice your belly moving out a little as you breathe in, and coming gently back in toward your spine as you breathe out.

Pause.

We often tighten up our abdomen when we don't want to feel emotions, and just breathe with our chest. Breathing using your belly can help let out emotions that are stuck inside. If you feel comfortable with it right now, feel free to take another 4–5 breaths focusing on the movements of your belly. Or if you would rather, just breathe in any way that feels comfortable to you right now, noticing what moves as you breathe.

Pause to allow students to breathe for 4–5 more rounds.

Whatever you notice, and however you are breathing right now, is just fine. You might want to congratulate yourself for taking the time to notice.

WRAP-UP

GUIDED MEDITATION AND CLOSING BELL (1 MINUTE)

We're going to end class by sitting silently for 1 minute. Feel free to close your eyes or look down to help you concentrate only on yourself.

If you like, you can even put your head down and rest it on your arms.

Pause.

Notice your feet resting on the floor, your legs relaxed on the seat. Notice where your arms and hands are. Maybe you can allow your arms and shoulders to relax a bit more.
Notice how you're breathing.

You might even allow the muscles of your face to relax as you breathe.

Long pause, allow students to sit silently for remainder of the minute.

I will now ring the bell one last time. Listen to the bell and when you can't hear it anymore, please look up at me.

Ring bell and allow it to vibrate to completion.

CONNECTION QUESTIONS (3 MINUTES)

How is everyone feeling?

What environments would be ideal places for someone to be with and observe strong emotions that they are feeling?

Ask students if they have any questions about what we did today or about TLS or mindfulness in general, and thank them for their participation.

LESSON 3.10: PRACTICING MAKING CHOICES

In this lesson, students will be introduced to Seated Hip Stretch Pose. Physically, this pose:

❖ Releases tension in the hips
❖ Stretches the hamstring and gluteus muscles

Lesson objectives are (a) students will learn that they can get better at making good choices for themselves through practice, and (b) students will practice making healthy choices for themselves.

STUDENT OVERVIEW

REVIEW EXPECTATIONS (2 MINUTES)

Review the expectations for TLS sessions, including:

❖ Students clear desks of all distractions including books, papers, food, cell phones, and music.
❖ One-mic rule: one person talks at a time. If students have questions, they can raise a hand or ask at the end of class. Assure students that there will be a few minutes dedicated to questions at the end of each session.
❖ Students focus on their own body and breath. That means not making comments about self or others, not touching others, and not distracting others from their experience.
❖ Students try their best to participate at all times. (However, participation may look different for each student. For some students, it may mean doing only the breathing for as long as they need, until they choose to engage with the movement. Allow students to come to the practice at their own pace, as long as they are not being distracting or disrespectful toward others. Engaging with one's body and mind through TLS is always a choice, and every day is a different experience.)

ACTIVATE BACKGROUND KNOWLEDGE (3 MINUTES)

In response to the class environment each day, you may wish to provide this information to students when you feel it would be best received—that may be at the beginning of class, woven into the mindful movement, or before the silent sitting.

In TLS, we have been working on building mental, emotional, and physical awareness and balance. Each of these aspects of the self has its own intelligence and can help us make choices. We can use our intellectual intelligence to reason through options and consider consequences. We can use our emotional intelligence by gathering information from our emotional reactions to different options. Or we can tap into our bodies: has anyone here ever made a decision based on a "gut reaction"? What does this mean? (Get a few answers from students.) We have a collection of nerves in the gut that is so big that it's second only to the brain. They actually call it the second brain! Sometimes the "gut feelings" we have can give us information about the safety of a situation or whether or not we should trust someone. So the body has its own intelligence, we just have to pause long enough to listen. As human beings we have access to all 3 types of intelligence.

Activation Question 3.10

Thinking about our different forms of intelligence, including intellectual, emotional, and physical, or gut feelings, which ones do you tend to focus on more when faced with a decision? Who here tends to make decisions based on on gut feelings, or intuition?

Pause to allow students to raise hands.

Based on reasoning, or thinking things through? (Pause) Based on how you feel emotionally?

Give students a chance to reflect, and choose a few students to share their responses with the class.

When faced with a decision to make, wouldn't it be better to use all of our intelligences instead of just listening to one of them? This might mean if you tend to respond more to emotions, pausing to think things through before taking action. Or if you tend to focus only on thinking, connecting with your breathing and how your body feels when considering different options. You could also expand your intelligence to include learning from the experiences of people you trust.

In TLS today, you'll have lots of opportunities to make choices for yourself. As you do this, you can experiment with tapping into how your body feels, how you feel emotionally, and what you think is the best choice for you at the time.

ACTION, BREATHING, CENTERING

OPENING BELL AND FOCUSED BREATHING (2 MINUTES)

We will start our time together today by trying to focus our attention on a sound. I would like to ask you all to listen to the sound of the bell I am going to ring.

Try to keep your attention on the sound of the bell for as long as you can, and when you can't hear it anymore, please raise your hand.

Ring bell or singing bowl.

❖ Allow to vibrate to completion and until all students have raised their hands.
❖ Then ask students to do the same thing, this time closing their eyes or looking down at their desks to focus just on their hearing, and ring the bell again.
❖ Wait until all students have raised their hands.

That was very good. Now I'll lead you in a breathing exercise:

- *You can keep your eyes closed, or just look down.*
- *Let all the air out of your lungs.*
- *Now breathe in, breathe out.*

Lead class in simple breathing, encouraging them to breathe deeply and smoothly.

Continue for 3–4 rounds.

Then tell students that you are going to do the bell exercise one more time.

Ring the bell again, and students raise their hands when they can no longer hear it.

MINDFUL MOVEMENT AND POSE OF THE DAY (6 MINUTES)

Mountain

Let's all stand up in Mountain Pose.

Press your hands together at your chest, and either close your eyes or look down at the place where your hands meet. As you breathe in, lift the top of your head up toward the ceiling. As you breathe out, let your shoulders and arms relax. Breathe in and stand tall, reaching your head toward the ceiling. Breathe out and feel your feet on the floor, wiggling your toes if that helps you feel them. Take 1 more deep breath: standing tall, feeling your feet on the floor and shoulders relaxed.

Pause to allow students to breathe and focus.

Sun Breaths

We're going to practice some Sun Breaths now.

When we do Sun Breaths, we match our movement with our breathing. There are two options for the movement.
- *You can raise your arms out to the sides and up as you breathe in, and lower them as you breathe out.*

- *Or you can use your hands: opening your hands as you breathe in, and closing them into fists as you breathe out.*

You can experiment and choose which one you prefer for today.
- *Breathing in: raising your arms or opening your hands.*
- *Breathing out: lowering your arms or closing your hands.*

Do a few more rounds, trying to match your movement with your breath.

You can choose to match your movements to mine, or follow your own rhythm.

Demonstrate movement and breathing for 3–4 more rounds.

Standing Backbend with Clasp

Next we are going to do a Standing Backbend as a movement.
- *Inhale and reach up toward the ceiling. On the exhale, you can choose to either clasp your hands behind your back or press your hands to your lower back.*
- *Inhale as you draw your shoulder blades together and lift your chest.*
- *Exhale and return to standing, releasing your hands and relaxing your shoulders.*

Maybe you felt some muscles in your upper back working to bring your shoulder blades together. You might check that out as we repeat the movement with the breath 3 times.

Ask a student to lead the breaths for 3 rounds of movement.

Good! Shake out your arms and shoulders and return to Mountain Pose.

Eagle

Let's extend our arms straight forward for Eagle Pose. Cross the right arm on top of the left.

Here there are a few options for the arms:
- *The first option is to cross the arms above the elbows, and keep twisting the arms around each other until you can press the palms of the hands together.*
- *The other option is to cross your arms once and wrap your hands around your shoulder blades for a big hug.*

Whichever arm option you choose, check in with your body to make sure it feels okay to sustain it for several breaths, and make modifications if needed. Stand up a little straighter as you breathe in. Breathe out and try lowering your shoulders down, away from your ears.

Now as you do this, come into Chair Pose by bending your knees forward with your feet flat on the floor. To do the full Eagle Pose, cross your left leg on top of your right and balance on your bent right leg. If you prefer to focus just on the arms, stay in Chair Pose or stand with your legs straight as you do this. Either option is fine, just do what is best for you today. (Student name), can you lead us in 3 breaths?

To come out of the pose, untwist everything and straighten your legs. Take a couple of Trunk Twists to release tension.

Lead students in a few Trunk Twists. Then do Eagle Pose on the opposite side: left arm on top of right, right leg on top of left. Do some Trunk Twists again when you are done with the second side.

Have students take a seat.

Seated Hip Stretch—Pose of the Day

The pose of the day is Seated Hip Stretch. Seated Hip Stretch can release stress and muscle tension in the hips, where a lot of people carry stress. It can also help prevent back pain due to tightness in the hips. In Seated Hip Stretch, only you know if you can feel a stretch, so it's up to you to listen to your body and go further or back off as needed.

Scoot forward to sit at the edge of your seat with your feet resting on the floor.

If students have a desk in front of them, have them slide the chair away from the desk or sit sideways so that they have room to lift their legs in front of them and lean forward.

If it feels okay, cross your right ankle over your left thigh, right above the knee. Flex the right foot and notice if by doing that you engage some of the muscles in your leg and around your knee. Try to keep your foot flexed the whole time. You might already feel a stretch in your right hip. If so, experiment with sitting up straighter and keeping your breath moving as you hold the pose. Let your right knee sink down toward the floor.

If you don't quite feel a stretch here, try bending forward at the waist, leading with your chest, until you feel a stretch in your hip or thigh. Let your right knee sink toward the floor. Pay attention to what you feel in your body—you are the only one who knows if you are feeling a healthy stretch, or if you are going too far and hurting yourself! If you notice things loosen up, you might experiment with leaning a little further forward. Be gentle and keep your attention on your body and breath.

(Student name), *can you lead us in 3 breaths?*

Once the 3 breaths are done, have students gently switch legs. Lead them through the same pose with the left leg lifted, reminding them to keep the left foot flexed. Then have students rest both feet on the floor for 3 breaths, and notice any sensations or changes in the way the hips feel.

Proceed to the Mindful Breathing section.

MINDFUL BREATHING (3 MINUTES)

We're going to practice a breathing technique we did a few sessions ago. You can choose whether to pause for a second at the top of the inhale, which can boost your energy, or at the bottom of the exhale, which can help you feel more calm, or neither.

Find a way to sit comfortably, and either close your eyes or just look down to help you focus on yourself. Before we start, take a moment to notice what you might need right now: do you feel like you need more energy, or more relaxation, or neither? You might even notice if you are using your reasoning to decide what you need, or your emotions, or the sensations in your body. Just notice as you let your breathing get deeper.

Pause.

Breathing in a little deeper, and breathing out a little longer.

Pause.

On your next breath:

- *See if you can notice the very moment when the inhale turns into an exhale.*
- *Breathe out, and notice the moment when the exhale turns into an inhale.*

Pause.

Now, if you would like a little energy boost, try pausing for a second after each inhale, noticing what it feels like to be full of breath before you let it out.

If you would like some relaxation, pause for a second after each exhale, noticing what it feels like to be still and empty of breath.

If you feel pretty balanced already, just keep noticing the top and the bottom of each inhale and exhale.

Choose which option is best for you right now, and try it for about a minute. If you feel distracted, aggitated, or out of breath, feel free to take a break: breathing deeply and noticing your feet in contact with the floor and your body against your chair. We'll start now.

Pause, and let students try the breathing for 1 minute, giving verbal cues if needed to help students stay present.

Good job! Please go back to breathing normally and notice how you feel right now. Notice how it feels to make a choice and take the action that's best for you.

WRAP-UP

GUIDED MEDITATION AND CLOSING BELL (1 MINUTE)

We're going to end class by sitting silently for 1 minute, just noticing your breathing and how your body feels.

Feel free to close your eyes or look down to help you concentrate only on yourself.

If you like, you can even put your head down and rest it on your arms.

Pause.

Notice your feet resting on the floor, your legs relaxed on the seat.

Notice where your arms and hands are. Maybe you can allow your arms and shoulders to relax a bit more.

Notice how you're breathing.

You might even allow the muscles of your face to relax as you breathe.

Long pause, allow students to sit silently for remainder of the minute.

I will now ring the bell one last time. Listen to the bell and when you can't hear it anymore, please look up at me.

Ring bell and allow it to vibrate to completion.

CONNECTION QUESTIONS (3 MINUTES)

How is everyone feeling?

Why do you think you are given so many choices when practicing TLS?

Ask students if they have any questions about what we did today or about TLS or mindfulness in general, and thank them for their participation.

LESSON 3.11: IMAGINING POSSIBILITIES

In this lesson, students will be introduced to King Dancer Pose. Physically, this pose:

❖ Strengthens and tones the ankles, legs, and back
❖ Stretches the shoulders and quadriceps
❖ Improves balance and focus

Lesson objectives are (a) students will reflect upon the people in their lives whom they might affect by learning to manage their emotions better, and how the world would be different if most people were able to manage their stress and have more self-control, and (b) students will practice centering themselves with the idea that it benefits not only themselves but others as well.

STUDENT OVERVIEW

REVIEW EXPECTATIONS (2 MINUTES)

Review the expectations for TLS sessions, including:

❖ Students clear desks of all distractions including books, papers, food, cell phones, and music.
❖ One-mic rule: one person talks at a time. If students have questions, they can raise a hand or ask at the end of class. Assure students that there will be a few minutes dedicated to questions at the end of each session.
❖ Students focus on their own body and breath. That means not making comments about self or others, not touching others, and not distracting others from their experience.
❖ Students try their best to participate at all times. (However, participation may look different for each student. For some students, it may mean doing only the breathing for as long as they need, until they choose to engage with the movement. Allow students to come to the practice at

their own pace, as long as they are not being distracting or disrespectful toward others. Engaging with one's body and mind through TLS is always a choice, and every day is a different experience.)

ACTIVATE BACKGROUND KNOWLEDGE (3 MINUTES)

In response to the class environment each day, you may wish to provide this information to students when you feel it would be best received—that may be at the beginning of class, woven into the mindful movement, or before the silent sitting.

In other schools, students who have practiced TLS have reported feeling less stressed and having more self-control than the students who didn't practice. Imagine if most people felt less stress and had more self-control. What would that look like? How would your school be different? How would your family, your community, or the world be different? Of course, you can't control how other people manage their emotions and stress. But you can control how you do. You can do it for yourself and for the good of everyone.

Activation Question 3.11

How do you think your school, your community, or the world would be different if people felt less stress and had more self-control?

Give students a chance to reflect and choose a few students to share their responses with the class.

Today as you practice TLS, imagine whom you are practicing for. You might choose to practice for yourself, or you might dedicate your practice to other people in your life that would benefit from you feeling less stressed and more balanced.

ACTION, BREATHING, CENTERING

OPENING BELL AND FOCUSED BREATHING (2 MINUTES)

We will start our time together today by trying to focus our attention on a sound. I would like to ask you all to listen to the sound of the bell I am going to ring.

Try to keep your attention on the sound of the bell for as long as you can, and when you can't hear it anymore, please raise your hand.

Ring bell or singing bowl.

❖ Allow to vibrate to completion and until all students have raised their hands.
❖ Then ask students to do the same thing, this time closing their eyes or looking down at their desks to focus just on their hearing, and ring the bell again.
❖ Wait until all students have raised their hands.

That was very good. Now I'll lead you in a breathing exercise:
- *You can keep your eyes closed, or just look down.*
- *Let all the air out of your lungs.*
- *Now breathe in, breathe out.*

Lead class in simple breathing, encouraging them to breathe deeply and smoothly.

Continue for 3–4 rounds.

Then tell students that you are going to do the bell exercise one more time.

Ring the bell again, and students raise their hands when they can no longer hear it.

MINDFUL MOVEMENT AND POSE OF THE DAY (6 MINUTES)

Mountain

Let's all stand up in Mountain Pose. Place your feet flat on the floor. Notice if you can feel your feet making contact with the floor. Lift the very top of your head up toward the ceiling. Notice how you're breathing.

If needed, review the elements of Mountain Pose:

❖ Feet parallel and hip-width distance apart
❖ Shoulders relaxed
❖ Standing tall

Press your hands together at your chest, and either close your eyes or look down at the place where your hands meet. Can someone lead us in 3 breaths, saying, "breathe in, breathe out"?

Choose a student to lead the breaths, making sure the student leads them slowly to allow for deep breathing.

Crescent Moon

Let's try Crescent Moon.
There are a few options for your arms:

• *You can reach your arms up straight and clasp your hands together.*
• *Or you can hook your thumbs together with your palms facing forward.*
• *Or place your hands on your hips.*
• *Each time we breathe in, we reach higher or stand taller.*
• *When we breathe out we lean to the right side, just enough to feel a gentle stretch in your side.*
• *Breathe in, come back to center standing up tall.*

- *Breathe out, lean to the left side.*
- *Try to match the movement to your breath.*

Try to keep the weight balanced between your right and left foot as you lean—notice if this requires any adjustments in your hips.

Can someone lead the breath for us?

Choose a student to lead the breath.
Allow students to try out 2 rounds per side.

Next time you breathe out, let your arms relax at your sides.

Thank the student for leading the breath.

This time we'll hold the pose for 3 breaths per side. Notice your breathing. Notice if you feel a stretch in your side.

Choose a student to lead the class in 3 breaths as you lead Crescent Moon to the right. Once the 3 breaths to the right are over:

- Breathe in to come to standing tall;
- Breathe out to go to the other side.
- Take 3 breaths on the left side.
- Then breathe in to stand tall, breathe out to relax and release.

Just stand in Mountain Pose with your arms hanging at your sides. Notice if you feel anything different in your body: maybe some warmth in your waist or your arms, or maybe your heart is beating faster than before. Close your eyes if you want. Take a moment to notice what you feel.

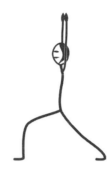

Forward Warrior

As we get ready to do Forward Warrior, you might want to bring to mind the person to whom you are dedicating your practice today. As you're ready, bring your right leg straight back for Forward Warrior.

- *Keep your right leg straight and the toes pointed slightly forward as you bend your left leg, bringing the knee right over the ankle.*
- *If your knee goes past your ankle, you can widen your stance by bringing your right foot farther back.*
- *Notice how it feels in your leg as you press your right heel onto the floor behind you with your right leg straight.*
- *Your hips and chest are facing the front.*
- *Now, when you breathe in, straighten both legs and reach your arms up like you're going to touch the ceiling.*
- *When you breathe out, bend your front leg and bring your hands to your chest.*

Keep your back leg straight if it feels okay.

Let's try this 2 more times, straightening and bending the front leg. You might notice your front quad working as you bend, or a more intense stretch in your back leg.

Lead the class in 2 more rounds of movement and breath.

Now we'll stay in the pose with the front knee bent for 2 more breaths. Keep breathing to center yourself as you notice any sensations you feel in the pose, such as warmth, fatigue, stretching, or something else.

Breathing deeply for 2, and 1 more breath: 1.

Warrior III

From Forward Warrior, we'll lift into either Bird Pose or Warrior III, your choice.

- *Extend your arms out to the sides.*
- *When you're ready, lean forward and lift your right leg off the floor.*
- *Experiment with pulling in your belly gently and reaching your right heel back.*
- *If you lose your balance, it's helpful to smooth out your breath before you try it again.*
- *Keep your breath flowing.*

Pause.

- *Either stay in Bird, or try extending the arms forward into Warrior III.*
- *Can someone lead us in 3 breaths?*

Choose a student to lead the breaths.

Come out of the pose by lowering the right leg into Forward Warrior, then bringing it forward to Mountain Pose.

Lead students through Forward Warrior with the left foot back, Bird, and Warrior III.

When finished, bring everyone back to Mountain Pose, and have one student lead 3 mindful breaths.

King Dancer—Pose of the Day

The pose of the day is King Dancer. King Dancer is a challenging balancing pose. It stretches the hips and shoulders, which are where most people carry stress. Practicing King Dancer helps to focus the mind and build self-awareness.

To do King Dancer, we start by coming into Baby Dancer. Notice both of your feet flat on the floor. Then start to move the weight into your right foot, lifting the left foot lightly off the floor.

Keeping your knees close together, experiment with lifting and lowering your left lower leg. Notice the muscles in the back of your thigh working to lift the leg. Maybe you can grab onto your left ankle with your left hand. If that doesn't work for you, try grabbing onto your pant leg or simply lift the left foot up off the floor—without using your hand—and balance there.

- *Point your knee down toward the floor and feel yourself stand up tall, reaching up through the top of your head.*
- *If you engage your core muscles, tightening your abs, it can help protect your back and help you balance.*
- *Keep the breath flowing.*
- *When you're ready, reach the right arm forward. You can always touch a desk or chair, if you need more support.*
- *If your left hand is grabbing your foot or ankle, start to kick into your hand to raise your leg up.*
- *Once your leg comes up higher, you might notice your body lean forward slightly.*

You also might notice a stretching in your left shoulder.
- *If you feel any pain or crunching in your lower back, try lowering the left leg a bit.*
- *Keep drawing your belly in gently as you breathe, standing tall on your right leg. (Student name), can you lead us in 3 breaths please?*

Once students finish 3 breaths, lead them in slowly transitioning to the other side. Once both sides have been done, invite students to take 3 breaths standing tall in Mountain Pose.

Instruct students to take a seat. Proceed to the Mindful Breathing section.

MINDFUL BREATHING (3 MINUTES)

We'll now do a progressive relaxation, which can help release excess tension and stress in the body and mind. You might take a moment to remember whom you are practicing for today, whether yourself or someone else who will benefit from you feeling more relaxed.

Close your eyes if it feels okay, or just look down at your desk. Notice the rhythm of your breath right now. Your breath will have a different rhythm at different times.

Pause to allow students to notice their breath.

As you notice your breath, let each breath get a little deeper.

Pause.

Allow your breath to fill up your lungs completely, and then empty them completely.

Pause to let them breathe deeply for a few rounds.

Now I'll lead you in a progressive relaxation—as I name different areas of your body, you can try tensing or tightening them up, and then relaxing them as you exhale. Alternatively, you can just focus your attention on each area as I name it, and try to relax that area a little more as you breathe out.

Bring your attention to your feet. As you inhale,—if it feels okay— tense up your feet and toes, squeezing them inside your shoes. As you exhale, relax your feet and toes. Again, inhale, tense your feet and toes. Exhale let your feet and toes soften and relax.

Bring your attention to your legs this time, as well as your feet. As you inhale, tense up your legs, the calves as well as the thighs. Notice the muscles tighten up, and then as you exhale let the muscles soften and release. Inhale tensing your legs, exhale relaxing your legs and feet.

Lead students through the exercise of tensing on the inhale and releasing on the exhale, for 2 breaths per area of the body. These areas include:

❖ Belly, chest, and back
❖ Hands, shoulders, and arms
❖ Face and neck.

Finish with 2 rounds of tensing/releasing of the whole body. Then invite students to breathe normally, noticing any tension that still might be present in any area of their body. Remind students that it's not bad to still have tension, but the point is to be aware of it being here. If we'd like, and if it's ready, we can use our mindful awareness to release some of the tension.

WRAP-UP

GUIDED MEDITATION AND CLOSING BELL (1 MINUTE)

We're going to end class by sitting silently for 1 minute, just noticing your breathing and how your body feels.

Feel free to close your eyes or look down to help you concentrate only on yourself.

If you like, you can even put your head down and rest it on your arms.

Pause.

Notice your feet resting on the floor, your legs relaxed on the seat.

Notice where your arms and hands are. Maybe you can allow your arms and shoulders to relax a bit more.

Notice how you're breathing.

You might even allow the muscles of your face to relax as you breathe.

Long pause, allow students to sit silently for remainder of the minute.

I will now ring the bell one last time. Listen to the bell and when you can't hear it anymore, please look up at me.

Ring bell and allow it to vibrate to completion.

CONNECTION QUESTIONS (3 MINUTES)

How is everyone feeling?

Can you think of anyone you know who would benefit from doing TLS? Have you taught any TLS to a friend or family member?

Ask students if they have any questions about what we did today or about TLS or mindfulness in general, and thank them for their participation.

LESSON 3.12: REVIEW AND RETEACHING

The purpose of this lesson is to review and reteach any essential skills before moving on to Unit 4. Although this lesson is optional, we encourage instructors to review their fidelity checklists and instructor notes, and formulate a lesson plan based on what they think students would benefit from most. If content was covered equally well, instructors may want to attempt to reteach lessons during which students did not appear well engaged and attempt new strategies to motivate and engage students. Or instructors may choose to review a lesson during which a high percentage of students were absent. After reviewing your notes, make a plan for what you intend to reteach and why.

UNIT 3 REVIEW FORM

UNIT 3. Lesson	% Implementation	% Students absent	Overall engagement
3.1: Your Environment Affects Your Thoughts and Feelings			
3.2: You Can Manage Your Thoughts and Feelings			
3.3: Centering Yourself			
3.4: Your Thoughts and Feelings Affect Your Actions			
3.5: Acting vs. Reacting			
3.6: Your Actions Affect Your Brain			
3.7: Using Tools to Calm Down			
3.8: Using Tools to Energize			
3.9: Being with Emotions			
3.10: Practicing Making Choices			
3.11: Imagining Possibilities			

_____ I choose to reteach lesson(s) because _____.

_____ All students have mastered skills. No reteaching is necessary.

Healthy Relationships

UNIT OVERVIEW

In TLS, we focus a lot on self, building self-awareness, self-regulation, and self-knowledge. However, TLS is not meant to be selfish. When we practice dynamic mindfulness, we become stronger and can be our best selves more often. As a result, we are more able to reach out to those we care about and to our communities. The intent of this unit is to reinforce what we have learned so far, and to apply it to our personal relationships and the larger community in which we live.

In TLS as in life, true success and joy come not through force or manipulation, but from paying attention to and accepting ourselves—just as we are—in this moment. In practicing dynamic mindfulness, we take personal responsibility for our well-being and take action to meet our needs without aggression or violence. Practicing acceptance and nonviolence toward ourselves is the first step to being able to practice them toward others.

As we become more self-aware, we notice how our thoughts and feelings are affected by others and how we, in turn, affect how others feel. We come to understand more deeply how we are all dependent on each other. At the same time, mindfulness shows us how much we have in common, allowing us to see others as people just like ourselves. Through mindfulness, we develop empathy, self-regulation, and a deep understanding of our interdependence, so that we can strengthen our relationships and make positive changes in the world in which we live.

Objectives

❖ Understand how having healthy relationships relates to emotion regulation, self-awareness, and stress resilience

❖ Understand the impact of behavior (thoughts, words, and actions) on self and others

❖ Enhance empathy for self and others

❖ Develop an understanding that we are all connected and interdependent

LESSON 4.1: YOUR BEHAVIOR AFFECTS YOUR ENVIRONMENT

In this lesson, students will practice linking Eagle Pose with Warrior III. The benefits of these poses include:

❖ Promote circulation of the blood in the hips
❖ Relieve stiffness in the shoulders
❖ Strengthen the legs, abdomen, and back
❖ Improve balance and concentration

Lesson objectives are (a) students will reflect upon the impact their behavior has on their family, school, and community, and (b) students will practice noticing how the behavior of others in yoga class affects them, and practice recentering themselves when they get distracted.

STUDENT OVERVIEW

REVIEW EXPECTATIONS (2 MINUTES)

Review the expectations for TLS sessions, including:

❖ Students clear desks of all distractions including books, papers, food, cell phones, and music.
❖ One-mic rule: one person talks at a time. If students have questions, they can raise a hand or ask at the end of class. Assure students that there will be a few minutes dedicated to questions at the end of each session.
❖ Students focus on their own body and breath. That means not making comments about self or others, not touching others, and not distracting others from their experience.
❖ Students try their best to participate at all times. (However, participation may look different for each student. For some students, it may mean doing only the breathing for as long as they need, until they choose to engage with the movement. Allow students to come to the practice at

their own pace, as long as they are not being distracting or disrespectful toward others. Engaging with one's body and mind through TLS is always a choice, and every day is a different experience.)

ACTIVATE BACKGROUND KNOWLEDGE (3 MINUTES)

In response to the class environment each day, you may wish to provide this information to students when you feel it would be best received—that may be at the beginning of class, woven into the mindful movement, or before the silent sitting.

The way you behave has a big impact on the people around you. Sometimes you might not think so, but every person is important, and together we create the environments that we share. Knowing that our behavior as an individuals can positively or negatively affect the world around us can help us feel more connected with others. Understanding how our behavior effects our shared environment can help us to be more mindful of our actions and influence our schools, neighborhoods, and communities in positive ways.

Activation Question 4.1

Can you think of something that you do that affects the environment around you? What impact does your behavior have?

Give students a chance to reflect, and choose a few students to share their responses with the class.

Today, you might notice that if those around you are peaceful and focused during TLS, their energy will affect you, and vice versa. Understanding how our actions affect our environment can help us understand how as individuals we can make a positive impact.

ACTION, BREATHING, CENTERING

OPENING BELL AND FOCUSED BREATHING (2 MINUTES)

We will start our time together today by trying to focus our attention on a sound. I would like to ask you all to listen to the sound of the bell I am going to ring.

Try to keep your attention on the sound of the bell for as long as you can, and when you can't hear it anymore, please raise your hand.

Ring bell or singing bowl.

❖ Allow to vibrate to completion and until all students have raised their hands.

❖ Then ask students to do the same thing, this time closing their eyes or looking down at their desks to focus just on their hearing, and ring the bell again.

❖ Wait until all students have raised their hands.

That was very good. Now I'll lead you in a breathing exercise:
- *You can keep your eyes closed, or just look down.*
- *Let all the air out of your lungs.*
- *Now breathe in, breathe out.*

Lead class in simple breathing, encouraging them to breathe deeply and smoothly.

Continue for 3–4 rounds.

Then tell students that you are going to do the bell exercise one more time.

Ring the bell again, and students raise their hands when they can no longer hear it.

MINDFUL MOVEMENT AND POSE OF THE DAY (6 MINUTES)

When teaching this lesson, take a few occasions to pause and bring students' attention to the energy and/or noise level in the class. Invite students to notice whether the behavior or energy of those around them affects their own ability to focus. (For example, there might be a lot of side conversations that distract students, or the overall energy might be focused and grounded.)

This lesson's Mindful Movement includes forward folding poses. You may wish to position students in a circle around the room before beginning the Mindful Movement section in order to avoid students having someone behind them.

Mountain

Let's all stand up in Mountain Pose. Place your feet flat on the floor. Notice if you can feel your feet making contact with the floor. Lift the very top of your head up toward the ceiling. Notice how you're breathing.

If needed, review the elements of Mountain Pose:

❖ Feet parallel and hip-width distance apart
❖ Shoulders relaxed
❖ Standing tall

If you'd like, press your hands together at your chest, and either close your eyes or look down at the place where your hands meet. Can someone lead us in 3 breaths, saying, "breathe in, breathe out"?

Choose a student to lead the breaths, making sure the student leads them slowly to allow for deep breathing.

Shoulder Stretch

As you breathe in, stretch your arms out to the sides as far as it feels comfortable to you. As you breathe out, cross your right arm straight over your chest, and use your left arm to pull it close. Keep your breath flowing, and notice any stretching or opening you might feel on your right shoulder. (Slowly) Hold it for 3. . . .

Letting your shoulders relax a little . . . 2. Breathing . . . 1.

On your next big breath in, stretch your arms out to the sides again. Feel how wide apart you can reach your hands.

As you breathe out, reach your left arm straight across your chest, pulling it in with your right arm. Keep breathing and notice if this shoulder feels the same or different than the other one did.
- *Holding for 3.*
- *Relaxing the shoulders a little for 2.*
- *And 1.*

Good job, shake out your arms.

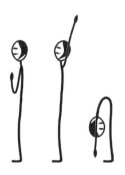

Half Sun Salutation

Let's practice some Sun Salutations. We'll start in Mountain Pose with the hands together at the chest.
- *On your next inhale, raise your arms high reaching toward the ceiling.*
- *If it feels okay, you can reach your arms back a little. Notice any sensations in your upper back and shoulders.*
- *On the exhale fold forward as far as feels comfortable. You can fold forward a lot, feeling a stretch in the back of the legs. Or if you feel more comfortable you can just fold forward a little, letting your arms and neck relax and your upper back round.*
- *Take a breath here and notice where you feel a stretch—maybe*

in your neck, or your back, or the back of your legs. Find a position where you feel a stretch but it's not too much for you.

If students are looking around and giggling, ask the class if that behavior creates an environment that makes it easier or harder for people to relax and concentrate in this pose.
Pause.

- *When you inhale, place your hands on the fronts of your legs and experiment with flattening out your back like a tabletop. Feel the muscles in your back working as you do this.*
- *When you exhale, relax and fold forward again.*
- *Inhale, come back to standing, reaching the arms up.*
- *Exhale, hands to the front of the chest, Mountain Pose.*

That was 1 round.

We are going to repeat that series 3 times, but with only 1 breath per movement. Try to keep your movement connected to your breath, and feel free to pause for a rest if you need to.

Ready?
- *On your next inhale, raise your arms high and maybe a little back.*
- *Exhale, fold forward.*
- *Inhale, flat back.*
- *Exhale, fold forward.*
- *Inhale, reach your arms straight up.*
- *Exhale, hands to chest.*

Repeat 2 more times, having a student lead:
When you finish, instruct students to stay in Mountain Pose and notice how they are breathing, notice if their heart is beating faster, maybe notice the energy in their bodies.

Have one student lead everyone in 3 breaths in Mountain Pose.

Eagle

For Eagle Pose, we'll start by extending our arms forward. Cross the right arm on top of the left.

Here there are a few options for the arms:

(1) The first option is to cross the arms above the elbows, and keep twisting the arms around each other until you can press the palms of the hands together.

(2) The other option is to cross your arms once, and wrap your hands around your shoulder blades for a big hug.

Choose the option that works best for you. Once you are there, breathe in and stand up a little straighter. Breathe out and notice if you can release your shoulders down away from your ears

Now for the legs, there are two options. Option one is to bend your knees while doing your best to keep them lined up with your ankles. Option two is to bend your legs and cross your left leg on top of your right, balancing on your right leg. Either option is fine, just do what you feel will help you the most today.

(Student name), can you lead us in 3 breaths?

Take 3 breaths here, led by a student.

To come out of the pose, untwist everything and straighten your legs.

Let's take a couple of Trunk Twists to release tension.

Lead students in a few Trunk Twists.

Then do Eagle Pose on the opposite side: Left arm on top of right, right leg on top of left.

Do some Trunk Twists again when you are done with the second side.

Warrior III

We're going to practice Warrior III, but we'll start with just holding it for 1 breath. Try your best to match your movement with your breathing here.

- *Breathe in, and lift your arms as high as feels comfortable.*
- *Breathe out, lean your upper body forward and extend your right leg back, lifting it off the floor.*
- *Breathe in, and place both feet back on the floor and arms up.*
- *Breathe out, and release the arms down.*

Let's do the other side.

Remember, looking at a spot on the floor can help you keep your balance.

- *Breathe in, arms lift up.*
- *Breathe out, lean forward and lift the left leg.*

Notice your standing foot pressing flat on the floor.

- *Breathe in, both feet on the floor and stand up straight.*
- *Breathe out, arms down.*

Can someone lead us in the breathing as we do this 2 more times on each leg?

Have one student say, "breathe in, breathe out" as you lead students in 2 more rounds of the sequence.

Warrior III with Eagle Arms—Pose of the Day

Now for the pose of the day, let's combine those two poses, Eagle arms with Warrior III legs.

Practicing moving from one pose to the next will help improve focus and build endurance, mentally and physically. As you do this challenging sequence, you might be tempted to look around, laugh, or make comments to others. Think about what kind of environment you want to create for our practice, and choose actions that will help create that environment. (If you want laughter in your environ-ment, just make sure you're not laughing at others!)

We'll start by coming into Eagle Pose with the left arm on top.

Choose the version of Eagle arms you would like to do:

(A) Arms twisted up and palms together, or

(B) Arms crossed and hands grabbing your shoulder blades.

As you're ready, bend your legs into Chair, and if it feels okay, cross your right leg over the left. Keep your breath moving

Pause for a few breaths.

Now we'll experiment with switching to Warrior III legs. It will help if you keep breathing and focus on how your body feels rather than thinking too much.

- *When you feel you can, uncross your right leg and slowly extend it straight behind you.*
- *Keep breathing.*
- *If you lose your focus and come out of it, just try again.*
- *If you notice tension in your body as you try to balance, see if you can let some of it go without falling out of the pose.*

(Student name), can you lead us in 3 breaths?

Pause.

Thank you. As you breathe in, put both feet on the floor and release your arms.

Ask students if anyone noticed they were holding their breath during the pose. Encourage them to try to keep the breath flowing, to practice staying calm during challenging situations.

Lead students in the poses on the other side, holding Warrior III with Eagle Arms for 3 breaths. When students are done, invite them to shake out their arms and legs or do some Trunk Twists, then come to seated.

Proceed to the Mindful Breathing section.

MINDFUL BREATHING (3 MINUTES)

Take a moment to sit comfortably with your back straight. Either close your eyes or look slightly down to help you focus on yourself. Bring your attention to your breathing. Without changing the way you breathe, just notice how you're breathing right now. Notice if you're breathing through your nose or through your mouth.

Pause.

Notice if your breath is deep or shallow, long or short.

Pause.

Notice if your breath is smooth or uneven.

Pause.

Does your breath feel cooler as you breathe in and warmer as you breathe out?

Pause.

As you breathe, your breath affects your body. It actually moves different parts of your body as it comes in and out. Notice what parts of your body are being moved by your breath.

Pause.

Can you notice your chest move as you breathe?

Pause.

What about your ribs?

Pause.

Maybe you can even feel your back move, as your ribs go all the way around to the back of your body.

Can you feel your breath move your belly?

Pause.

Maybe you even feel your shoulders move a little. Take another 4 or 5 breaths, focusing on all the ways your breath moves your body.

Pause to allow students to breathe 5 more rounds.

Good job.

WRAP-UP

GUIDED MEDITATION AND CLOSING BELL (1 MINUTE)

We're going to end class by sitting silently for 1 minute, just noticing your breathing and how your body feels.

Feel free to close your eyes or look down to help you concentrate only on yourself.

If you like, you can even put your head down and rest it on your arms.

Pause.

Notice your feet resting on the floor, your legs relaxed on the seat.

Notice where your arms and hands are. Maybe you can allow your arms and shoulders to relax a bit more.

Notice how you're breathing.

You might even allow the muscles of your face to relax as you breathe.

Long pause, allow students to sit silently for remainder of the minute.

I will now ring the bell one last time. Listen to the bell and when you can't hear it anymore, please look up at me.

Ring bell and allow it to vibrate to completion.

CONNECTION QUESTIONS (3 MINUTES)

How is everyone feeling?

Is there a certain place where you feel the most relaxed and happy?
If so, what makes that particular environment so peaceful for you?

Ask students if they have any questions about what we did today or about TLS or mindfulness in general, and thank them for their participation.

LESSON 4.2: UNDERSTANDING YOUR HABITS

In this lesson, students will practice linking Side Warrior and Half Moon Poses. Benefits of these poses include:

- ❖ Release tension in the hips
- ❖ Strengthen leg muscles, knees and ankles
- ❖ Tone the nervous system
- ❖ Improve balance and focus

Lesson objectives are (a) students will learn that it is important to recognize the thoughts behind their behavior if they want to change their habits, and (b) students will practice slowing down their breathing and movement in order to slow down their thoughts and become more aware of them.

STUDENT OVERVIEW

REVIEW EXPECTATIONS (2 MINUTES)

Review the expectations for TLS sessions, including:

- ❖ Students clear desks of all distractions including books, papers, food, cell phones, and music.
- ❖ One-mic rule: one person talks at a time. If students have questions, they can raise a hand or ask at the end of class. Assure students that there will be a few minutes dedicated to questions at the end of each session.
- ❖ Students focus on their own body and breath. That means not making comments about self or others, not touching others, and not distracting others from their experience.
- ❖ Students try their best to participate at all times. (However, participation may look different for each student. For some students, it may mean doing only the breathing for as long as they need, until they choose to engage with the movement. Allow students to come to the practice at

their own pace, as long as they are not being distracting or disrespectful toward others. Engaging with one's body and mind through TLS is always a choice, and every day is a different experience.)

ACTIVATE BACKGROUND KNOWLEDGE (3 MINUTES)

In response to the class environment each day, you may wish to provide this information to students when you feel it would be best received—that may be at the beginning of class, woven into the mindful movement, or before the silent sitting.

We don't always understand why we behave the way we do. Taking a closer look at the thoughts and feelings we have can give us clues about the beliefs, fears, and hopes that influence our behavior. Getting the root of why you behave a certain way is the first step in having a choice of whether to continue with that behavior. This is especially true with habits, which tend to be hard to break if you don't understand the thoughts or emotions behind them.

Activation Question 4.2

Is there something you do (a behavior), but you don't understand why you do it?

Give students a chance to reflect, and choose a few students to share their responses with the class.

In TLS, we take time to be aware of our thoughts and emotions by slowing down our movement and breathing. This awareness will help give us clues to understanding the thoughts and feelings behind our behavior.

ACTION, BREATHING, CENTERING

OPENING BELL AND FOCUSED BREATHING (2 MINUTES)

We will start our time together today by trying to focus our attention on a sound. I would like to ask you all to listen to the sound of the bell I am going to ring.

Try to keep your attention on the sound of the bell for as long as you can, and when you can't hear it anymore, please raise your hand.

Ring bell or singing bowl.

❖ Allow to vibrate to completion and until all students have raised their hands.
❖ Then ask students to do the same thing, this time closing their eyes or looking down at their desks to focus just on their hearing, and ring the bell again.
❖ Wait until all students have raised their hands.

> *That was very good. Now I'll lead you in a breathing exercise:*
> • *You can keep your eyes closed, or just look down.*
> • *Let all the air out of your lungs.*
> • *Now breathe in, breathe out.*

Lead class in simple breathing, encouraging them to breathe deeply and smoothly.

Continue for 3–4 rounds.

Then tell students that you are going to do the bell exercise one more time.

Ring the bell again, and students raise their hands when they can no longer hear it.

MINDFUL MOVEMENT AND POSE OF THE DAY (6 MINUTES)

Mountain

Let's all stand up in Mountain Pose. Press your hands together at your chest, and either close your eyes or look down at the place where your hands meet. Pause.

As you breathe in, lift the top of your head up toward the ceiling. As you breathe out, let your shoulders and arms relax. Breathe in and stand tall, reaching your head toward the ceiling. Breathe out and feel your feet on the floor, wiggling your toes if that helps you feel them. Take 1 more deep breath: standing tall, feeling your feet on the floor and shoulders relaxed.

Pause to allow students to breathe and focus.

Shoulder Movements

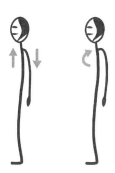

We are going to do some movements to release tension in the shoulders.
- *Let your arms hang at your sides.*
- *On your next inhale, shrug your shoulders up toward your ears.*
- *On the exhale, let them drop. Let's do that 3 more times.*

Imagine bringing tension into that area and letting it go, as your shoulders drop.

For the next movement, we are going to rotate our shoulders in small circles. Even if it feels boring, try slowing down the movement enough to allow for deep breathing:
- *As you inhale rolling the shoulders up and back, and*
- *As you exhale bringing them down and forward.*

Repeat the movement 3 times.
Then reverse direction and repeat 3 times.

Side Warrior—Half Moon—Pose of the Day

The poses of the day are Side Warrior to Half Moon. Practicing these two poses together helps build self-awareness and control over our actions. To do Side Warrior:

- *Start in Mountain Pose and take your left leg back.*
- *Press your left heel to the floor and face your hips and chest to the left.*
- *When you bend your right leg, make sure your knee bends straight forward, no further forward than your ankle.*
- *When you're ready, raise your arms to shoulder height and look over the fingers of your right hand. Notice your spine straight up and down as you hold Side Warrior.*
- *Now as we breathe in, we'll straighten our legs and reach our arms up, palms together.*
- *As we breathe out, we'll bend our front leg and bring our arms back out to the sides, palms down.*

Let's do this 2 more times with the breath.

Lead 2 more rounds of breathing with the movement. Encourage students to notice any sensations of stretching or effort in their leg muscles as they bend and straighten.

Good. Now we'll come into Half Moon.

- *Bend your right leg and look down at a spot on the floor in front of you.*
- *You can choose to touch the floor with your right hand or just reach it downward.*
- *When you breathe in, experiment with lifting your left leg off the floor and your left arm toward the ceiling. Try to find your balance.*
- *Keep your breath moving. Taking deep breaths can help you stay calm and focused.*
- *If you fall out of balance, notice where your mind was when you were trying to balance.*

Take a deep breath to help you focus on your body and breathing, and try it again. Trying is more important than doing it perfectly.

Let's try to hold it for 3 breaths:
- *3: Feel your standing foot on the floor.*
- *2: Still breathing.*
- *1! Next time you breathe in, take your left foot to the floor and stand up straight.*

Breathe out and bring your left leg forward to Mountain Pose. Take a breath, and feel both feet on the floor.

Lead the students in the Side Warrior–Half Moon sequence with the right leg back.

Try to hold the poses for the same amount of time on both sides. Finish in Mountain Pose and take 3 breaths.

Trunk Twists

Shake out your arms and bring your feet a little farther apart. If there is enough room, let your arms just relax and swing as you twist from side to side. Notice how your hands and fingertips feel as you twist. If there isn't enough room for that, you can bend your arms at chest height. Pause.

As you twist to each side, lift your opposite heel. If you want to twist more, breathe out each time you turn to the side.

Pause for about 30 seconds as you continue twisting.

Now let your twists get smaller and smaller until you are still.

When you're ready, come back to Mountain Pose with your palms together at your chest and take a few breaths, noticing how your body feels.

Have another student lead 3 breaths.

When done, have students take a seat. Proceed to the Mindful Breathing section.

MINDFUL BREATHING (3 MINUTES)

If you want to understand the thoughts behind your actions, you have to be able to notice your thoughts. That's not as easy as it sounds! If you let yourself follow one thought or another, you can't actually see what your thoughts are because you're lost in them. But if you stay focused on your breath, it gets easier to notice your thoughts as they come and go. Using your hands to keep track of your breaths is a good trick for keeping your mind focused on your breath, so you don't get carried away by your thoughts.

Take a look at your hands.
- *When you breathe in, touch your index finger to your thumb.*
- *When you breathe out, touch your middle finger to your thumb.*
- *When you breathe in, touch your ring finger to your thumb.*
- *When you breathe out, touch your pinky finger to your thumb.*
- *Keep doing this as you breathe, one finger per breath. You can close your eyes as you do this, or look down at your desk.*

We're going to practice this for 1 minute. If thoughts come up, notice them but try to keep your attention on your fingers and your breath. If you get distracted or aggitated, take a deep breath, maybe stretch or look around, and when you are ready start again with a deep inhale.

Allow students to practice for 1 minute, providing verbal cues to help them remain present.

If you'd like, relax your hands. If you noticed any negative thoughts in your head, or thoughts you don't need right now, imagine breathing them out on the exhale. Deep breath in, and then breathe negative thoughts out. Do this 2 more times.
- *Deep breath in, negative thoughts out.*
- *In, out.*

Good, you can go back to breathing normally, if you wish.

WRAP-UP

GUIDED MEDITATION AND CLOSING BELL (1 MINUTE)

We're going to end class by sitting silently for 1 minute, just noticing your breathing and how your body feels.

Feel free to close your eyes or look down to help you concentrate only on yourself.

If you like, you can even put your head down and rest it on your arms.

Pause.

Notice any habits you have with your body, like crossing your legs or leaning to one side. Experiment with centering your body so that the right side and left side are doing the same thing.

Pause.

Notice how you're breathing.

Maybe you can allow the muscles of your face, shoulders, or legs relax a little, as you breathe.

Long pause, allow students to sit silently for remainder of the minute.

I will now ring the bell one last time. Listen to the bell and when you can't hear it anymore, please look up at me.

Ring bell and allow it to vibrate to completion.

CONNECTION QUESTIONS (3 MINUTES)

How is everyone feeling?

Would anyone please share one healthy "habit" or behavior you have?

Ask students if they have any questions about what we did today or about TLS or mindfulness in general, and thank them for their participation.

LESSON 4.3: BUILDING HEALTHY RELATIONSHIPS

In this lesson, students will practice connecting Warrior III and Forward Warrior Poses.

Benefits of these poses include:

❖ Strengthen the muscles in the legs, ankles, and back
❖ Stretch the hamstrings and calves
❖ Improve balance and concentration

Lesson objectives are (a) students will learn the importance of understanding the effect that their actions have on people they care about, and (b) students will practice making choices and noticing the impact of those choices in their bodies.

STUDENT OVERVIEW

REVIEW EXPECTATIONS (2 MINUTES)

Review the expectations for TLS sessions, including:

❖ Students clear desks of all distractions including books, papers, food, cell phones, and music.
❖ One-mic rule: one person talks at a time. If students have questions, they can raise a hand or ask at the end of class. Assure students that there will be a few minutes dedicated to questions at the end of each session.
❖ Students focus on their own body and breath. That means not making comments about self or others, not touching others, and not distracting others from their experience.
❖ Students try their best to participate at all times. (However, participation may look different for each student. For some students, it may mean doing only the breathing for as long as they need, until they choose to engage with the movement. Allow students to come to the practice at

their own pace, as long as they are not being distracting or disrespectful toward others. Engaging with one's body and mind through TLS is always a choice, and every day is a different experience.)

ACTIVATE BACKGROUND KNOWLEDGE (3 MINUTES)

In response to the class environment each day, you may wish to provide this information to students when you feel it would be best received—that may be at the beginning of class, woven into the mindful movement, or before the silent sitting.

Imagine all the different relationships you can have in your life: teacher/student, parent/child, boss/employee, friends, romantic partners, and so on. Your words and actions affect all the people you interact with. Realizing the effect your actions have on those you interact with can help you be more mindful of your words and actions, and is an integral skill for building healthy relationships.

Activation Question 4.3

In your opinion, what makes a relationship "healthy" or "unhealthy"?

Give students a chance to reflect, and choose a few students to share their responses with the class.

In TLS, we build awareness of ourselves and the impact of our actions. By tuning into our own bodies and emotions, we strengthen our capacity for empathy, or the ability to understand and share the feelings of others, and we build our skills for treating ourselves and others with respect.

ACTION, BREATHING, CENTERING

OPENING BELL AND FOCUSED BREATHING (2 MINUTES)

We will start our time together today by trying to focus our attention on a sound. I would like to ask you all to listen to the sound of the bell I am going to ring.

Try to keep your attention on the sound of the bell for as long as you can, and when you can't hear it anymore, please raise your hand.

Ring bell or singing bowl.

❖ Allow to vibrate to completion and until all students have raised their hands.

❖ Then ask students to do the same thing, this time closing their eyes or looking down at their desks to focus just on their hearing, and ring the bell again.

❖ Wait until all students have raised their hands.

That was very good. Now I'll lead you in a breathing exercise:
- *You can keep your eyes closed, or just look down.*
- *Let all the air out of your lungs.*
- *Now breathe in, breathe out.*

Lead class in simple breathing, encouraging them to breathe deeply and smoothly.

Continue for 3–4 rounds.

Then tell students that you are going to do the bell exercise one more time.

Ring the bell again, and students raise their hands when they can no longer hear it.

MINDFUL MOVEMENT AND POSE OF THE DAY (6 MINUTES)

This lesson's Mindful Movement includes forward folding poses. You may wish to position students in a circle around the room before beginning the Mindful Movement section in order to avoid students having someone behind them.

Mountain

Let's all stand up in Mountain Pose. Press your hands together at your chest, and either close your eyes or look down at the place where your hands meet. Pause.

As you breathe in, lift the top of your head up toward the ceiling. As you breathe out, let your shoulders and arms relax. Breathe in and stand tall, reaching your head toward the ceiling. Breathe out and feel your feet on the floor, wiggling your toes if that helps you feel them. Take 1 more deep breath: standing tall, feeling your feet on the floor, and shoulders relaxed.

Pause to allow students to breathe and focus.

Standing Backbend with Clasp

We are going to do a standing back bend as a movement.
- *Inhale, and reach up.*
- *Exhale, and clasp your hands behind your back or press your hands to your lower back.*
- *Inhale as you take your shoulders back, maybe straightening your arms if your hands are clasped.*
- *Notice your shoulder blades coming together and your chest lifting. You might even take a minute to notice the effect on your back when you bend back more or less, and choose the amount that's just right for you.*

- *Exhale and return to standing, releasing your arms to your sides. Let's repeat this movement with the breath 3 times.*

Ask a student to lead the breaths.

Good! Shake out your arms and shoulders and return to Mountain Pose.

Triangle

Next we'll try Triangle.

Take your left leg back. For this pose, your chest and belly are facing the left side. Your right foot is facing forward and your left foot is turned slightly inward. In Triangle, keep both legs straight or slightly bent.

Take your hands to your hips. Breathe in and press your right hip back toward the left leg. Notice your left hip rise up higher than your right hip.
- *When you're ready, reach your arms out to the sides, reaching forward with your right hand.*
- *If you reach farther forward, do you get more of a stretching feeling in the legs?*
- *Breathe in here.* Pause.
- *Breathe out, and lower your right hand to somewhere on your right leg.*
- *Lift your left arm to the sky, palm facing the left.*

Now you're in Triangle. Notice both feet pressing into the floor. Notice if you can open up your chest more by reaching your top arm back. You can either look up at your left hand or let your head hang down. Notice how each option feels for you, and choose the one that feels better. Keep your breath flowing.

(Student name), *can you lead us in 3 breaths please?*

Good. As you breathe in, lift up to stand up straight. Breathe out and bring your left leg forward to Mountain Pose. As you breathe here, notice if one side of your body feels different than the other.

Pause to allow students to breathe and notice how they feel. Then lead students through Triangle Pose with the right leg back. Finish in Mountain Pose with 3 breaths, inviting students to notice their energy level and how they are feeling after that pose.

Warrior III—Forward Warrior—Pose of the Day

The poses of the day are Warrior III connected with Forward Warrior.

When we connect the poses and transition mindfully from one pose to the next, we build self-awareness, which can help us in our relationships with others. By practicing breathing through challenging transitions, we get better at using our breathing during difficult conversations or conflicts with others. We'll start in Warrior III, then transition straight to Forward Warrior, then back to Warrior III. Try to keep your attention on your breathing and how your body feels even as we move from one pose to the other.

Start in Mountain Pose. When you breathe in, lift your arms up high. As you breathe out, lift your right leg up straight behind you and tilt your upper body forward. You might choose to lift your right leg a few inches off the floor, or you might choose to lift it higher, bringing your legs and arms to the level of your hips. Try pulling your hands and your right heel away from each other, stretching the fingers and toes.

Take a few breaths to steady yourself. If you need to, you can touch a desk to catch your balance, then try lifting your hand away from the desk again. Keep breathing.

Now keep breathing deeply as you step your right leg way back onto the floor behind you and bend your left knee. Feel your right foot flat on the floor. For Forward Warrior you can lift your arms up by your ears, or press your hands together at your chest. Breathe to steady yourself. You might try bending your left leg more and noticing the muscles on the top of your thigh engage. Keep your breath moving. Pause.

Now we'll lift the back leg up once more and see if we can balance in Warrior III. Keep your attention on your breath as you transition. Good. Notice if you can be aware of where your back foot is in the air. Be aware of your sense of balance, making small adjustments or touching a chair or desk if necessary.

- *Let's breathe here for 3.* Pause.
- *Notice your arms reaching forward, maybe wiggling your fingers, 2.* Pause. *And one.*
- *Lift back into Mountain Pose, reaching up.*
- *And exhale, release.*
- *Shake out your arms and legs if you'd like.*
- *We'll take a few breaths in Mountain Pose and try the other side.*

Lead students through 3 breaths in Mountain Pose, and then the whole Warrior III–Forward Warrior series with the left leg back. Encourage students to be mindful of their breath during the transitions. Take 3 breaths in Mountain Pose when finished.

Rag Doll Roll-Up

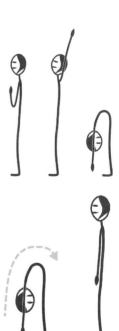

We'll end with Rag Doll Pose to relax the back and stretch the legs, rolling up nice and slow when we finish.

- *When you breathe in, raise your arms up toward the ceiling.*
- *When you breathe out, fold forward at the hips.*

You have a choice here:

- *To release tension in the lower back and hips, you can fold forward until you feel a stretch in the back of your legs or your back.*

- *Or if you'd rather focus on releasing tension in the neck and shoulders, just lean forward a little, letting your chin come toward your chest and your arms hang down.*
- *Try to let your neck relax and your head be heavy.*
- *Notice any stretching or tension in your neck, shoulders, back, or thighs. Experiment with letting go of some of the tension each time you exhale.*

(Student name), can you lead us in 3 breaths?

Pause as the student leads the breathing.

We will now practice rolling up slowly to Mountain Pose. Keep your legs bent and your back rounded, and see how slowly you can roll up to standing. Take your time! Take several breaths to roll up, if you'd like. The last thing to come up will be your head. Pause.

Once you are back in Mountain Pose, let your shoulders release downward. Notice your arms hanging down below your shoulders. Notice if you got dizzy, or any other sensations you feel. Maybe you notice your breath coming in and out.

Pause.
When you're ready, find a comfortable seat.
Proceed to the Mindful Breathing section.

MINDFUL BREATHING (3 MINUTES)

An important skill for healthy relationships is being able to center yourself before speaking, especially if you're dealing with conflict. Let's practice a breathing technique that is helpful for centering.

Sit comfortably with your back straight, and let your eyes close if you'd like, or just look down. Notice the rhythm of your breath. Notice it moving in and out. Pause.

If it feels okay, bring one hand to your belly. Notice if your abdomen (the belly area) moves as your breathe. If not, try to relax the muscles around your abdomen.

Pause.

You'll probably notice your belly pushing your hand out a little as you breathe in.
- *Draw it gently back in toward your spine as you breathe out.*
- *Your belly doesn't have to expand a lot—just notice any small movement that might happen as you breathe.*
- *Breathe in and out.*

If students have a hard time with this breath, encourage them to relax the muscles around their belly and breathe deeply, not worrying about whether the belly is moving "correctly."
Pause to allow students to breathe for 3 to 4 rounds.

Notice how your body feels as a whole. If you have any stress or tension in your shoulders or face, you might experiment with releasing some of the tension as you breathe out.

Now if your hand is on your belly, take it off. See if you can feel your belly moving without using your hand, just feeling it from the inside. Breathing in belly expands, breathing out belly contracts. Pause.

Paying attention to your breathing and how it feels in your body is a good technique for centering yourself.

Pause to allow students to breathe about 3 more rounds.

Good job. Come back to breathing normally and notice how you feel. Do you feel a little more centered than before we did the breathing?

WRAP-UP

GUIDED MEDITATION AND CLOSING BELL (1 MINUTE)

We're going to end class by sitting silently for 1 minute, just noticing your breathing and how your body feels.

Feel free to close your eyes or look down to help you concentrate only on yourself.

If you like, you can even put your head down and rest it on your arms.

Pause.

Notice your feet resting on the floor, your legs relaxed on the seat.

Notice where your arms and hands are. Maybe you can allow your arms and shoulders to relax a bit more.

Notice how you're breathing.

You might even allow the muscles of your face to relax as you breathe.

Long pause, allow students to sit silently for remainder of the minute.

I will now ring the bell one last time. Listen to the bell and when you can't hear it anymore, please look up at me.

Ring bell and allow it to vibrate to completion.

CONNECTION QUESTIONS (3 MINUTES)

How is everyone feeling?

Who here has ever done or said something without realizing the impact it would have on someone else?

Do you think practicing mindfulness helps you build awareness of your actions and words?

Ask students if they have any questions about what we did today or about TLS or mindfulness in general, and thank them for their participation.

LESSON 4.4: WHAT DOES "KARMA" MEAN TO YOU?

In this lesson, students will practice connecting Eagle, Warrior III, and Forward Warrior Poses. Benefits of these poses include:

- ❖ Strengthen the muscles in the legs, abdomen, and back
- ❖ Relieve stiffness in the shoulders
- ❖ Promote circulation in the hips
- ❖ Improve balance and concentration

Lesson objectives are (a) students will discuss "karma" as a concept expressing interconnectedness, and consider ways in which we are connected to each other, and (b) students will practice noticing their breathing, which connects us to one another.

STUDENT OVERVIEW

REVIEW EXPECTATIONS (2 MINUTES)

Review the expectations for TLS sessions, including:

- ❖ Students clear desks of all distractions including books, papers, food, cell phones, and music.
- ❖ One-mic rule: one person talks at a time. If students have questions, they can raise a hand or ask at the end of class. Assure students that there will be a few minutes dedicated to questions at the end of each session.
- ❖ Students focus on their own body and breath. That means not making comments about self or others, not touching others, and not distracting others from their experience.
- ❖ Students try their best to participate at all times. (However, participation may look different for each student. For some students, it may mean doing only the breathing for as long as they need, until they choose to engage with the movement. Allow students to come to the practice at

their own pace, as long as they are not being distracting or disrespectful toward others. Engaging with one's body and mind through TLS is always a choice, and every day is a different experience.)

ACTIVATE BACKGROUND KNOWLEDGE (3 MINUTES)

In response to the class environment each day, you may wish to provide this information to students when you feel it would be best received—that may be at the beginning of class, woven into the mindful movement, or before the silent sitting.

> *Today we're going to talk about karma. In our culture, the word "karma" has come to mean, "what goes around comes around." But in reality, it's not that simple. Traditionally, karma is the law of cause and effect. In the context of relationships, it means that your words and actions affect others, and vice versa.*

> *We are all connected. If I hurt you, I am also hurting myself. If I do something positive for someone else, it will affect how I feel in a positive way. It works the other way around too: if you feel more relaxed and confident, that feeling will have a positive effect on those around you as you interact with them.*

Activation Question 4.4

Do you believe in "karma"? Why or why not?

Give students a chance to reflect, and choose a few students to share their responses with the class.

> *One thing that shows us we are all connected is the breath— everyone on the planet shares the same air. Notice this connection as we practice TLS today.*

ACTION, BREATHING, CENTERING

OPENING BELL AND FOCUSED BREATHING (2 MINUTES)

We will start our time together today by trying to focus our attention on a sound. I would like to ask you all to listen to the sound of the bell I am going to ring.

Try to keep your attention on the sound of the bell for as long as you can, and when you can't hear it anymore, please raise your hand.

Ring bell or singing bowl.

❖ Allow to vibrate to completion and until all students have raised their hands.
❖ Then ask students to do the same thing, this time closing their eyes or looking down at their desks to focus just on their hearing, and ring the bell again.
❖ Wait until all students have raised their hands.

That was very good. Now I'll lead you in a breathing exercise:
  • *You can keep your eyes closed, or just look down.*
  • *Let all the air out of your lungs.*
  • *Now breathe in, breathe out.*

Lead class in simple breathing, encouraging them to breathe deeply and smoothly.

Continue for 3–4 rounds.

Then tell students that you are going to do the bell exercise one more time.

Ring the bell again, and students raise their hands when they can no longer hear it.

MINDFUL MOVEMENT AND POSE OF THE DAY (6 MINUTES)

This lesson's Mindful Movement includes forward folding poses. You may wish to position students in a circle around the room before beginning the Mindful Movement section in order to avoid students having someone behind them.

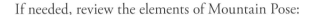

Mountain

Let's all stand up in Mountain Pose. Place your feet flat on the floor. Notice if you can feel your feet making contact with the floor. Lift the very top of your head up toward the ceiling. Notice how you're breathing.

If needed, review the elements of Mountain Pose:

❖ Feet parallel and hip-width distance apart
❖ Shoulders relaxed
❖ Standing tall

If you'd like, press your hands together at your chest, and either close your eyes or look down at the place where your hands meet. Can someone lead us in 3 breaths, saying, "breathe in, breathe out"?

Choose a student to lead the breaths, making sure the student leads them slowly to allow for deep breathing.

Half Sun Salutation

Let's practice some Half Sun Salutations. We'll start in Mountain Pose with the hands together at the chest.

• *On your next inhale, raise your arms high reaching toward the ceiling.*
• *If it feels okay, you can reach your arms back a little. Notice any sensations in your upper back and shoulders.*

- *On the exhale, fold forward as far as feels comfortable. You can fold forward a lot, feeling a stretch in the back of the legs. Or if you feel more comfortable you can just fold forward a little, letting your arms and neck relax and your upper back round.*
- *Take a breath here and notice where you feel a stretch—maybe in your neck, or your back, or the back of your legs. Find a position where you feel a stretch but it's not too much for you.*

Pause.

- *When you inhale, place your hands on the fronts of your legs and experiment with flattening out your back like a tabletop. Feel the muscles in your back working as you do this.*
- *When you exhale, relax and fold forward again.*
- *Inhale, come back to standing, reaching the arms up.*
- *Exhale, hands to the front of the chest, Mountain Pose.*

That was 1 round.

We are going to repeat that series 3 times, but with only 1 breath per movement. Try to keep your movement connected to your breath, and feel free to pause for a rest if you need to.

Ready?
- *On your next inhale, raise your arms high and maybe a little back.*
- *Exhale, fold forward.*
- *Inhale, flat back.*
- *Exhale, fold forward.*
- *Inhale, reach your arms straight up.*
- *Exhale, hands to chest.*

Repeat 2 more times, inviting a student to lead. When you finish, instruct students to stay in Mountain Pose and notice how they are breathing, notice if their heart is beating faster, notice the energy in their bodies. Have one student lead everyone in 3 breaths in Mountain Pose.

Eagle—Warrior III—Forward Warrior—Pose of the Day

Today we'll link Eagle Pose, Warrior III, and Forward Warrior in a series. Transitioning mindfully between poses helps us to develop self-awareness and flexibility when we face changes and transitions in life. It also helps us see how things are connected in our own bodies.

We'll start by coming into Eagle Pose with the left arm on top. Choose the version of Eagle arms you would like to do:
- *Either arms twisted up and palms together, with elbows bent or*
- *Arms crossed in a hug, hands grabbing your shoulder blades.*

As you're ready, bend your legs into Chair, and if it feels okay, cross your right leg over the left. Find a spot to focus your eyes on. Keep your breath moving as you find your balance.

Pause for a few breaths.

Now we'll experiment with switching to Warrior III legs. It will help to keep breathing and focus on how your body feels rather than thinking too much.
- *When you feel you can, uncross your right leg and slowly extend it straight behind you. Keep breathing. See if you can keep your arms wrapped up like in Eagle!*
- *If you lose your focus and come out of the pose, just try again.*
- *If it feels ok, press your right leg straight behind you.*
  - *Keep breathing out any tension you don't need.*

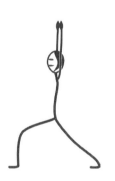

(Student name), *can you lead us in 3 breaths?* Pause.

Good! Now we'll transition to Forward Warrior by taking the right leg to the floor behind you. If you managed to keep your arms wrapped up until now, go ahead and unwind them, either reaching them up or pressing your palms together at your chest. Notice the right foot flat on the floor and right leg straight. Maybe bend your left leg a little more. Take a deep breath here—you did it! When you're ready, come back to Mountain Pose. Take a few breaths with your hands pressed together at your chest. Can you feel your heart beating? How is your breathing?

Lead students through the whole series on the other side, starting with Eagle Pose with the right arm on top and left leg crossed over the right. Once you are finished, allow students to breathe silently in Mountain Pose, letting their heartbeat and breathing come back to a normal rhythm.

Seated Twist

Let's all take a seat. Sit facing the front with your feet on the floor, and if it feels okay, slide forward so you are sitting at the front edge of your seat.

Pause.

The last pose we'll do today is a Seated Twist.
- *As you breathe in, see if you can sit up a little straighter.*
- *As you breathe out, turn to face the right. It might help you twist more if you take your right hand to the back of your seat and your left hand to your right thigh.*

Keep twisting as you take 3 or 4 breaths.
- *Breathe in and see if you can sit up straighter in the twist, breathe out and maybe twist a little more.*
- *Keep your breath flowing.*
- *Notice if your shoulders are tensed up near your ears. You might try lowering them down to release the tension.*
- *Take 1 more breath here.*

Great! As you breathe in, come back to face forward.

You can use the metaphor of a sponge to explain the twist. When you twist a wet sponge, the water comes out. When you put a twisted sponge in the water and let it untwist, it fills with new water. That's what we do when we twist: we flush out old fluids and toxins and bring fresh fluids into the area.

❖ Lead students in the seated twist on the other side.

❖ You can also have a student say "breathe in, breathe out" as they twist.

❖ After students return to face forward, have them take a deep breath and notice any sensations they feel in their bodies after twisting.

Proceed to the Mindful Breathing section.

MINDFUL BREATHING (3 MINUTES)

Karma is all about connection: we affect one another through our actions and words. Remembering that our actions and words are affected by our thoughts and feelings, let's practice a breathing technique that allows us to slow down and build awareness of our thoughts and feelings.

If it feels okay, allow your arms and legs to relax, making yourself comfortable. You can close your eyes or just look down at your desk. Notice your breath as it comes in and goes out. Pause.

Experiment with breathing in a little bit more deeply each time, and breathing out a little bit more each time.

Pause for 2 to 3 breaths.

Now when you're ready, breathe in, and notice the moment when the inhale turns into an exhale. Pause.

• *Breathe out, and notice the moment when the exhale becomes an inhale.* Pause.
• *Breathing in, noticing the very top of the inhale.* Pause.
• *Breathing out, noticing the very bottom of the exhale.* Pause.

Continue to breathe, noticing the end point of each breath and when the new breath starts. If it feels comfortable to you, you can experiment with pausing for a second before starting each new inhale or exhale.

We will practice this for 1 minute. I will ring the bell to start and stop.

- *During the minute, try to keep your mind focused on the breathing.*
- *If at any time your mind wanders, notice where it went and bring your focus back to your breath. Do this as many times as you need to.*
- *If you feel overwhelmed at any moment, feel free to take a breath and stretch out or look around, and come back to the breathing when you're ready.*
- *You can start now.*

Ring the bell. Allow students to breathe silently for 1 minute. Then ring the bell to signify the end of the minute.

WRAP-UP

GUIDED MEDITATION AND CLOSING BELL (1 MINUTE)

We're going to end class by sitting silently for 1 minute, just noticing your breathing and how your body feels.

Feel free to close your eyes or look down to help you concentrate only on yourself.

If you like, you can even put your head down and rest it on your arms.

Pause.

Notice your feet resting on the floor, your legs relaxed on the seat.

Notice where your arms and hands are. Maybe you can allow your arms and shoulders to relax a bit more.

Notice how you're breathing.

You might even allow the muscles of your face to relax as you breathe.

Long pause, allow students to sit silently for remainder of the minute.

I will now ring the bell one last time. Listen to the bell and when you can't hear it anymore, please look up at me.

Ring bell and allow it to vibrate to completion.

CONNECTION QUESTIONS (3 MINUTES)

How is everyone feeling?

Do you consider "karma," or the idea that our actions affect others, before you act?

Ask students if they have any questions about what we did today or about TLS or mindfulness in general, and thank them for their participation.

LESSON 4.5: YOUR ROLE IN CREATING YOUR SCHOOL CULTURE

In this lesson, students will practice connecting Side Warrior, Half Moon, and Bird Poses.

Benefits of these poses include:

❖ Strengthen the legs, knees, and ankles
❖ Release tension in the hips
❖ Tone the nervous system
❖ Improve balance and focus

Lesson objectives are (a) students will recognize how their actions affect their school climate, and (b) students will practice centering themselves so that they have more control over their actions.

STUDENT OVERVIEW

REVIEW EXPECTATIONS (2 MINUTES)

Review the expectations for TLS sessions, including:

❖ Students clear desks of all distractions including books, papers, food, cell phones, and music.
❖ One-mic rule: one person talks at a time. If students have questions, they can raise a hand or ask at the end of class. Assure students that there will be a few minutes dedicated to questions at the end of each session.
❖ Students focus on their own body and breath. That means not making comments about self or others, not touching others, and not distracting others from their experience.
❖ Students try their best to participate at all times. (However, participation may look different for each student. For some students, it may mean doing only the breathing for as long as they need, until they choose to engage with the movement. Allow students to come to the practice at

their own pace, as long as they are not being distracting or disrespectful toward others. Engaging with one's body and mind through TLS is always a choice, and every day is a different experience.)

ACTIVATE BACKGROUND KNOWLEDGE (3 MINUTES)

In response to the class environment each day, you may wish to provide this information to students when you feel it would be best received—that may be at the beginning of class, woven into the mindful movement, or before the silent sitting.

> *It's easy to get lost in the crowd and feel like what you do doesn't make a difference at your school. Sometimes you get busy doing your own things and don't think beyond yourself. Sometimes you don't even realize the impact your actions have on your school climate. But once you try to have a positive influence at your school, you can see that you do have a voice, and what you do makes a difference. Knowing that you can influence your school culture can be exciting and challenging. Seeing the results of your actions can make you more inspired to learn and feel more connected to your school.*

Activation Question 4.5

> *Have you ever seen or been a part of making a change at your school? (Like improving food, cleaning up the campus, and so on.) Can anyone give an example?*

Give students a chance to reflect, and choose a few students to share their responses with the class.

> *Your actions and where you focus your attention affect your classroom environment and culture as well! Keep that in mind as you make choices during TLS today, and choose actions that influence your class culture in a positive way, whatever that means to you.*

ACTION, BREATHING, CENTERING

OPENING BELL AND FOCUSED BREATHING (2 MINUTES)

We will start our time together today by trying to focus our attention on a sound. I would like to ask you all to listen to the sound of the bell I am going to ring.

Try to keep your attention on the sound of the bell for as long as you can, and when you can't hear it anymore, please raise your hand.

Ring bell or singing bowl.

❖ Allow to vibrate to completion and until all students have raised their hands.

❖ Then ask students to do the same thing, this time closing their eyes or looking down at their desks to focus just on their hearing, and ring the bell again.

❖ Wait until all students have raised their hands.

> *That was very good. Now I'll lead you in a breathing exercise:*
> - *You can keep your eyes closed, or just look down.*
> - *Let all the air out of your lungs.*
> - *Now breathe in, breathe out.*

Lead class in simple breathing, encouraging them to breathe deeply and smoothly.

Continue for 3–4 rounds.

Then tell students that you are going to do the bell exercise one more time.

Ring the bell again, and students raise their hands when they can no longer hear it.

MINDFUL MOVEMENT AND POSE OF THE DAY (6 MINUTES)

Mountain

Let's all stand up in Mountain Pose. Place your feet flat on the floor. Notice if you can feel your feet making contact with the floor. Lift the very top of your head up toward the ceiling. Notice how you're breathing.

If you'd like, press your hands together at your chest, and either close your eyes or look down at the place where your hands meet. Can someone lead us in 3 breaths, saying, "breathe in, breathe out"?

Choose a student to lead the breaths, making sure the student leads them slowly to allow for deep breathing.

Breath of Joy

Next we'll do a breathing exercise that can help give you energy. It's called the Breath of Joy. We breathe in 3 parts, raising the arms up.

Demonstrate taking 3 inhales in a row and lifting the arms higher with each inhale, until they are overhead.

Then we let the arms drop with one big exhale.

Demonstrate letting your breath out strongly and letting the arms drop.

Let's try it 3 times.

Lead students in 3 Breaths of Joy.

When finished, have students shake out their arms and hands and notice how they feel. Return to Mountain Pose for 3 breaths.

Shoulder Isolations

We are going to do some movements to release tension in the shoulders.

- *Let your arms hang at your sides.*
- *Try making circles with just your right shoulder, without moving any other part of your body. Keep breathing as you do this.*
- *Notice if it's hard or easy to keep the other parts of your body still as you move. Maybe make the circles bigger—is your shoulder warming up?* Pause.
- *Let's switch now, making circles with only the left shoulder.*
- *Feel your feet on the floor, standing tall and still as your shoulder moves.*
- *Deep breaths in* (pause) *and out.*

Pause.

Okay let's combine them: right, left, both.

Demonstrate making circles with first the right shoulder, then the left, then both. After a few rounds, make the circles faster. If you'd like, reverse the direction of the circles and/or the shoulder that goes first. Finish in Mountain Pose, noticing any sensations in the shoulders.

Side Warrior—Half Moon—Bird—Pose of the Day

The poses of the day are Side Warrior, Half Moon, and Bird, all connected together. Connecting these poses helps us build self-control and body awareness.

To do Side Warrior, start in Mountain Pose and take your left leg back. Press your left heel to the floor and face your hips and chest to the left. When you bend your right leg, make sure your knee bends straight forward over your ankle.

When you're ready, raise your arms to shoulder height and look over the fingers of your right hand. Notice your spine straight up and down. Looks good! Now as you breathe in, straighten your legs. If it feels okay, reach your arms up, palms together. As you breathe out, bend your front leg and bring your arms back out to the sides, palms down. Let's do this 2 more times with the breath.

Good. Now we'll come into Half Moon.

Bend your right leg and look down at a spot on the floor in front of you. If you'd like, touch the floor with your right hand, or just reach it downward. When you breathe in, experiment with lifting your left leg off the floor and your left arm toward the ceiling. Try to find your balance. Keep your breath moving.

- *Taking deep breaths can help calm and focus your mind.*
- *If you fall out of balance, take a deep breath, focus your eyes on a spot on the floor, and try again. Trying is more important than doing it perfectly.*
- *We'll be here for 3 breaths, then we'll transition right into Bird.*
- *3, feel your standing foot on the floor.*
- *2, still breathing.*
- *1. Now we'll come straight into Bird.*

Experiment with slowly lowering your left hip toward the floor so that it is the same level as your right hip, facing your chest toward the floor. Reach both arms back behind you to come into Bird, pulling the left heel back to help you find stability

Are you still breathing? If you feel your left hip still floating upward, you might focus on lowering the outer part of your left thigh toward the floor. Notice how that makes the pose feel for you.

- *Notice if you feel a stretch or tightening muscles in your standing leg, or somewhere else.*
- *Let's breathe here for 3.*
- *Belly in slightly. 2.*

- *Reach out through your back heel. 1.*
- *Slowly lower your left foot to the floor and come into Mountain Pose.*

Ahh, good job! Let's do one Rag Doll Pose to release the back before coming into the other side. Breathing in, arms reaching up. Breathing out, folding forward. Let your breath flow in and out. Does one leg feel different from the other? Experiment with letting your shoulders relax in this posture. (Student name), can you lead us in 3 breaths?

Once the breaths are done, invite students to slowly roll up to Mountain Pose. Lead the students in the Side Warrior–Half Moon–Bird sequence with the right leg back. Finish by doing Rag Doll Pose and rolling up to Mountain Pose. Take 3 breaths in Mountain Pose.

Seated Hip Stretch

As you're ready, scoot forward to sit at the edge of your seat with your feet resting on the floor.

If students have a desk in front of them, have them slide the chair away from the desk or sit sideways so that they have room to lift their leg in front of them.

If it feels okay, cross your right ankle over your left thigh, right above the knee.
- *Flex the right foot and notice if by doing that you engage some of the muscles in your leg and around your knee.*
- *Try to keep your foot flexed the whole time. You might already feel a stretch in your right hip here. If so, experiment with sitting up straighter with your sitting bones flat on the chair and keeping your breath moving as you hold the pose.*
- *Continue to let your right knee sink down toward the floor.*
- *If you don't quite feel a stretch here, you might try bending for-*

ward at the waist, leading with your chest, until you feel a stretch in your hip or thigh.

- *Let your right knee sink toward the floor. Pay attention to what you feel in your body— you are the only one who knows if you are feeling a stretch, or if you are going too far and hurting yourself!*

Be gentle and keep your attention on your body and breath. (Student name), *can you lead us in 3 breaths?*

Once the 3 breaths are done, have students gently switch legs. Lead them through the same pose with the left leg lifted. Then have students rest both feet on the floor, and hands on the lap, for 3 breaths, tuning in to any sensations or changes in the way the hips feel.

Proceed to the Mindful Breathing section.

MINDFUL BREATHING (3 MINUTES)

Close your eyes if that feels comfortable, and notice the rhythm of your breathing. Pause.

Allow your breath to get a little deeper each time you breathe in, and a little longer each time you breathe out. Pause.

We're going to practice observing the sounds in our environment. For the next 30 seconds, I would like you to focus on the sounds you hear. Notice any sound that occurs, loud or soft, without judging it as a bad sound or a good sound. Just notice sounds as they come and go. I'll ring the bell to start and end the 30 seconds.

Ring bell. Wait for 30 seconds and ring bell again.

Whenever you want to make a change, it's important first to notice what is here, without reacting to it, like we just did. Then you can decide if and how you would like to make a change.

Now we'll practice focusing our attention inside. To help you do this, we'll do some focused breathing first.

- *First, just notice how you are breathing. Is your breath slow or fast, deep or shallow? If you would like, you can deepen your breaths.*
- *Follow your breath as you breathe in.*
- *Notice when you get to the end of the inhale.*
- *Follow your breath as you slowly breathe out.*
- *Notice when you get to the end of the exhale.*
- *Breathing in deeply. Pause.*
- *Breathing out slowly.*

Pause while students breathe a few more rounds.

For the next 30 seconds, focus only on yourself: on your breathing, on your heart beating, or on how your body feels. Just like before, you don't need to judge how you feel, or decide if it's good or bad. Just notice what is here for you right now.

Ring bell. Wait for 30 seconds and ring bell again.

Good job everyone.

WRAP-UP

GUIDED MEDITATION AND CLOSING BELL (1 MINUTE)

We're going to end class by sitting silently for 1 minute, just noticing your breathing and how your body feels.

Feel free to close your eyes or look down to help you concentrate only on yourself.

If you like, you can even put your head down and rest it on your arms.

Pause.

Notice your feet resting on the floor, your legs relaxed on the seat.

Notice where your arms and hands are. Maybe you can allow your arms and shoulders to relax a bit more.

Notice how you're breathing.

You might even allow the muscles of your face to relax as you breathe.

Long pause, allow students to sit silently for remainder of the minute.

I will now ring the bell one last time. Listen to the bell and when you can't hear it anymore, please look up at me.

Ring bell and allow it to vibrate to completion.

CONNECTION QUESTIONS (3 MINUTES)

How is everyone feeling?

Do you think having TLS at your school affects the school culture? Why or why not?

Ask students if they have any questions about what we did today or about TLS or mindfulness in general, and thank them for their participation.

LESSON 4.6: SHARING WHAT YOU LEARN

In this lesson, students will practice connecting Warrior III and Half Moon Poses.

Benefits of these poses include:

❖ Strengthen the muscles in the legs, abdomen, and back
❖ Stretch the hamstrings
❖ Improve balance and concentration
❖ Strengthen the knees
❖ Tone the nervous system

Lesson objectives are (a) students will build confidence and motivation to practice TLS on their own and teach it to those they care about, and (b) students will practice noticing the effects of different breathing and movement exercises.

STUDENT OVERVIEW

REVIEW EXPECTATIONS (2 MINUTES)

Review the expectations for TLS sessions, including:

❖ Students clear desks of all distractions including books, papers, food, cell phones, and music.
❖ One-mic rule: one person talks at a time. If students have questions, they can raise a hand or ask at the end of class. Assure students that there will be a few minutes dedicated to questions at the end of each session.
❖ Students focus on their own body and breath. That means not making comments about self or others, not touching others, and not distracting others from their experience.
❖ Students try their best to participate at all times. (However, participation may look different for each student. For some students, it may mean doing only the breathing for as long as they need, until they choose to

engage with the movement. Allow students to come to the practice at their own pace, as long as they are not being distracting or disrespectful toward others. Engaging with one's body and mind through TLS is always a choice, and every day is a different experience.)

ACTIVATE BACKGROUND KNOWLEDGE (3 MINUTES)

In response to the class environment each day, you may wish to provide this information to students when you feel it would be best received—that may be at the beginning of class, woven into the mindful movement, or before the silent sitting.

> *You don't have to be a professional to teach others what you learn in TLS. In fact, they say that the best way to get good at something is to teach it to others. Teaching others builds skills and confidence. By sharing these tools for managing stress with your family, you can help them improve their health, and you can have a positive effect on your home environment. TLS can also be a helpful tool for supporting your friends during challenging times.*

Activation Question 4.6

> *Have you ever taught something you learned from TLS to a family member or friend?*

Give students a chance to reflect, and choose a few students to share their responses with the class.

> *While we practice TLS today, notice what parts about it you like. You might try practicing on your own sometime or teaching these parts to others!*

ACTION, BREATHING, CENTERING

OPENING BELL AND FOCUSED BREATHING (2 MINUTES)

We will start our time together today by trying to focus our attention on a sound. I would like to ask you all to listen to the sound of the bell I am going to ring.

Try to keep your attention on the sound of the bell for as long as you can, and when you can't hear it anymore, please raise your hand.

Ring bell or singing bowl.

- Allow to vibrate to completion and until all students have raised their hands.
- Then ask students to do the same thing, this time closing their eyes or looking down at their desks to focus just on their hearing, and ring the bell again.
- Wait until all students have raised their hands.

    That was very good. Now I'll lead you in a breathing exercise:
    - *You can keep your eyes closed, or just look down.*
    - *Let all the air out of your lungs.*
    - *Now breathe in, breathe out.*

Lead class in simple breathing, encouraging them to breathe deeply and smoothly.

Continue for 3–4 rounds.

Then tell students that you are going to do the bell exercise one more time.

Ring the bell again, and students raise their hands when they can no longer hear it.

MINDFUL MOVEMENT AND POSE OF THE DAY (6 MINUTES)

For the Mindful Movement today, it's important that none of the students have someone standing behind them. You may wish to position students in a circle around the room before beginning the Mindful Movement section.

Mountain

Let's all stand up in Mountain Pose. Press your hands together at your chest, and either close your eyes or look down at the place where your hands meet. As you breathe in, lift the top of your head up toward the ceiling. As you breathe out, let your shoulders and arms relax. Breathe in and stand tall, reaching your head toward the ceiling. Breathe out and feel your feet on the floor, wiggling your toes if that helps you feel them. Take 1 more deep breath: standing tall, feeling your feet on the floor, and shoulders relaxed.

Pause to allow students to breathe and focus.

Flamingo

We'll do Flamingo next. Breathe in and feel yourself standing tall, reaching the top of your head toward the ceiling.

- *When you exhale, bend your right leg and raise your knee up toward your chest. You can help keep your leg up by wrapping your hands around your shin or under your thigh.*
- *To help with balance, look at a spot that's not moving, like a spot on the floor or the wall in front of you.*
- *It can also help to draw the belly in toward the spine as you breathe out to balance.*

As you balance, you can make circles with your right foot. We're warming up the ankle here. Keep your breath flowing.

Pause.

You might notice you can stand up a little taller. If you'd like, switch the direction of your circles. Pause.

If you notice you are tensing up your shoulders, see if it feels okay to let them relax and sink down. Pause.

On your next inhale, we'll switch legs. Right foot down, left leg up.

Repeat the ankle rolls on the left side, giving the same cues.

Now we'll try switching from side to side with each breath.
- *Inhale, place both feet firmly on the floor and stand tall.*
- *Exhale and raise the right leg. Inhale, both feet down.*
- *Exhale, left leg up.*
- *See if you can stand up tall still.*

(Student's name) can you say, "breathe in, breathe out" as we do this 2 more times on each side?

When students are finished, invite them to shake out their legs and stand in Mountain Pose.

Rag Doll Roll-Up

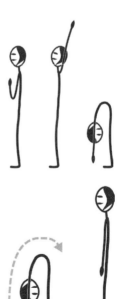

Let's stretch out now with a forward fold. When you breathe in, raise your arms up toward the ceiling. When you breathe out, fold forward. You have a choice here: you can fold forward at the hips until you feel a stretch in the back of your legs or your back. Or if you'd rather, you can just bend forward a little, letting your chin come toward your chest and your arms hang down. If you notice any tension in your neck, shoulders, back, or thighs, see if you can release some of it with each exhale. Take a moment to notice if you like this pose or not. If not, maybe there is a way you can modify it to make it feel more comfortable, like bending your legs more or folding forward more or less.

Let your breath flow in and out as you stay here. (Student name), *can you lead us in 3 breaths?*

We will now practice rolling up slowly to Mountain Pose. Let your back stay rounded and see how slowly you can roll up to standing. Take your time! Take several breaths to roll up if you'd like. The last thing to come up will be your head. Pause.

Once you are back in Mountain Pose, let your shoulders release downward. Notice your arms hanging down below your shoulders. Notice if you got dizzy, or any other sensations you feel. Maybe you notice your breath coming in and out.

Warrior III—Half Moon—Pose of the Day

For the pose of the day, we'll practice Warrior III, and then we'll try going straight from Warrior III to Half Moon Pose. It can be challenging to link these poses together and keep your balance at the same time! It's good practice for maintaining focus and building body awareness.

- *From Mountain Pose, breathe in and lift your arms as high as you can.*
- *Breathe out, lean your upper body forward and extend your right leg back, lifting it off the floor. You can choose to lift your right foot a few inches off the floor, or try lifting it higher, even as high as your hips. Pull your right heel back to lengthen out your right leg.*

- *We'll hold here for 3 counts: 3.*
- *See if pulling your belly in a little helps you balance: 2.*
- *Still breathing: 1.*

Now we'll transition to Half Moon.
- *For Half Moon, lift your right hip so it stacks on top of your left hip.*
- *Lift your right arm up toward the ceiling so your right shoulder*

stacks on top of your left shoulder. You can let your left arm reach down toward the floor if you'd like, or you can touch your hand to a chair or desk to help you catch your balance.

• *Feel yourself reaching out through your right heel and up with your right fingers. (Student name), can you please lead us in 3 breaths?*

After the 3 breaths are done, invite students to lift back up to standing. Have them take 3 breaths in Mountain Pose with their hands at their chest, and then lead them through the sequence on the other side. End with 3 breaths in Mountain Pose.

Trunk Twists

Shake out your arms and bring your feet a little farther apart. Let your arms just relax and swing as you twist from side to side if there's room. Notice how your hands and fingertips feel as you twist. If you don't have room to let your arms swing, you can bend them at chest height as you twist. Pause.

Lift the opposite heel as you twist to each side. To twist more, breathe out each time you turn to the side. Pause.

Now let your twists get smaller and smaller. Notice the moment when the movement stops and your body is completely still, except for your breathing.

Pause.

Notice your feet flat on the floor. How do your arms and shoulders feel?

Invite students to take a seat. Proceed to the Mindful Breathing section.

MINDFUL BREATHING (3 MINUTES)

Find a way to sit comfortably with your back straight. To help you focus inward, you can close your eyes or look down at your desk. Notice your breath as it comes in and goes out.

Pause.

We'll practice some rhythmic breathing. This is a simple breathing technique you could share with someone else in your home if they are dealing with stress or have a hard time sleeping.
- *Breathing in to a count of 4, and*
- *Out to a count of 8.*

Feel free to go with your own counting if I go too fast or too slow. Let all the air out of your lungs. Pause.
- *Breathe in 1, 2, 3, 4.*
- *Breathe out 1, 2, 3, 4, 5, 6, 7, 8.*
- *Breathe in 1, 2, 3, 4.*
- *Breathe out 1, 2, 3, 4, 5, 6, 7, 8.*
- *Now count silently to yourself: Breathing in for 4*—Pause—*and out for 8.* Pause.
- *In deeply, and out slowly.*

Pause.

Now I'm going to be quiet and let you practice 4 or 5 rounds on your own. If thoughts or feelings come up, just notice what they are and come back to your breathing.

Pause, allow students to breathe on their own for 4 to 5 rounds.

Continue to do the rhythmic breathing for as long as you'd like, or if you're ready, go back to breathing normally. Notice how you are feeling. Remember that the breath is a tool that you and others you care about can use anytime, anywhere, to help you manage stress and feel more centered.

WRAP-UP

GUIDED MEDITATION AND CLOSING BELL (1 MINUTE)

We're going to end class by sitting silently for 1 minute, just noticing your breathing and how your body feels.

Feel free to close your eyes or look down to help you concentrate only on yourself.

If you like, you can even put your head down and rest it on your arms.

Pause.

Notice your feet resting on the floor, your legs relaxed on the seat.

Notice where your arms and hands are. Maybe you can allow your arms and shoulders to relax a bit more.

Notice how you're breathing.

You might even allow the muscles of your face relax as you breathe.

Long pause, allow students to sit silently for remainder of the minute.

I will now ring the bell one last time. Listen to the bell and when you can't hear it anymore, please look up at me.

Ring bell and allow it to vibrate to completion.

CONNECTION QUESTIONS (3 MINUTES)

How is everyone feeling?

Of the movements and breathing exercises that we've done in TLS so far, which ones do you like best?

Ask students if they have any questions about what we did today or about TLS or mindfulness in general, and thank them for their participation.

LESSON 4.7: RECOGNIZING THAT YOU ARE COMPLETE

In this lesson, students will practice connecting King Dancer and Twisting Flamingo Poses. Benefits of these poses include:

* ❖ Strengthen and tone the ankles, legs, and back
* ❖ Stretch the shoulders and quadriceps
* ❖ Improve balance and focus
* ❖ Increase flexibility in the spine

Lesson objectives are (a) students will recognize that they are complete just the way they are, even though they may receive messages from the media and other people that tell them otherwise, and (b) students will practice bringing their attention back to the present through awareness of the breath and the body.

STUDENT OVERVIEW

REVIEW EXPECTATIONS (2 MINUTES)

Review the expectations for TLS sessions, including:

* ❖ Students clear desks of all distractions including books, papers, food, cell phones, and music.
* ❖ One-mic rule: one person talks at a time. If students have questions, they can raise a hand or ask at the end of class. Assure students that there will be a few minutes dedicated to questions at the end of each session.
* ❖ Students focus on their own body and breath. That means not making comments about self or others, not touching others, and not distracting others from their experience.
* ❖ Students try their best to participate at all times. (However, participation may look different for each student. For some students, it may mean doing only the breathing for as long as they need, until they choose to engage with the movement. Allow students to come to the practice at

their own pace, as long as they are not being distracting or disrespectful toward others. Engaging with one's body and mind through TLS is always a choice, and every day is a different experience.)

ACTIVATE BACKGROUND KNOWLEDGE (3 MINUTES)

In response to the class environment each day, you may wish to provide this information to students when you feel it would be best received—that may be at the beginning of class, woven into the mindful movement, or before the silent sitting.

In order to sell us stuff, advertisers send us the message that we are not okay the way we are—that we need to buy certain products or look a certain way in order to be complete. These messages come at us through TV, magazines, music videos, billboards, and web ads. Have you ever heard anyone say, "I would be so happy if I only had that car, or those shoes, etc."? But even if they buy the shoes, the quick shot of happiness soon wears off, and they are on to something else that they wish they had.

What the media doesn't tell you is this truth: in this moment, each of you is complete, just the way you are. Take a breath and notice that—each one of you is unique, and traveling your own path of life.

Activation Question 4.7

Do you get messages from the media or others around you that tell you that you should look or act in a certain way? Can you give an example?

Give students a chance to reflect, and choose a few students to share their responses with the class.

As we practice and throughout the day today, try to notice any negative thoughts that creep into your awareness, either about yourself or others. Remember that a lot of these thoughts don't even come

*from you, but rather are messages from outside. Maybe this aware-
ness can help you have more choice about what thoughts you buy
into and what thoughts you discard.*

ACTION, BREATHING, CENTERING

OPENING BELL AND FOCUSED BREATHING (2 MINUTES)

*We will start our time together today by trying to focus our atten-
tion on a sound. I would like to ask you all to listen to the sound of
the bell I am going to ring.*

*Try to keep your attention on the sound of the bell for as long as you
can, and when you can't hear it anymore, please raise your hand.*

Ring bell or singing bowl.

❖ Allow to vibrate to completion and until all students have raised their
   hands.
❖ Then ask students to do the same thing, this time closing their eyes or
   looking down at their desks to focus just on their hearing, and ring the
   bell again.
❖ Wait until all students have raised their hands.

> *That was very good. Now I'll lead you in a breathing exercise:*
> • *You can keep your eyes closed, or just look down.*
> • *Let all the air out of your lungs.*
> • *Now breathe in, breathe out.*

Lead class in simple breathing, encouraging them to breathe deeply and
smoothly.

Continue for 3–4 rounds.

Then tell students that you are going to do the bell exercise one more time.

Ring the bell again, and students raise their hands when they can no longer
hear it.

MINDFUL MOVEMENT AND POSE OF THE DAY (6 MINUTES)

For the Mindful Movement today, it's important that none of the students have someone standing behind them. You may wish to position students in a circle around the room before beginning the Mindful Movement section.

Mountain

Let's all stand up in Mountain Pose. Press your hands together at your chest, and either close your eyes or look down at the place where your hands meet. As you breathe in, lift the top of your head up toward the ceiling. As you breathe out, let your shoulders and arms relax. Breathe in and stand tall, reaching your head toward the ceiling. Breathe out and feel your feet on the floor, wiggling your toes if that helps you feel them. Take 1 more deep breath: standing tall, feeling your feet on the floor and shoulders relaxed.

Pause to allow students to breathe and focus.

Wrist-Cross Crescent

Cross your right wrist over your left in front of you.
- *Feel the backs of your hands pressing together.*
- *When you're ready, lift your arms above your head.*
- *Breathe in, maybe lift your arms a little higher.*
- *Breathe out, lean to the left just far enough to feel a stretch in your right side.*
- *Breathing in we lift up straight, breathing out we lean to the left again.*

Moving slowly with the breath: in, out, and in we stand up straight again.

Now bring your arms forward and cross them more, more, more, until your arms are crossed above the elbows. Give yourself a big hug, grabbing onto your shoulder blades with your hands. Take a big breath in. Breathe out and see if you can keep your grip on your shoulder blades as you lower your shoulders down away from your ears. Take 1 more breath here: you might feel a stretch in the upper back or shoulders. Good!

Eagle

Now we'll add the legs and come into Eagle Pose. Bend both legs as much as feels comfortable while keeping your heels on the floor. Stay here or cross your left leg over your right. Keep your breath moving!

Remind students to look at a spot on the floor to help them balance.

Either keep your arms here in the hug, or wrap them around each other for Eagle arms. Notice if any judgmental or critical thoughts come up about what the pose should look like, and know that wherever you are at right now is perfect. We'll be here for 3 breaths:

- *See if you can relax your shoulders a little more. That's 3.*
- *Perhaps sitting up a little straighter. 2.*
- *For the last breath maybe sink the hips lower and see if the thigh muscles work a little harder: 1.*

Good job! Untwist yourself and shake out your arms and legs.

Lead students in whole sequence of Wrist-Cross Crescent and Eagle with the left wrist crossed over the right, leaning to the right, and then crossing the right leg over the left. When done, take Mountain Pose and have a student lead everyone in taking 3 breaths, feeling their feet on the floor and reaching their head toward the ceiling.

King Dancer—Twisting Flamingo—Pose of the Day

The poses of the day are King Dancer followed by Twisting Flamingo. There are lots of options for doing these poses. It's up to you to choose what options work for you today. Choosing options helps us celebrate what our bodies can do today, rather than comparing ourselves to others, as we continue improving our balance, focus, strength, and flexibility.

To do King Dancer, we start by coming into Baby Dancer.
- *Notice your feet flat on the floor. Then start to move the weight into your right foot, lifting the left foot lightly off the floor.*
- *Keeping your knees close together, experiment with lifting and lowering your left lower leg. Notice the muscles in the back of your thigh working to lift the leg.*
- *Now one option here is to reach back and grab onto your left ankle with your left hand.*
- *Another option is to grab onto your pant leg or lift the left foot up off the floor without using your hand, maybe resting the foot on a chair behind you.*
- *Point your knee down toward the floor and feel yourself stand up tall, reaching up through the top of your head.*
- *If you engage your core muscles, tightening your abs, it can help protect your back and help you balance.*
- *Keep your breath flowing.*
- *Stay here, or if you'd like to do King Dancer, reach the right arm forward. You can always touch a desk or chair if you need more support.*
- *If your left hand is grabbing your foot or ankle, start to kick into your hand to raise your leg up. Once your leg comes up higher, you might notice your body lean forward slightly.*
- *You also might notice a stretching in your left shoulder. If you feel any pain or crunching in your lower back, try lowering the left leg a bit and drawing your abdominal muscles in.*

- *Breathing, standing tall on your right leg. (Student name,) can you lead us in 3 breaths, please?* Pause.
- *Now still breathing, we'll slowly transition to Flamingo and then Twisting Flamingo.*
- *Come back through Baby Dancer, pointing your knee down.*
- *If you can, without touching your left foot to the floor, let go of your foot and lift the knee up toward your chest.*
- *Grab onto your shin or under your thigh to help support your leg. Take a few breaths to steady your focus.*
- *Notice if your standing leg is feeling tired. Maybe you can stand up a little straighter to relieve the muscles in your leg. Or if you need to take a rest, shake out your legs and then join us again.*
- *Stay here, or if you would like to do the twist, take your left knee into your right hand.*
- *If your body feels wobbly, take a few breaths to center yourself before you move on.*
- *Now twist your chest to face the left side of the room, keeping your left knee pointed forward.*
- *Reach your left arm back toward the wall behind you. Pause. Breathe.*
- *Notice if you can stand up straighter.*
- *Stay here for a few breaths, or if you want an extra challenge, begin to turn your head until you're looking behind you at your left thumb.*

(Student name), *could you lead us in 3 breaths please?*

Once students finish 3 breaths, lead them in slowly transitioning to Mountain Pose and then to the other side.

Do Baby Dancer, King Dancer, Flamingo, and Twisting Flamingo with the right leg lifted, offering the same options on this side. Once both sides have been done, invite students to take 3 breaths, standing tall in Mountain Pose.

As you breathe, feel your feet on the floor, wiggling your toes if that helps, and reach your head toward the ceiling. Notice your body stretching tall, and notice that in this moment you are complete and perfect, just as you are.

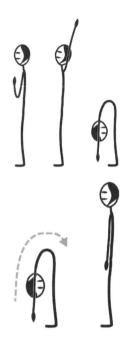

Rag Doll Roll-Up

Let's finish with one forward fold to release the muscles in the back. When you breathe in, raise your arms up toward the ceiling. When you breathe out, fold forward. Let your arms and head hang down toward the floor. You have a choice here: you can fold forward at the hips until you feel a stretch in the back of your legs or your back. Or if you'd rather, you can just bend forward a little, letting your chin come toward your chest and your arms hang down. Notice any stretching or tightness in your neck, shoulders, back, or thighs. Let your breath flow in and out as you stay here. (Student name), *can you lead us in 3 breaths?*

We will now practice rolling up slowly to Mountain Pose.

Let your back stay rounded and see how slowly you can roll up to standing. Take your time! Take several breaths to roll up if you'd like. The last thing to come up will be your head. Pause.

Once you are back in Mountain Pose, let your shoulders release downward. Notice your arms hanging down below your shoulders. Notice if you got dizzy, or any other sensations you feel, like your pulse or tingling or blood flow. Maybe you just notice your breath coming in and out. Pause.

Go ahead and find a comfortable seat.

Proceed to the Mindful Breathing section.

MINDFUL BREATHING (3 MINUTES)

Take a moment to make yourself comfortable, sitting with your back straight and feet resting on the floor. Notice the rhythm of your breath right now. Your breath will have a different rhythm at different times.

Pause to allow students to notice their breath.

As you notice your breath, let each breath get a little deeper. Pause.

Close your eyes if it feels okay, or just look down at your desk. Allow your breath to fill up your lungs completely, and then empty them completely.

Pause to let students breathe deeply for a few rounds.

Continue to make full, complete inhales and full, complete exhales. Notice if you are still sitting up straight, or if you forgot about your posture. If you'd like, place a hand on your upper chest. Can you feel your chest move as you breathe? Pause.

- *Now place your hand on your belly if that feels okay. Do you notice your belly moving as you breathe?*
- *Try to relax the muscles around your belly and breathe deeply to allow it to expand a little as you breathe in.* Pause.
- *Now if you'd like, let both hands rest on your lap or on your desk.*

Without using your hands, can you notice different parts of your body moving as you breathe? Pause.

- *Maybe you feel your belly and chest moving. Maybe you can even notice some movement in your shoulders. Maybe even the ribs in your back move—the ribs go all the way around from the front to the back.* Pause.

Whatever you feel is just fine—that's just how you are breathing in this moment. Let's take another 30 seconds just noticing what moves as we take full, complete breaths.

Pause for 30 seconds.

Good concentration.

WRAP-UP

GUIDED MEDITATION AND CLOSING BELL (1 MINUTE)

We're going to end class by sitting silently for 1 minute, just noticing your breathing and how your body feels.

Feel free to close your eyes or look down to help you concentrate only on yourself.

If you like, you can even put your head down and rest it on your arms.

Pause.

Notice your feet resting on the floor, your legs relaxed on the seat.

Notice where your arms and hands are. Maybe you can allow your arms and shoulders to relax a bit more.

Notice how you're breathing. As you breathe, notice that in this moment you are complete, just as you are.

Long pause, allow students to sit silently for remainder of the minute.

I will now ring the bell one last time. Listen to the bell and when you can't hear it anymore, please look up at me.

Ring bell and allow it to vibrate to completion.

CONNECTION QUESTIONS (3 MINUTES)

How is everyone feeling?

Does owning certain stuff or wearing certain brands of clothes make you feel better about yourself?

Does not having certain things make you feel badly about yourself?

Ask students if they have any questions about what we did today or about TLS or mindfulness in general, and thank them for their participation.

LESSON 4.8: CONNECTING WITH YOUR BEST SELF

In this lesson, students will practice connecting Warrior III, Flamingo, and Extended Flamingo Poses. Benefits of these poses include:

- ❖ Strengthen the muscles in the legs, abdomen, and back
- ❖ Stretch the hamstrings
- ❖ Improve balance and concentration
- ❖ Release tension in the lower back

Lesson objectives are (a) students will build awareness of how they feel and act when they are at their best, and (b) students will practice centering themselves (connecting with their best selves) using the breath and body awareness.

STUDENT OVERVIEW

REVIEW EXPECTATIONS (2 MINUTES)

Review the expectations for TLS sessions, including:

- ❖ Students clear desks of all distractions including books, papers, food, cell phones, and music.
- ❖ One-mic rule: one person talks at a time. If students have questions, they can raise a hand or ask at the end of class. Assure students that there will be a few minutes dedicated to questions at the end of each session.
- ❖ Students focus on their own body and breath. That means not making comments about self or others, not touching others, and not distracting others from their experience.
- ❖ Students try their best to participate at all times. (However, participation may look different for each student. For some students, it may mean doing only the breathing for as long as they need, until they choose to engage with the movement. Allow students to come to the practice at their own pace, as long as they are not being distracting or disrespectful

toward others. Engaging with one's body and mind through TLS is always a choice, and every day is a different experience.)

ACTIVATE BACKGROUND KNOWLEDGE (3 MINUTES)

In response to the class environment each day, you may wish to provide this information to students when you feel it would be best received—that may be at the beginning of class, woven into the mindful movement, or before the silent sitting.

Have you ever lost control of your actions, or seen someone else "lose it" and do or say things they didn't mean? Remember that when you get really stressed out, your brain loses its ability to think clearly. No wonder people sometimes lose it when they're under stress! When you are experiencing stress and difficult emotions, it can sometimes be difficult to be the person you want to be.

Take a moment to close your eyes if that feels comfortable and imagine yourself at your best.

Activation Question 4.8

What are you like when you're "your best self"? How do you feel? How do you interact with others? (You are your "best self" when you are being the person you want to be, when you are at your best.)

Give students a chance to reflect, and choose a few students to share their responses with the class.

In TLS, we practice ways to manage our emotions so that we can be our best selves more of the time. Every one of us is capable of being the person we want to be. The better you get at managing stress and difficult emotions, the more often you can be at your best.

ACTION, BREATHING, CENTERING

OPENING BELL AND FOCUSED BREATHING (2 MINUTES)

We will start our time together today by trying to focus our attention on a sound. I would like to ask you all to listen to the sound of the bell I am going to ring.

Try to keep your attention on the sound of the bell for as long as you can, and when you can't hear it anymore, please raise your hand.

Ring bell or singing bowl.

❖ Allow to vibrate to completion and until all students have raised their hands.

❖ Then ask students to do the same thing, this time closing their eyes or looking down at their desks to focus just on their hearing, and ring the bell again.

❖ Wait until all students have raised their hands.

That was very good. Now I'll lead you in a breathing exercise:
- *You can keep your eyes closed, or just look down.*
- *Let all the air out of your lungs.*
- *Now breathe in, breathe out.*

Lead class in simple breathing, encouraging them to breathe deeply and smoothly.

Continue for 3–4 rounds.

Then tell students that you are going to do the bell exercise one more time.

Ring the bell again, and students raise their hands when they can no longer hear it.

MINDFUL MOVEMENT AND POSE OF THE DAY (6 MINUTES)

Mountain

Let's all stand up in Mountain Pose. Place your feet flat on the floor. Notice if you can feel your feet making contact with the floor. Stand up tall, lifting the very top of your head up toward the ceiling. Notice how you're breathing.

Press your hands together at your chest, and either close your eyes, or look down at the place where your hands meet. Can someone lead us in 3 breaths, saying, "breathe in, breathe out"?

Choose a student to lead the breaths, making sure the student leads them slowly to allow for deep breathing.

Shoulder Isolations

Let your arms rest at your sides. When you're ready, start to make circles with your right shoulder. Try not to move anything else.

Pause while students do 4 to 5 circles.

Now try it with your left shoulder. Remembering to breathe in (pause) and out.

Pause while students do 4 to 5 circles.

Relax both shoulders. Now we'll combine the 2: one circle with right, one with left, one with both. Right, left, both.

Repeat 4 to 5 times, going faster if you want.

Now reverse: left, right, both.

Repeat 4 to 5 times.

Shake out your arms and let them relax.

Warrior III—Flamingo—Extended Flamingo—
Pose of the Day

For the pose of the day, we'll connect Warrior III, Flamingo, and Extended Flamingo. As we move from pose to pose, we stay connected with our breathing, and in doing so, we learn to be more mindful of our bodies and our emotions, even when we feel pressure or stress.

From Mountain Pose:
- *Breathe in and lift your arms as high as feels comfortable.*
- *Breathe out, lean your upper body forward and extend your right leg back, lifting it off the floor. You can choose to lift your right foot a few inches off the floor, or try lifting it higher, even as high as your hips. See what happens when you reach your right heel back, lengthening your right leg.*
- *We'll hold here for 3 counts as we breathe: 3.*
- *See if tightening your abs a little helps you balance: 2.*
- *Still breathing: 1.*

Now we'll transition to Flamingo. Maybe you can do it without putting your foot down.

When you're ready, start to straighten up your upper body and, at the same time, bend your right leg. Lift your right knee upward, and grab it at the shin or under the thigh.

Let's take a moment to steady ourselves. Breathing, perhaps finding a spot to focus your eyes on. Good.

Now stay here if you'd like, or transition to Extended Flamingo by straightening out the right leg little by little. It doesn't matter how much you can straighten your leg—however the pose looks for you today, give it your best. Maybe standing a little straighter. Maybe relaxing the shoulders or the face.

(Student name), can you lead us in 3 breaths please? Pause. When you're ready, gently lower your leg back to Mountain Pose.

Invite students to take 3 breaths in Mountain Pose, and then lead them through the sequence with the left leg lifted.

End in Mountain Pose.

Shake-Out

Now we'll shake out any tension that's left over. If it feels okay, the next time you breathe in, tense up all your body, from your feet to your head. Squeeze all your muscles, starting with your feet, your ankles, legs, belly, arms, shoulders, and face. Hold it!

Pause.

Breathe out, and relax and release. Try it again. Breathe in and squeeze all your muscles: feet, ankles, legs, belly, shoulders, arms, face . . . hold it!

Pause.

Breathe out, and relax and release. One more time: breathe in and squeeze all your muscles, even the little ones! Even the ones deep inside! Hold it!

Pause.

Breathe out, relax and release. Now let's shake out our arms and legs counting down from 5.

- Demonstrate shaking your right arm and hand as you say: "5, 4, 3, 2, 1."
- Shake your left arm and hand as you say: "5, 4, 3, 2, 1."
- Shake your right leg, counting down from 5. Repeat with your left leg.
- Then repeat the whole sequence counting down from 4.

- Again counting down from 3, from 2, and 1—the last round will consist of one quick shake per limb.

Come back to being very still in Mountain Pose. Take 3 full breaths here, noticing any tingling, lightness, or other sensations in your arms, legs, or hands.

Invite students to have a seat. Invite them notice if they feel more relaxed now, and if they still notice places of tension in the body.

Proceed to the Mindful Breathing section.

MINDFUL BREATHING (3 MINUTES)

Sometimes it's difficult to connect with your best self because stress and other strong emotions can get in the way. Using a breathing technique like the "Count Down to Calm Down" breath can help you calm your nervous system and reconnect with the person you want to be, beneath all the stressful emotions. Let's practice it.

Make sure you're sitting comfortably with your back straight. You can close your eyes or look down to help you focus on yourself. Notice how you're breathing. Notice if you can feel your belly move as you breathe. If not, you can try relaxing the muscles around your belly so that it moves out a little on the inhale and in toward your spine on the exhale. Practice this a few times, letting the belly get a little bigger as you breathe in, and drawing it gently inward as you breathe out.

Pause.

We're going to do 10 belly breaths just like this, counting down from 10. Breathe in a way that is comfortable to you, noticing the movement of your belly as you breathe. If you need to take a rest at any time you can do so, and join us again as you're ready.
- *Take a breath in.* Pause. *Breathe out. 10.* Pause.
- *In.* Pause. *Out. 9.*

Count down slowly to 1, giving students plenty of time to inhale and exhale fully for each count. Give reminders to help students focus on the movement in their body as they breathe. After you finish, invite students to return to normal breathing and notice how they are feeling.

WRAP-UP

GUIDED MEDITATION AND CLOSING BELL (1 MINUTE)

We're going to end class by sitting silently for 1 minute, just noticing your breathing and how your body feels.

Feel free to close your eyes or look down to help you concentrate only on yourself.

If you like, you can even put your head down and rest it on your arms.

Pause.

Notice your feet resting on the floor, your legs relaxed on the seat.

Notice where your arms and hands are. Maybe you can allow your arms and shoulders to relax a bit more.

Notice how you're breathing.

You might even allow the muscles of your face to relax as you breathe.

Long pause, allow students to sit silently for remainder of the minute.

I will now ring the bell one last time. Listen to the bell and when you can't hear it anymore, please look up at me.

Ring bell and allow it to vibrate to completion.

CONNECTION QUESTIONS (3 MINUTES)

How is everyone feeling?

Are there certain people, activities, or environments that bring out the best in you? What are they?

Ask students if they have any questions about what we did today or about TLS or mindfulness in general, and thank them for their participation.

LESSON 4.9: SEEING THE GOOD IN YOURSELF AND OTHERS

In this lesson, students will practice connecting Tree and King Dancer Poses. Benefits of these poses include:

❖ Strengthen and tones the ankles, legs, and back
❖ Stretch the shoulders and quadriceps
❖ Improve balance and focus

Lesson objectives are (a) students will reflect on the positive within themselves and recognize the positive in others, and (b) students will practice shifting their focus from negative to positive aspects of their experience.

STUDENT OVERVIEW

REVIEW EXPECTATIONS (2 MINUTES)

Review the expectations for TLS sessions, including:

❖ Students clear desks of all distractions including books, papers, food, cell phones, and music.
❖ One-mic rule: one person talks at a time. If students have questions, they can raise a hand or ask at the end of class. Assure students that there will be a few minutes dedicated to questions at the end of each session.
❖ Students focus on their own body and breath. That means not making comments about self or others, not touching others, and not distracting others from their experience.
❖ Students try their best to participate at all times. (However, participation may look different for each student. For some students, it may mean doing only the breathing for as long as they need, until they choose to engage with the movement. Allow students to come to the practice at their own pace, as long as they are not being distracting or disrespectful

toward others. Engaging with one's body and mind through TLS is always a choice, and every day is a different experience.)

ACTIVATE BACKGROUND KNOWLEDGE (3 MINUTES)

In response to the class environment each day, you may wish to provide this information to students when you feel it would be best received—that may be at the beginning of class, woven into the mindful movement, or before the silent sitting.

We can be very critical of ourselves and of those around us without even realizing it. Since the days when humans lived closely with nature and had to be constantly on the lookout for predators, the human brain is wired to focus on the negative. We often have to consciously shift our focus to notice the positive, even when it's right in front of us. As you enter into adulthood, you are still forming your perception of yourself. Taking time to look for the positive qualities in yourself and others can affect your mood and build your self-esteem. If we could all try and see the good in others and ourselves despite our differences, imagine how much more peaceful the world would be!

Activation Question 4.9

What is one thing that you like about yourself? It can be a personality trait or something you do well.

Give students a chance to reflect, and choose a few students to share their responses with the class.

When we practice TLS, we also practice taking time to celebrate what we have and what we can do in this moment. We see that we can relax and be content with ourselves, even as we work toward our goals.

ACTION, BREATHING, CENTERING

OPENING BELL AND FOCUSED BREATHING (2 MINUTES)

We will start our time together today by trying to focus our attention on a sound. I would like to ask you all to listen to the sound of the bell I am going to ring.

Try to keep your attention on the sound of the bell for as long as you can, and when you can't hear it anymore, please raise your hand.

Ring bell or singing bowl.

❖ Allow to vibrate to completion and until all students have raised their hands.

❖ Then ask students to do the same thing, this time closing their eyes or looking down at their desks to focus just on their hearing, and ring the bell again.

❖ Wait until all students have raised their hands.

That was very good. Now I'll lead you in a breathing exercise:
- *You can keep your eyes closed, or just look down.*
- *Let all the air out of your lungs.*
- *Now breathe in, breathe out.*

Lead class in simple breathing, encouraging them to breathe deeply and smoothly.

Continue for 3–4 rounds.

Then tell students that you are going to do the bell exercise one more time.

Ring the bell again, and students raise their hands when they can no longer hear it.

MINDFUL MOVEMENT AND POSE OF THE DAY (6 MINUTES)

Mountain

Let's all stand up in Mountain Pose. Press your hands together at your chest, and either close your eyes or look down at the place where your hands meet. As you breathe in, lift the top of your head up toward the ceiling. As you breathe out, let your shoulders and arms relax. Breathe in and stand tall, reaching your head toward the ceiling. Breathe out and feel your feet on the floor, wiggling your toes if that helps you feel them. Take 1 more deep breath: standing tall, feeling your feet on the floor and shoulders relaxed.

Pause to allow students to breathe and focus.

Arm Movements

Press your hands together at your chest. (Demonstrating.) *When we breathe in, we'll take the hands forward, still pressed together, and then apart and out to the sides. When we breathe out, we'll bring the hands back together and then in to the chest. Now we'll slow down the exhale, which helps us calm the nervous system. When the stress response is activated, we look for the negative because we're searching for danger. Calming the mind can help us focus on the positive. The next time you reach forward and out, breathe in for 4 counts.*

Count to 4.

Bring the hands together and in, and breathe out for 8.

Count to 8.

Lead students in the movement and counting for 1 to 2 more rounds.

Now as you do it, count silently in your head. In for 4. Pause. *Out for 8.*

Pause as students continue for a few more rounds, then return to Mountain Pose.

Standing Backbend as a Movement

We are going to do a standing back bend as a movement. When you inhale, if it feels alright, reach your arms up straight. When you exhale, bring your hands to your lower back. Support your lower back as you inhale, and if it feels comfortable, open up your chest and lean back. Only go so far back as it is still comfortable to you. On the exhale, return to standing. Let's repeat this movement 3 times.

When finished, invite students to return to Mountain pose for 3 deep breaths.

Arched Lunge

Next we'll do Arched Lunge.
- *Let's start by coming into Lunge with the left leg back, and right leg forward.*
- *The front leg is bent with the knee right above the ankle. Do you feel your front quad working as you bend? If the knee goes farther forward than the ankle, it's best to make your stance wider so you don't hurt your knee.*
- *Straighten your back leg as much as feels comfortable, and notice if you feel a stretch in your left hip flexor, in the upper front part of your thigh.*

Raise arms above your head, noticing if it feels better to hold them straight or bend them a little. Make sure you're still breathing! Maybe you can feel your feet against the floor, or the muscles working in your legs. Pause.
- *Now as you're ready, bring your hands to rest against the back of your head, with elbows out.*
- *If that doesn't feel good, another option is to bring your palms together at your chest.*
- *As you breathe in, lift your chest up and take your shoulders back.*

- *Pay attention to what you feel in your back, so that you don't arch too far. Tighten the muscles in your abs to help protect your back.*

Keep breathing for 3. Pause.
- *Notice the space across the front of your chest—2.* Pause.
- *And 1.*
- *Lift up and forward to come out of the arch. And when you're ready, bring your back leg forward to Mountain Pose. Bring your hands to your chest. Can you feel your heart beating? If it's beating a little faster, notice if it slows as we stand here and rest.*

(Student name), *can you lead us in 3 breaths please?*

After resting in Mountain Pose, lead students through Lunge and Arched Lunge on the other side. Try to have students hold the pose for the same amount of time on both sides. Then come back to Mountain Pose for 3 breaths, noticing any changes in their energy or breathing.

Tree—King Dancer—Pose of the Day

For the pose of the day, we'll do Tree Pose and then try to come right into King Dancer without putting the foot down. Both Tree and King Dancer are balancing poses—what do balancing poses help you do? Focus your mind! If you keep your breath moving as you try the pose, you can also build body awareness and control. Remember, whatever your body can do today is perfect—that's why TLS is called a practice.
- *Start in Mountain Pose. Make sure your left foot is planted firmly on the floor.*
- *When you're ready, bring your right foot to your ankle, or to your calf, or to your thigh.*
- *Press the sole of the foot into the left leg and point the right knee out to the side.*

- *If it feels okay, bring your hands to your chest as you balance in Tree. Keep breathing.*
- *If you fall out of the pose it's no big deal—just focus your eyes on one spot in front of you and try again.*

(Student name), *can you lead us in 3 breaths?* Pause.

Now we'll transition straight to Baby Dancer and then maybe King Dancer.
- *Slowly reach down to your right foot and grab your ankle, if you can.*
- *If you can't reach your ankle, grab your pant leg or simply bend your leg behind you.*
- *Point your knee down toward the floor. Take a moment to settle here in Baby Dancer. Still breathing.*

You might be able to stand up a little straighter.

Notice if you feel a stretch in the front of your right thigh.
- *You can stay here, or if you'd like you can reach your left hand forward. If you're holding your ankle, press your ankle into your hand, beginning to reach your knee behind you.*
- *Keep breathing and standing tall.*
- *As you kick your foot back, you might find yourself leaning forward a bit.*

If you feel pain or crunching in your lower back, back off a bit, and lift your belly inward to take some of the curve out of the back.
- *Breathing for 3. Maybe you notice a stretch in your right shoulder.*
- *2. Noticing the strength in your legs.*
- *1. Gently come out of the pose when you're ready.*
- *Shake it out.*

Come into Mountain Pose and take a few deep breaths.

Notice how you feel: does one side of your body feel different than the other?

Lead students through the sequence with the left leg raised. End in Mountain Pose with 3 breaths. Invite students to have a seat.

Proceed to the Mindful Breathing section.

MINDFUL BREATHING (3 MINUTES)

Sit in a comfortable way with your back straight. You can close your eyes, or just look down to help you focus inward.

- *Notice how you are breathing.*
- *Notice if the breath is short or long, deep or shallow.*
- *Notice if it's even or uneven.* Pause.
- *The next time you inhale, make your inhale last just a little bit longer.*
- *When you exhale, make your exhale last for a little bit longer.*
- *If it feels good, keep lengthening each inhale and exhale a little bit more each time.*

Pause.

- *Inhaling as fully as feels comfortable, and breathing out completely.* Pause.
- *Try to maintain this full, complete breathing for 3–4 more breaths.* Pause.
- *Now, place your right hand on your heart toward the left side of your chest, and your other hand can rest on your belly if that feels alright.*
- *As you take full breaths, try to imagine something about yourself that you are thankful for.*

It can be something simple, like appreciating the beating of your own heart, or it can be someone you care about, or something that brings you joy.

Pause.

Once you have something you are thankful for in your mind, continue breathing full, complete breaths.

As you breathe, if negative thoughts come up, you can picture breathing them out on an exhale. Let that one thing you are thankful for be the focus of your attention as you take 3 more full breaths, breathing out slowly.

Pause and take 3 slow breaths.

Good. Now if you'd like, you can keep concentrating on breathing full breaths, or you can go back to breathing normally.

WRAP-UP

GUIDED MEDITATION AND CLOSING BELL (1 MINUTE)

We're going to end class by sitting silently for 1 minute, just noticing your breathing and how your body feels.

Feel free to close your eyes or look down to help you concentrate only on yourself.

If you like, you can even put your head down and rest it on your arms.

Pause.

Notice your feet resting on the floor, your legs relaxed on the seat.

Notice where your arms and hands are. Maybe you can allow your arms and shoulders to relax a bit more.

Notice how you're breathing.

You might even allow the muscles of your face to relax as you breathe.

Long pause, allow students to sit silently for remainder of the minute.

I will now ring the bell one last time. Listen to the bell and when you can't hear it anymore, please look up at me.

Ring bell and allow it to vibrate to completion.

CONNECTION QUESTIONS (3 MINUTES)

How is everyone feeling?

Let's take a moment to give appreciation either to another student or to the group for something they did well in class today. Can someone volunteer to go first?

Ask students if they have any questions about what we did today or about TLS or mindfulness in general, and thank them for their participation.

LESSON 4.10: WE ARE ALL CONNECTED

In this lesson, students will practice Forest Pose. Benefits of this pose include:

❖ Strengthens and firms the legs and abdominal muscles
❖ Helps to focus the mind
❖ Improves balance and concentration
❖ Builds sense of connection with others

Lesson objectives are (a) students will learn about ways in which all people are connected, and (b) students will practice paying attention to the breath, heartbeat, and body sensations as aspects of our experience that we all have in common.

STUDENT OVERVIEW

REVIEW EXPECTATIONS (2 MINUTES)

Review the expectations for TLS sessions, including:

❖ Students clear desks of all distractions including books, papers, food, cell phones, and music.
❖ One-mic rule: one person talks at a time. If students have questions, they can raise a hand or ask at the end of class. Assure students that there will be a few minutes dedicated to questions at the end of each session.
❖ Students focus on their own body and breath. That means not making comments about self or others, not touching others, and not distracting others from their experience.
❖ Students try their best to participate at all times. (However, participation may look different for each student. For some students, it may mean doing only the breathing for as long as they need, until they choose to engage with the movement. Allow students to come to the practice at their own pace, as long as they are not being distracting or disrespectful

toward others. Engaging with one's body and mind through TLS is always a choice, and every day is a different experience.)

ACTIVATE BACKGROUND KNOWLEDGE (3 MINUTES)

In response to the class environment each day, you may wish to provide this information to students when you feel it would be best received—that may be at the beginning of class, woven into the mindful movement, or before the silent sitting.

People say we are all connected to one another, but how do we know if that's true? For one, you can observe your breath. We get energy and life from the air we breathe—without it we can't survive. And all of us, no matter how different, breathe air from the same atmosphere. We are connected by our breath.

Another way we can see we are connected is by observing the effects of our actions— you've probably noticed that the way you interact with others affects the way they feel and what they think, and vice versa. We pick up on each other's energy—excitement can be contagious, or someone can "kill your vibe." Even on a larger and environmental scale, we have learned that when we do something here, it can affect people many miles away.

Activation Question 4.10

Can you name something that everyone in this room has in common?

Give students a chance to reflect, and choose a few students to share their responses with the class.

Yes, we all have breath, a heartbeat, emotions, and the ability to feel our bodies as we move. In TLS, even though we focus inward, it actually helps us celebrate our connectedness and all the things we have in common.

ACTION, BREATHING, CENTERING

OPENING BELL AND FOCUSED BREATHING (2 MINUTES)

We will start our time together today by trying to focus our attention on a sound. I would like to ask you all to listen to the sound of the bell I am going to ring.

Try to keep your attention on the sound of the bell for as long as you can, and when you can't hear it anymore, please raise your hand.

Ring bell or singing bowl.

❖ Allow to vibrate to completion and until all students have raised their hands.

❖ Then ask students to do the same thing, this time closing their eyes or looking down at their desks to focus just on their hearing, and ring the bell again.

❖ Wait until all students have raised their hands.

   That was very good. Now I'll lead you in a breathing exercise:
   - *You can keep your eyes closed, or just look down.*
   - *Let all the air out of your lungs.*
   - *Now breathe in, breathe out.*

Lead class in simple breathing, encouraging them to breathe deeply and smoothly.

Continue for 3–4 rounds.

Then tell students that you are going to do the bell exercise one more time.

Ring the bell again, and students raise their hands when they can no longer hear it.

MINDFUL MOVEMENT AND POSE OF THE DAY (6 MINUTES)

The pose of the day for this lesson invites students to touch hands for support. You may wish to position students in a circle around the room before beginning the Mindful Movement section to facilitate this. If physical contact would not be safe or helpful for your class, please have students do Tree Pose individually, or invite a student to lead a balancing pose of their choice.

Mountain

Let's all stand up in Mountain Pose. Place your feet flat on the floor. Notice if you can feel your feet making contact with the floor. Lift the very top of your head up toward the ceiling. Notice how you're breathing.

If you'd like, press your hands together at your chest, and either close your eyes or look down at the place where your hands meet. Can someone lead us in 3 breaths, saying, "breathe in, breathe out"?

Choose a student to lead the breaths, making sure the student leads them slowly to allow for deep breathing.

Crescent Moon

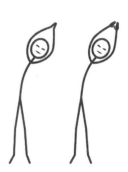

Breathing in, reach your arms up as high as feels comfortable. Either clasp your hands together, hook your thumbs together with your palms facing forward, or place your hands on your hips if you'd rather not lift your arms up right now.

- *Each time we breathe in, we reach our hands up and stand tall.*
- *As we breathe out, we lean to the right side.*
- *Breathe in, reach up tall through the center.*
- *Breathe out, lean to the left side.*
- *Continue to match the movement to your breath. Can someone lead the breath for us?*

Have students try out 2 rounds per side while one student leads the breathing.

The next time you breathe out, let your arms relax at your sides.

Thank the student for leading the breath.

This time we'll hold the pose for 3 breaths per side. Notice if you start to feel heat or stress in your body, or if you get the urge to come out of the pose before the 3 breaths are over.

If it feels okay to hold the pose, keep breathing, and either focus your attention on your breath or look around at other people to give or get some moral support.

- Once the 3 breaths to the right are over, breathe in to come to standing tall, and breathe out to go to the other side.
- Take 3 breaths on the left side.
- Then breathe in to stand tall, breathe out to relax and release.

Just stand in Mountain Pose with your arms hanging at your sides. Notice if you feel anything different in your body: maybe some warmth in your waist or your arms, or maybe your heart is beating faster than before. Close your eyes if you want.
   Take a moment to just notice what you feel.

Standing Backbend

Now place your hands together at your chest. We'll do one Standing Backbend.

- *As you breathe in, feel your upper chest rise up toward your thumbs.*
- *As you breathe out, pull your belly in a little and bring your shoulders back.*
- *Keep breathing and trying to lift your upper chest toward your hands. Either keep your hands at your chest, or on your next breath in, raise the arms high above the head. Either option is fine.*
- *Arching back, you can look up at the ceiling or forward. Pay*

attention to the sensations in your back and find an amount of arching that feels okay to you. Try to balance out the arch so that you don't feel it too much in your lower back—pulling your abs in or backing off the arch if needed.

- *See if you can hold this for 3 breaths.*
- *2 more breaths.*
- *Last one.*
- *When you're ready, breathe in and use your abdominal muscles to lift yourself out of the backbend.*
- *If your arms are raised, return them to your chest.*
- *Is your heart beating any faster?*
- *How is your breathing?*

Lunge

Next we'll practice Lunge Pose together. Remember, Lunge is a lot like Forward Warrior, but with the back heel lifted up toward the ceiling.

- *Let's start with the left leg back, and right leg forward.*
- *Place your legs farther apart for more of a stretch. You can move them closer together if you feel like that's too much.*
- *Start to bend the front leg, lining up the knee right above the ankle.*
- *Bend and straighten the front leg a few times, noticing if you feel more of a stretch the more you bend it.*
- *Try to keep your back leg straight if that feels okay.*

Now, keeping the front leg bent, bring the hands together at the chest. Breathe in, feeling your chest lift up toward your hands. Breathe out, maybe you can sink down more in your stance. Can someone lead us in 2 more breaths?

Choose a student to lead a few breaths. Then try the other side. Try to have students hold the pose for the same amount of time on both sides. Then come back to Mountain Pose for 3 breaths.

Forest—Pose of the Day

The pose of the day is called Forest pose. Unlike other dynamic mindfulness poses, which are individual, Forest is a group pose. In order to do the pose, we need everyone in the group. We use our connection with each other to make the pose more stable.

- *To do Forest, make sure that if you reach your arms out to the sides you can touch the palms of your hands to the hands of the people next to you. If touching palms with your neighbor doesn't work for you today, take a step inside the circle and do the pose with your hands together at your chest, feeling the support of your classmates who are holding the circle around you with their arms.*

Pause to allow students to space themselves out.

- *Come into Mountain Pose with your arms at your sides.*
- *Plant your right foot steadily on the floor.*
- *Begin to experiment with lifting your left foot off the floor.*
- *You can bring your left foot to your ankle, your calf, or your thigh to come into Tree Pose.*
- *Extend your arms to the sides, and touch the palms of your hands to your neighbors' hands.*
- *If you are feeling steady, offer your steady hands to help your neighbors balance.*
- *If you're feeling wobbly, use the gentle support of your neighbors' hands to steady yourself.*
- *If you are in the center of the circle, just know that your classmates are around you holding the circle steady while you balance.*
- *If you fall, just try again. You can look at a spot on the floor to help you balance, or look up to notice everyone balancing together, or alternate between the two.*

(Student name), *can you lead us in 3 breaths?*

Pause as student leads the breathing.

Good! Gently lower your leg and lower your arms. How did it feel to be supported by your classmates?

Lead students through Forest with the right leg lifted. End with 3 breaths in Mountain Pose with the hands pressed together at the chest.

Invite students to have a seat. Proceed to the Mindful Breathing section.

MINDFUL BREATHING (3 MINUTES)

We spend a lot of time focused on what makes other people different from us. But we can also choose to focus on how we're the same. Two things that everyone has are breath and heartbeat.

- *If it feels comfortable, bring your left hand to your belly and right hand to the left side of your chest.*
- *Feel free to close your eyes or look down to help you focus inside.*
- *With your right hand, notice any movements of your chest as you breathe.*
- *With your left hand, notice any movements of your belly as you breathe. Notice if one is moving more than the other.*

Pause for 3 to 4 breaths.

Now, with your right hand, see of you can find the beating of your own heart. It is normal to have a hard time doing this, but for the next 30 seconds, see if you can make the beating of your heart the loudest thing you hear.

Remain quiet for 30 seconds and allow students time to focus.

Is anyone having a hard time feeling their heartbeat? If so, why do you think that is?

Allow students to respond.

We can agree that all of our hearts are beating, so maybe it is that we are having trouble focusing our minds. It is important to remember that we have a choice of what we pay attention to. The heartbeat and the breath are tools that all of us have that can help us calm the mind and center ourselves.

Let's try one more time to focus on the beating of our hearts, letting all other noises and thoughts be in the background. Continue to breathe as you notice your heartbeat. If your breathing makes it harder to feel your heart beating in your chest, feel free to tune into the feeling of your heartbeat elsewhere in your body, like below your jawbone or in your wrist.

Allow students 30 seconds to 1 minute to focus, providing encouragement as needed to help students stay present.

WRAP-UP

GUIDED MEDITATION AND CLOSING BELL (1 MINUTE)

We're going to end class by sitting silently for 1 minute, just noticing your breathing and how your body feels.

Feel free to close your eyes or look down to help you concentrate only on yourself.

If you like, you can even put your head down and rest it on your arms.

Pause.

Notice your feet resting on the floor, your legs relaxed on the seat.

Notice where your arms and hands are. Maybe you can allow your arms and shoulders to relax a bit more.

Notice how you're breathing.

You might even allow the muscles of your face to relax as you breathe.

Long pause, allow students to sit silently for remainder of the minute.

I will now ring the bell one last time. Listen to the bell and when you can't hear it anymore, please look up at me.

Ring bell and allow it to vibrate to completion.

CONNECTION QUESTIONS (3 MINUTES)

How is everyone feeling?

Can you think of a group of people that you consider different from you? If you focus on what you have in common with them, might that change your perspective?

Ask students if they have any questions about what we did today or about TLS or mindfulness in general, and thank them for their participation.

LESSON 4.11: STRENGTHENING YOURSELF TO STRENGTHEN YOUR COMMUNITY

In this lesson, students will practice Flock of Birds. Benefits of this pose include:

❖ Strengthens the muscles in the legs, abdomen, and back
❖ Stretches the hamstrings
❖ Improves balance and concentration
❖ Builds connection with others

Lesson objectives are (a) students will understand the importance of taking care of themselves in order to be able to care for others and strengthen their community, and (b) students will practice taking time to listen to their bodies and clear their minds.

STUDENT OVERVIEW

REVIEW EXPECTATIONS (2 MINUTES)

Review the expectations for TLS sessions, including:

❖ Students clear desks of all distractions including books, papers, food, cell phones, and music.
❖ One-mic rule: one person talks at a time. If students have questions, they can raise a hand or ask at the end of class. Assure students that there will be a few minutes dedicated to questions at the end of each session.
❖ Students focus on their own body and breath. That means not making comments about self or others, not touching others, and not distracting others from their experience.
❖ Students try their best to participate at all times. (However, participation may look different for each student. For some students, it may mean doing only the breathing for as long as they need, until they choose to engage with the movement. Allow students to come to the practice at

their own pace, as long as they are not being distracting or disrespectful toward others. Engaging with one's body and mind through TLS is always a choice, and every day is a different experience.)

ACTIVATE BACKGROUND KNOWLEDGE (3 MINUTES)

In response to the class environment each day, you may wish to provide this information to students when you feel it would be best received—that may be at the beginning of class, woven into the mindful movement, or before the silent sitting.

> *Michael Jackson said it when he talked about starting with the "Man in the Mirror." In order to make a change in the world around you, you have to start with yourself first. Leading by example is the most powerful way to lead. But sometimes you have to take time out for yourself, to clear your mind, rest your body, or heal your heart, before you can give your time to others. It's important to take time for yourself because if you are strong, you can share your strength with other people.*

Activation Question 4.11

Can you name one thing you do for your family or friends, and one thing you do that is just for yourself?

Give students a chance to reflect, and choose a few students to share their responses with the class.

> *In TLS, we take time out to listen to our bodies and be with ourselves. This isn't because we're being selfish but because it helps us to be stronger and more focused, so that we can accomplish things that are important to us and be there for the people we care about.*

ACTION, BREATHING, CENTERING

OPENING BELL AND FOCUSED BREATHING (2 MINUTES)

We will start our time together today by trying to focus our attention on a sound. I would like to ask you all to listen to the sound of the bell I am going to ring.

Try to keep your attention on the sound of the bell for as long as you can, and when you can't hear it anymore, please raise your hand.

Ring bell or singing bowl.

❖ Allow to vibrate to completion and until all students have raised their hands.

❖ Then ask students to do the same thing, this time closing their eyes or looking down at their desks to focus just on their hearing, and ring the bell again.

❖ Wait until all students have raised their hands.

> *That was very good. Now I'll lead you in a breathing exercise:*
> * *You can keep your eyes closed, or just look down.*
> * *Let all the air out of your lungs.*
> * *Now breathe in, breathe out.*

Lead class in simple breathing, encouraging them to breathe deeply and smoothly.

Continue for 3–4 rounds.

Then tell students that you are going to do the bell exercise one more time.

Ring the bell again, and students raise their hands when they can no longer hear it.

MINDFUL MOVEMENT AND POSE OF THE DAY (6 MINUTES)

This lesson's Mindful Movement includes forward folding poses as well as students supporting each other by touching hands to shoulders. If physical contact would not be safe or helpful for your class, please have students do Bird Pose individually, or invite a student to lead a balancing pose of their choice.

You may wish to position students in a circle around the room before beginning the Mindful Movement section in order to avoid students having someone behind them.

Mountain

Let's all stand up in Mountain Pose. Press your hands together at your chest, and either close your eyes or look down at the place where your hands meet. As you breathe in, lift the top of your head up toward the ceiling. As you breathe out, let your shoulders and arms relax. Breathe in and stand tall, reaching your head toward the ceiling. Breathe out and feel your feet on the floor, wiggling your toes if that helps you feel them. Take 1 more deep breath: standing tall, feeling your feet on the floor and shoulders relaxed.

Pause to allow students to breathe and focus.

Half Sun Salutation

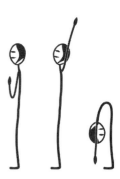

Let's practice some Half Sun Salutations. Doing these can help you get your focus and energy back when you're feeling scattered or stressed.
- *We'll start in Mountain Pose with hands together at your chest.*
- *On your next inhale, raise your arms high, reaching toward the ceiling. If it feels okay, you can reach your arms back a little.*
- *Notice the muscles in your upper back and shoulders as you reach back.*
- *On the exhale, fold forward. You can fold forward a lot, feeling a stretch in the back of the legs. Or if you feel more comfortable you can just fold forward a little, letting your arms and neck relax and your upper back round.*

When you inhale:
- *Flatten out your back like a tabletop.*
- *You can place your hands on the fronts of your legs to help support yourself.*
- *When you exhale, relax and fold forward again.*
- *Inhale, come back to standing, reaching the arms straight up.*
- *Exhale, hands to the front of the chest, Mountain Pose.*

That was 1 round.

We are going to repeat that series 3 times, but with only 1 breath per movement. Try to keep your movement connected to your breath, and feel free to pause for a rest if you need to. Ready?
- *On your next inhale raise your arms high and maybe a little back.*
- *Exhale, fold forward.*
- *Inhale, flat back.*
- *Exhale, fold forward.*
- *Inhale, reach your arms straight up.*
- *Exhale, hands to chest.*

Repeat 2 more times. When you finish, instruct students to stay in Mountain Pose and notice how they are breathing. Notice if their heart is beating faster. Notice how their body feels. Have one student lead everyone in 3 breaths in Mountain Pose.

Forward Warrior—Arched Warrior—Bird

Next we'll come into Forward Warrior, and then Arched Warrior and Bird. You might remember that Forward Warrior is a pose of strength and stability. Arched Warrior gives the added benefit of opening the chest, which can give us more energy if we're feeling tired or sad.
- *Bring the left leg back for Forward Warrior, pressing your left heel into the ground.*

- *If you'd like, extend the arms up to the ceiling, or you can take the hands together at the chest.*
- *Take a few breaths, bending your front leg and noticing if it feels okay to keep your back leg straight. Try to keep your breath smooth as you do this.*
- *If you feel an arch in your lower back, try to straighten it out by bringing your abs in and pointing your tailbone down.* Pause.
- *As you breathe in, straighten the front leg and reach up.*
- *As you breathe out, bend the front leg and bring the hands together at the chest. Let's do this 2 more times.*

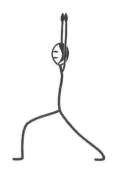

(Student name), *can you lead us in 2 more breaths?*

Great. The next time you breathe in:
- *Keep your front leg bent.*
- *Lift the center of your chest and reach your arms slightly back. If it feels better, you can keep your hands at your chest.*
- *Keep your breath smooth as you arch back. If you feel pain or your breath stops, back off a bit or take a rest.*
- *1 more breath.* Pause. *And come back to regular Forward Warrior.*
- *When you're ready, extend your arms out to the sides.*
- *Lean forward and lift your left leg off the floor for Bird.*
- *Lift the leg as high as feels comfortable.*
- *Breath is moving. Look at a still spot in front of you to steady your balance.*

(Student's name) *could you please lead us in 3 breaths?*

Pause as student leads the breathing.

Good.
- *Gently lower the leg, and then bring it forward again to Mountain Pose.*
- *Let's take 3 breaths here with the hands at the chest.*

- *Look down at your hands or close your eyes if that feels comfortable.*

Notice how you feel—does your mind feel focused, or distracted? How much energy do you have?

Choose a student to lead 3 breaths.

Once they are done, repeat the Front Warrior/Arched Warrior/Bird sequence with the right leg back. End in Mountain Pose again with 3 focusing breaths.

Flock of Birds—Pose of the Day

Sometimes it can be easier to accomplish something if we connect to support each other. Let's try it with Bird Pose. Everyone stand close enough so that you can reach each other's shoulders with your arms straight.

Demonstrate Bird pose and explain that with your arms extended straight, the fingers will rest on your neighbors' shoulders or arms.

We'll start by standing in Mountain Pose with your feet facing forward and your hands at your chest. During this pose, if you feel uncomfortable with people touching your shoulders today, you can signal this by keeping your palms pressed together at your chest. If you see that your neighbor has their hands at their chest, just extend your arm without touching them. You can still support the people next to you by taking deep, calming breaths as you balance.

- *Now take a breath in, and as you breathe out lift your left leg up behind you, leaning forward into Bird Pose.*
  - *If it feels okay, reach your hands out to the sides and gently place them on your neighbors' shoulders. Keep breathing!*
- *Experiment with lifting the leg up more or less, or leaning forward more or less.*

Try to find a place where you feel you can balance. (Student name), could you please lead us in 3 breaths?

Good. Slowly release the pose, and lower your arms down.

How was that? Was it easier to balance as a group, or individually?

Pause to allow students to respond.

Here's another question: if I'm not strong myself, and I'm all wobbly and falling all over the place (demonstrate a very wobbly Bird Pose), *am I going to be a help to the rest of the group?*

Pause to allow students to respond.

So I need to take care of myself before I can take care of the other people in my group.

Let's try it on the other side. Come into Mountain Pose.
- *This time take a moment to feel your feet firmly planted on the ground.*
- *Breathe in deep, and as you breathe out, lift your right leg slightly off the floor.*
- *Feel the strength in your standing leg.*
- *When you're ready, reach your hands out to the sides and gently place them on your neighbors' shoulders.*
- *Maybe lift the right leg up higher behind you as you lean forward.*

Ask a student to lead 3 breaths in Bird Pose. When students are done, ask them how sturdy the pose felt that time around. End with 3 breaths in Mountain Pose.

Invite students to have a seat. Proceed to the Mindful Breathing section.

MINDFUL BREATHING (3 MINUTES)

Find a comfortable way to sit with your back straight. Notice how you are breathing. Notice if the breath is short or long, deep or shallow. Notice if it's even or uneven. Pause.

- *The next time you inhale, make your inhale last just a little bit longer.*
- *When you exhale, make your exhale last for a little bit longer.*
- *If it feels good, keep lengthening each inhale a little bit more, and breathe out for a little bit longer each time.* Pause.
- *Inhaling as fully as feels comfortable, and breathing out completely.* Pause.
- *Try to maintain this full, complete breathing for a few more rounds.*
- *Take a break if needed, taking a few normal breaths, and then try another full, complete breath, breathing out long and slow.*

Longer pause.

As you breathe in, you are taking in oxygen that supports all the cells in your body.

The deeper you breathe, the more oxygen can nourish you. When you breathe out slowly, you signal to your nervous system that its okay to calm down. If it feels good to you, on your next inhale, imagine you are breathing in strength. On your exhale, breathe out peace, for yourself and everyone else. Breathing in strength, breathing out peace. In strength, out peace.

Pause to allow students to breathe for 3 or 4 more rounds on their own.

Now if you'd like, you can keep concentrating on breathing full breaths, or you can go back to breathing normally.

WRAP-UP

GUIDED MEDITATION AND CLOSING BELL (1 MINUTE)

We're going to end class by sitting silently for 1 minute, taking this time to focus all your attention on yourself. You could think of this as a mini vacation from the people around you, time to recharge your batteries.

Feel free to close your eyes or look down to help you concentrate only on yourself.

If you like, you can even put your head down and rest it on your arms.

Pause.

Notice your feet resting on the floor, your legs relaxed on the seat.

Notice where your arms and hands are. Maybe you can allow your arms and shoulders to relax a bit more.

Notice how you're breathing.

You might even allow the muscles of your face to relax as you breathe.

Long pause, allow students to sit silently for remainder of the minute.

I will now ring the bell one last time. Listen to the bell and when you can't hear it anymore, please look up at me.

Ring bell and allow it to vibrate to completion.

CONNECTION QUESTIONS (3 MINUTES)

How is everyone feeling?

Why do you think we did "flock of birds" for the pose of the day? Did you like this pose? Why or why not?

Ask students if they have any questions about what we did today or about TLS or mindfulness in general, and thank them for their participation.

LESSON 4.12: REVIEW AND RETEACHING

The purpose of this lesson is to review and reteach any essential skills from Unit 4. Although this lesson is optional, we encourage instructors to review their fidelity checklists and instructor notes, and formulate a lesson plan based on what they think students would benefit from most. If content was covered equally well, instructors may want to attempt to reteach lessons during which students did not appear well-engaged and attempt new strategies to motivate and engage students. Or instructors may choose to review a lesson during which a high percentage of students were absent. After reviewing your notes, make a plan for what you intend to reteach and why.

UNIT 4 REVIEW FORM

UNIT 4. Lesson	% Implementation	% Students absent	Overall engagement
4.1: Your Behavior Affects Your Environment			
4.2: Understanding Your Habits			
4.3: Building Healthy Relationships			
4.4: What Does "Karma" Mean to You?			
4.5: Your Role in Creating Your School Culture			
4.6: Sharing What You Learn			
4.7: Recognizing That You Are Complete			
4.8: Connecting With Your Best Self			
4.9: Seeing the Good in Yourself and Others			
4.10: We Are All Connected			
4.11: Strengthening Yourself to Strengthen Your Community			

_____ I choose to reteach lesson(s) because _____.

_____ All students have mastered skills. No reteaching is necessary.

ABOUT THE NIROGA INSTITUTE

Founded in 2005, Niroga is a 501(c)(3) nonprofit organization that brings TLS to individuals, families, and communities through the integrative practice of dynamic mindfulness, including mindful movement, breathing techniques, and meditation. The Sanskrit word, Niroga, means "freedom from disease" or integral health—health of body, mind, and spirit.

Niroga currently teaches 100 TLS sessions every week in 40 different sites, serving over 2,000 children and youth in schools and alternative schools, juvenile halls, and jails. We also conduct TLS training nationally and internationally for hundreds of educators and school-based behavioral health professionals, social workers, and violence prevention officials annually. In addition to helping them with personal sustainability (stress management, self-care, and healing from secondary trauma), they are enabled to apply TLS in professional practice, both individually and in groups.

Niroga programs are widely viewed as evidence-based and trauma-informed, and a cost-effective front-line prevention and intervention strategy for education and mental health, positive child and youth development, and violence reduction. Independent research with students in urban schools has demonstrated that TLS can reduce stress and increase emotional awareness and regulation, enhance school engagement and distress tolerance, and alter attitudes toward violence (Frank, 2012). These findings have multidimensional impacts on learning readiness and social/emotional learning, classroom climate, and the school wide learning environment, and they demonstrate that TLS can increase the personal capacity of students to deal with systemic inequities affecting their education, evidenced by the academic achievement gap and the school-to-prison pipeline.

For more information, contact:
Niroga Institute
111 Fairmount Avenue
Oakland, California 94611
Telephone: (510) 451–3004
info@niroga.org
www.niroga.org

INSTRUCTOR RESOURCES

The community of yoga researchers and practitioners is growing every day. Several levels of training are available through Niroga Institute for those interested in delivering in-class or mat-based TLS. Niroga currently trains educators, mental health professionals, community organizers, and others in the practice and sharing of TLS through dynamic mindfulness trainings. Dynamic mindfulness trainings offer an exploration of the scientific basis for TLS, an introduction to the practice for personal transformation and tips and practice for applying TLS in professional work. For certified yoga teachers interested in applying TLS to teaching youth, the Teaching Yoga to Youth training is offered. This training offers best practices for adapting yoga to the needs of youth, cultivating inclusion and diversity in yoga, and tips and practice for classroom management. For more information on the resources and trainings offered through the Niroga Institute, visit: http://niroga.org/training/

ACKNOWLEDGMENTS

There are numerous individuals and organizations that have contributed to the development of this curriculum. Dr. Jennifer Frank, Assistant Professor of education and affiliate of the Prevention Research Center at Pennsylvania State University, has guided the formulation of this curriculum since inception. Senior Niroga teachers including Danielle Ancin, Annika Malik, Jonathan Relucio, and Vanessa Zelmer contributed the content—integrating their extensive experience in conducting TLS sessions in a wide variety of settings.

Bidyut Bose, founder and executive director of Niroga Institute, provided insight on the structure and progression of TLS practice from intrapersonal to interpersonal throughout the 48 lessons presented. Erika Reynolds worked tirelessly on the stick figures and layout, making the entire curriculum eminently readable. Wendy Martinez Marroquin brought the curriculum to life with photographs of the practice in action. Judy Dunlap, Niroga cofounder and program director, as well as Angela Urata, Niroga operations director, provided indispensable logistical support. We are thankful for many reviewers, both internal and external to Niroga, who have provided valuable feedback on the curriculum, and this project would not have been possible without the generous contribution of Niroga board members and many individual donors.

REFERENCES

Frank, J. L. (2012). *Results of transformative life skills (TLS) evaluation.* State College: Pennsylvania State University Prevention Research Center.

Frank, J. L., Bose, B., & Schrobenhauser-Clonan, A. (2014). Effectiveness of a school-based yoga program on adolescent mental health, stress coping strategies, and attitudes toward violence: Findings from a high-risk sample. *Journal of Applied School Psychology, 30*(1), 29–49.

Frank, J. L., & Peal, A. (2015). *Transformative life skills/dynamic mindfulness research summary.* State College: Pennsylvania State University Prevention Research Center.

Jha, A., Krimpinger, J., & Baine, M. J. (2007). Mindfulness training modifies subsystems of attention. *Cognitive, Affective, and Behavioral Neuroscience, 7,* 109–119.

Luders, E., Toga A. W., Lepore, N., & Gaser, C. (2009). The underlying anatomical correlates of long-term meditation: Larger hippicampal and frontal volumes of grey matter. *Neuroimage, 45*(3), 672–678.

McGonigal, K. (2010, June). The big brain benefits of meditation. *Yoga Journal.* http://www.yogajournal.com/article/health/brain-meditation/

Ramadoss, R., & Bose, B. K. (2010). Transformative life skills: Pilot studies of a yoga model for reducing perceived stress and improving self-control in vulnerable youth. *International Journal of Yoga Therapy, 20,* 75–80.

Segal, Z. V., Williams, J. M. G., & Teasdale, J. D. (2002). *Mindfulness-based cognitive therapy for depression: A new approach to preventing relapse.* New York, NY: Guilford Press.

Tagney, J. P., Baumeister, R. F., & Boone, A. L. (2004). High self-control predicts good adjustment, less pathology, better grades, and interpersonal success. *Journal of Personality, 72*(2), 271–324.

van der Kolk, B. A., Stone, L., West, J., Rhodes, A., Emerson, D., Suvak, M., & Spinazzola, J. (2014). Yoga as an adjunctive treatment for posttraumatic stress disorder: A randomized controlled trial. *Journal of Clinical Psychiatry, 75*(6), 559–565.</REF>

INDEX